OLD GHOSTS
of new england

Night descends upon the famously haunted halls of
the University of Vermont in Burlington.

OLD gHOStS of New engLaND

A Traveler's Guide to the Spookiest Sites in the Northeast

C. J. FUSCO

The Countryman Press
Woodstock, Vermont

Cover photo © Erin Paul Donoran/ScenicNH.com

Book design and composition by Susan Livingston
Interior photographs by the author unless otherwise specified
Stereograph image on p. vi reprinted courtesy of the Library of Congress, Prints & Photographs Division, number LC-USZ62-68332

Published by The Countryman Press,
P.O. Box 748, Woodstock, VT 05091

Distributed by W. W. Norton & Company, Inc.,
500 Fifth Avenue, New York, NY 10110

Printed in the United States of America

10 9 8 7 6 5 4 3 2 1

acknowledgments

I would like to extend my thanks to my parents and brother for their love and support (and for watching *The X-Files* with me every week in junior high school); to my network of friends for providing an occasional much-needed distraction and escape; to those friends who came along with me to many of the locations discussed within this volume, or those who put me up for the night during my travels, especially Chris Greiner, Josh Kaplan, and Chris and Jen Duane; to my copyeditor, Dale Evva Gelfand, who seemed to work just as hard on this manuscript as I did; and to the writers, investigators, and media personalities who have paved the way for this work, especially the authors cited in this volume as well as Art Bell and George Noory, the longtime hosts of *Coast to Coast A.M.*

11   The Orphans at their Mother's Grave.

A stereograph spirit photo circa 1889

contents

part five
specters of steady habits:
haunted connecticut ... 129

part six
spirits by the sea:
haunted rhode island ... 179

Smith's Castle, North Kingstown, Rhode Island

INTRODUCTION
BUMP IN THE NIGHT

When I was a boy of about 10 or 11 growing up in Connecticut's Farmington Valley, the only movie that my parents forbade me from watching was *Poltergeist*. *Predator, Jaws, Aliens*—when I watched these comparatively gory and violent films at my friends' houses during sleepover parties, it didn't even seem to raise my parents' eyebrows; when I watched *Poltergeist* with my neighborhood friends one rainy summer afternoon, however, I was told very sternly that I was not to watch that movie again. Although its MPAA rating was only PG, I was told that *Poltergeist*—perhaps because it dealt in part with the impact of fairly realistic-seeming paranormal events on young children—was simply too scary and too intense for me. Of course, to a young and inquisitive (and maybe slightly contrarian) mind, this only made me want to watch the movie even more. As soon as my parents banned the *Poltergeist* videotape in our household, it became a kind of fetishized object in my mind. If my parents didn't want me to watch it, I reasoned, it must be good. Although my cinematic tastes at that point typically consisted of a steady diet of *Star Wars* and *Back to the Future,* my fascination with *Poltergeist* (and, perhaps a little more harmlessly, *Ghostbusters*) instilled within me a lifelong interest in matters of the paranormal and unexplained.

Poltergeist, of course, is the story of a typical suburban family that discovers that their previously tranquil home has become inhabited by mischievous entities that become more and more malicious as the movie progresses. The term *poltergeist*, from the German word for "noisy ghost," actually refers to a haunting in which objects are physically manipulated by an unseen entity. In general, paranormal experts differentiate between a poltergeist and a more traditional haunting in that whereas a traditional haunting seems to be the spirit of the dead (or the replay, like a hologram, of a past event that has been imprinted on the fabric of space and time), a poltergeist infestation typically seems to be a more malicious force that has somehow found its way into our world (or perhaps the involuntary, unconscious telekinetic abilities of a present, living person—usually an adolescent or preadolescent). This is the concept that the film *Poltergeist* uses as the jumping-off point for its plot: a young girl named Carol-Anne makes contact with benign spirits through the static in her television set; as she communicates with them, something malevolent forces its way into her home. This aspect of the plot, paranormal experts claim, is accurate: when an inexperienced person conducts a séance or plays with a Ouija board to contact presumably benign spirits of the dead, they run the risk of opening a door that lets through far more hostile and dangerous forces. Such forces, they argue, will often trick the uninitiated into thinking they are speaking to harmless spirits so they can gain entry into our world.

As an adult, I now understand why my parents were concerned about my viewing such a film. *Poltergeist* was directed by Tobe Hooper, of *Texas Chainsaw Massacre* fame, and written and produced by Steven Spielberg, who was said to be the creative force behind the movie. Indeed, watching *Poltergeist* today, it's easy to recognize the point of view of childlike innocence that seems to mark many of Spielberg's best films—*Close Encounters of the Third Kind, E.T.: The Extra-Terrestrial,* and *Jurassic Park* come immediately to mind. Perhaps this childlike innocence juxtaposed with the terrifying subject matter is what raised the ire of my parents so much more than the comparatively ridiculous *Predator,* the action-and-pyrotechnics-driven *Aliens,* or the scary yet difficult-to-relate-to *Jaws* (the shark can't get me if I don't go into the ocean, after all): the victims of the story told in *Poltergeist* were children, in a setting that was, for a child growing up in suburban Connecticut, troublingly familiar. It is historical fact that the original MPAA rating for *Poltergeist* was "R"—possibly for the reasons listed above—until Spielberg petitioned the governing body to have the rating lowered to "PG"; if his gory and intense 1975 film *Jaws* can be rated "PG," then certainly the bloodless and clean *Poltergeist* didn't deserve an "R" rating—such a rating would almost certainly damage potential box office receipts. Spielberg got his wish—and it's largely due to *Poltergeist* and Spielberg's later *Indiana Jones and the Temple of Doom* that the MPAA created the "PG-13" rating.

The reason why I relate the memory of my parents forbidding me from watching *Poltergeist* is that the prohibited film became not only a fetishized object, but also an object of some mystery. Inevitably, the inquisitive mind is drawn toward mysteries. My fate, of course, was sealed; a few years later, *The X-Files*—a show about investigating the same kind of mysteries touched on in the banned film of my youth—came along at the perfect time and was, undoubtedly, largely the cause for my various forays into Connecticut's supposedly haunted locales. I voraciously read stories of the "New England Gothic" by Poe, Lovecraft, Irving, and Hawthorne; raptly listened to local legends of hometown ghosts and haunted houses; and eventually organized trips to reputed haunted locales. For me, the possible existence of ghosts was an exciting prospect, and one for which I was constantly surrounded with evidence: I had a cousin whose purported psychic abilities allowed her to know that somebody had died before she had actually received the news; I had an aunt and uncle whose house was the nexus for a large variety of unexplained events; and I had experienced some strange circumstances at one abandoned settlement, including photographs that depict faintly glowing orbs. None of these experiences, however, has convinced me that the existence of ghosts, being the spirits of the dead, is a foregone conclusion. I do believe that people are experiencing something—there is overwhelming evidence that people see and hear things that they don't understand—but I don't claim to know exactly what those things are. As ghostly apparitions have been witnessed by uncountable sane individuals since the beginning of recorded history, it makes one think there must be something going on that we can't quite understand and can't quite explain.

Working on a book such as this one, I am asked fairly regularly what I believe. The short answer is, "I don't know"; the slightly longer answer is, "I believe that people are seeing something, but I won't be presumptuous enough to venture a guess as to what that might be"; the really long answer is that my beliefs on the matter are a strange amalgam of Christianity, various philosophies and spiritualist influences (such as Taoism), and Science (with a capital "S"). Do I believe in an afterlife? I believe that the prospect of life is a sad and lonely concept without the idea that some form of our consciousness continues on after we have ceased to exist on this physical plane.

I also believe that there is an enormous body of evidence in favor of some form of an afterlife. Besides eyewitness accounts, there are spirit photographs; electronic voice phenomenon (EVP) recordings, in which disembodied voices—often not heard by the investigator's naked ears—are captured on electronic recording equipment; inexplicable anomalies such as "cold spots" and objects that move without a human hand to guide them; and even video recordings that depict inexplicable sights and sounds, all of which can be plausibly considered evidence of an afterlife. It's interesting to consider the scientific fact that energy cannot be destroyed—it simply changes forms. As we all know, the workings of the human mind is basically the processing and transfer of energy; energy is, basically, the essence of consciousness. So what happens to this energy when a human life ends? We know it doesn't stay in the lifeless human body; if energy can't be destroyed, it must dissipate somewhere. Does it dissipate into the surrounding environment and become part of a bigger energy field—the Collective Unconscious, the Aether, the Tao, the Holy Spirit, the Force, whatever one might call it depending on one's personal belief system? It's also interesting to consider that what passes for evidence of an afterlife—the aforementioned photographs, temperature drops, EVP recordings, and the like—all measure some form of energy; if the evidence is credible, it's almost as if there is consciousness from within the various energy fields that are attempting to communicate with those of us still on the physical plane. It's possibly

At the Benton Homestead in Tolland, CT, is the grave of Jemima Barrow, who may still be pining for her lost love, Elisha Benton, more than two centuries after their deaths from smallpox during the Revolutionary War.

one area in which Science and Religion coincide; in this instance, they might both have it right.

But who's to say that what people perceive of as "ghosts" are really the spirits of the deceased. There is certainly evidence—say, the phantom Confederate troops that have been known to march through Gettysburg residents' homes in the middle of the night, taking absolutely no notice of the living residents who had been, until the intrusion, fast asleep—that some ghost sightings and hauntings might actually be imprints on space and time that are being played back almost in a holographic form; they aren't spirits in the sense of what we think of as ghosts, but rather some kind of audio/visual anomaly that we can't quite explain. Some contend that ghosts are actually glimpses into another dimension. Some contend that ghosts are not the spirits of the deceased but rather evil forces or demons trying to trick us. Some contend that many physical manifestations of a haunting—objects that move about of their own volition, things that go bump in the night—are actually the involuntary telekinetic abilities of living humans. Of course, it is very possible that much of what is reported as ghosts and hauntings are actually figments of overactive imaginations or possibly hallucinations. In fact, many such reported incidents probably are. Many more, however, remain unexplained. The average human actively uses only about 9 percent of their brain; the rest is a mystery. Until we figure out exactly what might be the function of the remaining 91 percent, it's likely that what we human beings experience as ghosts will remain unknown. But what I can say with some degree of certainty is that an awful lot of people are seeing and hearing something. Things do, in fact, go bump in the night.

If something strange is seen or heard once, it is usually written off as imagination; if that same strange thing is seen or heard a second time, the kernel of thought, "This place might be haunted!" tends to enter the inquisitive mind. As New England is a region of living history—the cradle of life for this country we call America and the oldest consistently settled area of the nation—it only makes sense that it would be one of the most haunted regions of the country. If a ghost is anything other than a figment of an excitable and overactive imagination—or, for that matter, a hallucination—then it holds true that the longer and deeper a region's history, the better the chance the region will be haunted. As many readers of this volume will no doubt attest, New England is filled with locales that are considered to be haunted. This book is meant as a traveler's guide for those like me who are curious about strange sights and sounds that people are experiencing. It is by no means a comprehensive or exhaustive book—the number of allegedly haunted locations in New England could easily fill a volume that's five or ten times this size. Rather, this book is a collection of the best-known and most haunted spots in New England that the average person can visit (with a few exceptions, private residences and other private property are excluded). This volume is a painstakingly researched compilation of the most haunted inns, restaurants, museums, churches, parks, lighthouses, bridges, and cemeteries—

organized by state and then by region—complete with detailed directions and contact information so that the novice ghost hunter can conduct their own investigations. And investigate you should; the only way that we will ever solve such mysteries of life and death is through the inquisitiveness of the human mind. Then, perhaps, we will someday finally understand the cause and the nature of those things that go bump in the night.

—C. J. Fusco

part one
poltergeists in the pines:
haunted maine

Portraits of Captain Nathaniel Lord and his wife—who may still
be wandering their former house in Kennebunkport
after nearly two centuries.

as this volume will show, certain types of structures have, and for good reason, become synonymous with the concept of ghostly haunting. Mansions, cemeteries, opera houses, colonial inns, prisons, asylums, and lighthouses almost as a rule carry with them some history of unexplainable sights and sounds. In Maine in particular, a plethora of lighthouses have become—along with Connecticut's covered bridges, the colorful foliage of Vermont and New Hampshire, and the red *B* on a blue Boston Red Sox cap—the symbolic images of New England life. Almost without exception, Maine lighthouses carry with them legendary tales of ghostly encounters.

Perhaps it is the lonely, isolated nature of these beacons—which are often located far enough offshore to make the concept of accessing the structures an improbability without the aid of some kind of boat—that give visitors an eerie feeling. Perhaps, too, the same factors make it possible for the spirits of lonely, isolated lighthouse keepers and their loved ones to stay on long after they otherwise would have passed. The fact that a majority of structures and places like the aforementioned lighthouses, mansions, and cemeteries, have garnered a reputation for uninvited guests makes one think that there must be something about them to give them a haunted reputation. Do the emotions elicited by these locations "trap" spirits in a way different than, say, a shopping mall? Do the emotions felt at these locations by visitors simply give them an eerie feeling that only makes them *think* that something strange is going on? Are people *really* experiencing paranormal phenomena? Or do certain types of places breed overactive imaginations and recurring hysteria? We may never know for sure whether people really do see ghosts—and, if so, what ghosts really might be—but it seems that far too many people are seeing far too many unexplained things to just chalk it up completely to imagination or insanity. The following accounts are illustrative of this.

DOWNEAST AND ACADIA

Mayor's Inn (Brewer)

The Mayor's Inn was once St. Joseph's parish rectory, and the building is rumored to still house one of its former residents. St. Joseph's beloved founding pastor, Father Moriarty—a priest with a sharp Irish wit who was said to be equally gifted in the art of delivering a sermon as the art of reprimanding wayward members of his parish—served the town of Brewer from 1926 until his death in 1969. In both its incarnations, inn and rectory, footsteps have been heard emanating from empty rooms, especially the bedroom that Father Moriarty once called his own. Other strange events have occurred, such as drawers opening and closing without human intervention and plates shattering in an empty kitchen. There was even one isolated incident in which a sleeping baby and its crib were inexplicably transported from the former priest's room to the end of the hallway—despite the still-closed doors in between.

If one is to believe the stories, it would appear that Father Moriarty not only continues to watch over his rectory but also the entire parish. According to Thomas A. Verde's book *Maine Ghosts & Legends*, a new Brewer resident outside doing yard work was approached by a Catholic priest, who asked why he hadn't yet seen her in church at St. Joseph's:

> The woman apologized, saying that with all the chaos of moving in, she hadn't had the time. The priest made her promise to be there with her family the following Sunday and continued on his way. When the woman told her neighbor about the incident, the neighbor was a bit surprised. It didn't sound like the behavior of the current pastor at St. Joseph's.
> "What was the priest's name?" asked the neighbor.
> "Father. Moriarty."[1]

The stories of Father Moriarty being trapped within his rectory, apparently unable to pass on to the other side, would be slightly unnerving from a Christian point of view if not for this particular anecdote. But the idea that Father Moriarty has remained on our

plane of existence to watch over his parish coincides with his behavior during life and corroborates current St. Joseph's Church
pastor Father Rice's theory that "all is well with Father Moriarty, and
. . . his spirit still dwells with us."[2]

How to find it: The former St. Joseph's rectory-turned-lodging-
house-Mayor's Inn is located at 531 North Main Street in Brewer.
From I-95, take exit 182 to ME 2 eastbound through Bangor. Go
right onto Oak Street. Just over the river, take a left onto North
Main Street (ME 9 and ME 178). St. Joseph's Church is at 531 North
Main Street.

Prospect Harbor Lighthouse (Prospect Harbor)

Personnel and guests of the stout Prospect Harbor Light—now
part of a U.S. Navy recreational facility—report that objects inside
often change locations. Most notably, a statue of a sea captain
kept in the lighthouse's bay window often shifts positions seemingly of its own volition. Perhaps more chilling are the apparitions
of two young children reportedly seen walking together along the
nearby beach. Local legend states that these children drowned just
offshore of the lighthouse in the early 1900s;[3] perhaps their ghosts
are responsible for the playful relocation of objects in the lighthouse.

How to find it: From US 1, take Pond Road (ME 195 south) for
about 5 miles to Prospect Harbor. Turn left onto Main Street and
then right again onto Corea Road. Where the road bears left toward the town of Corea, drive straight onto Lighthouse Point Road.
Follow to the gate of the U.S. Navy installation and Prospect Harbor Light. The lighthouse is a naval base and not open to the public, but views of the lighthouse are possible from the nearby beach,
especially at low tide, or from across the harbor on the grounds of
the Stinson Canning Company on ME 186 in Prospect Harbor.[4]

mIDcoast maINe

Appledore Island

History contends that Phillip Babb was the Isles of Shoals' constable and butcher—a man who held such social prominence that one of the coves on Appledore Island came to be named for him. Local legend, however, states that Babb was one of the murderous pirate Captain Kidd's men and a "desperately wicked"[5] man in his own right. Near Babb's Cove, individuals have reportedly encountered a figure dressed as a butcher, brandishing a large butcher's knife, who would run toward them crazily, as if in a fit of rage. The apparition often appears to be a living human until it gets closer, and it becomes clear that it has the "sunken eyes of a corpse."[6]

Another apparition reported on Appledore Island is somewhat more pleasant looking than that of Philip Babb: the ghost of a gorgeous young blond-haired woman is said to appear on the shore looking out yearningly toward the sea. Local legend states that she was one of the pirate Blackbeard's many young lovers, waiting for him to come back for her.[7] Blackbeard—born Edward Teach—was, of course, captured and beheaded off the coast of North Carolina in 1718.

How to find it: The small grouping of islands known as the Isles of Shoals can be found off the northeast coast of New Hampshire near Portsmouth and the southeast coast of Maine near Kittery. Appledore, also called Hog Island, is the largest of the Shoals and is home to many prominent organizations, including Cornell University's Shoals Marine Laboratory. Appledore is easily accessed via I-95 and US 1 along the New Hampshire/Maine border.

Bailey Island

All the islands that dot Maine's Casco Bay have had rumors of hauntings, but the summer escape of Bailey Island seems to be especially infested. The island's wildest story concerns a headless pirate that is Maine's version of *The Legend of Sleepy Hollow*: during the winter, a ghostly pirate, riding a winged white horse and flying along the road, has been said to appear to many otherwise sane and respectable individuals.

The most persistent bit of paranormal mischief has been occurring since the 1970s: every so often, for several days in a row, lobstermen find their traps tampered with by some unseen, possibly paranormal vandal:

> Every morning, when the fishermen made the rounds to check their traps, they found some of the hinged covers open and thrown back; inside, the tightly wrapped burlap bags of bait were gone. The fishermen ruled out human thieves because many of them sat up all night keeping watch nearby in their boats.
>
> What they did see convinced the fishermen that a ghost was to blame. In the dark of night, they saw a white phosphorescent ball, as big as a bushel basket, rolling rapidly over the surface of the water where the pot buoys were floating.[8]

Considering these incidents—as well as tales of multiple island residents who would wake up in the morning sopping wet, covered in ocean water, with no recollection of what had occurred the night before—perhaps it shouldn't be surprising that Bailey Island was once considered a coven for witches.

How to find it: To access Bailey Island and Maine's other various Casco Bay islands, take US 1 to Gurnet Road (ME 24) southbound. Follow ME 24 south from the mainland to Orrs Island and Bailey Island.

Beckett's Castle (Cape Elizabeth)

Meant to call to mind a British castle, the stone cottage built by writer Sylvester Beckett in 1874 stands on a tall bluff overlooking Casco Bay. During Beckett's life, the "castle" served as a meeting place and temporary home to many artists and thinkers of the late 19th century. According to several individuals who have resided in the castle since Beckett's death in 1882, Beckett's spirit is still very much at home in the cottage—and he might not be alone. A self-styled psychic named Alex Tanous, who investigated the castle, claims that several artists' entities are still in the house, the most dominant of which is said to be the ghost of Beckett himself.[9]

For years, the house has seen a variety of unexplained phenomena that suggest a presence attempting to exert control over the home. Residents have attempted to hang paintings on a nail only to find, in the morning, the painting wedged between the stove and the wall, with the picture side facing the wall—criticism, perhaps, of the artwork. Residents have also complained that the door leading from the master bedroom to the castle's Gothic-looking tower simply will not stay shut. One such resident, a man named Robert Lins, attempted to nail the door shut to end the problem once and for all only to see the nails forcibly shoot out of the doorframe and across the room, just barely missing the perplexed—and probably terrified—Mr. Lins.[10]

Tanous and a skeptical journalist named Lynne Campbell investigated Beckett's house in 1982, during which visit Tanous claims to have gone into a trance and channeled Beckett, speaking in a voice that was, according to witnesses, not his own. Thomas A. Verde's *Maine Ghosts & Legends* contains a record of what Beckett —allegedly speaking through Tanous—had communicated during the investigation:

> I was always raised to believe that there was no separation from those who passed on and those who remain. . . . Much of my writing reflects this because people would not understand what I was saying. You have asked why I stay here. Why should I leave that which I love most? It does not take away from my new life but rather enhances it, since you people believe so differently than I do. But then again, it is not a belief. The difference is that you are there and I am here.[11]

Campbell, trained in objectivity as a journalist, wasn't completely sold on Tanous's impressive performance as a medium; however, in a unique instance of electonic voice phenomenon (EVP), when Campbell played back the audiotape they were using to record the session, she was surprised to hear that static blocked out the section of the recording that should have included Tanous's channeling of Beckett. The beginning and ending of the static coincided directly with Tanous's entering and then exiting his trance.

How to find it: Beckett's Castle is on a tall bluff in Cape Elizabeth, with a picturesque view overlooking Casco Bay. Although at last word the property was vacant, the castle is a private residence, and trespassing is strictly prohibited.

Brunswick High School (Brunswick)

Although the school dates back to 1937, paranormal activity there started several decades later. Many janitors and teachers have reported loud slamming noises coming from empty corridors, stacks of books toppling over on their own, and lights turning themselves on just minutes after being turned off. The disturbances and unexplained activity is said to increase substantially just before something major happens in the lives of the student body, such as a car accident involving one of the kids. The staff refers to their apparent ghost as "Mimi"—according to local legend, the spirit of a student who fell to her death in the school gymnasium sometime around 1961.[12]

How to find it: Brunswick High School is located at 116 Maquoit Road in Brunswick. From I-295, take exit 28 onto US 1 eastbound. Go right onto Maine Street, and then continue straight onto Mere Point Road, which will become Maquoit Road. Stay straight on Maquoit Road. For more information, call 207-319-1910, or visit the school's Web site at www.brunswick.k12.me.us/bhs.

Canfield's Restaurant (Wiscasset)

Originally built in 1800 by Charles and Lydia Dana as a Maine coast bed & breakfast, Canfield's Restaurant is now, locals say, haunted by the ghost of Lydia Dana. The former owner is said to "turn teapots upside down, move chairs, unlatch doors, and smack people on the back."[13] None of the various reports indicates why people think that the ghost belongs to Mrs. Dana; it might just be one of those local legends that originates when people attempt to explain the unexplainable.

How to find it: Canfield's Restaurant is located on Main Street (US 1) in Wiscasset on Montsweag Bay. To access US 1, which runs along the Maine coastline, take I-295 to exit 28 onto US 1. About 30 miles along US 1 is High Point and the town of Wiscasset. For more information, call 207-882-5238.

East Wind Inn (Tenants Harbor)

Built in 1860 as a Masonic Temple—where local legends state that bizarre and esoteric rituals were conducted for the latter part of the 19th century—the building standing at Tenants Harbor in Maine is now a casual and peaceful seaside inn. Well, peaceful except for the third floor, where accounts state a variety of unexplained disturbances have been occurring since at least the mid-1970s. Guests staying in the third floor's rooms 12 and 14 have reported the sensation of being held down in their bed by an unseen assailant, and mournful crying has purportedly been heard echoing down the third floor's corridors even when the hotel is completely vacant.[14] On a few isolated occasions, witnesses have claimed to see a gray apparition climbing the staircase up to the third floor or staring sadly out a window at the ocean.

How to find it: The East Wind Inn is located at 21 Mechanic Street in Tenant's Harbor. From I-295, take exit 28 onto US 1 northbound. Turn right onto ME 131; after about 9 miles, bear left onto Mechanic Street. For more information, or to make reservations, call 207-372-6366 or 800-241-8439, or visit the inn's Web site at www.east windinn.com.

High Point (Belfast)

It is said that the slight, manacled apparition of Barbara Houndsworth haunts the rocky coast of High Point. Sometime in the early 18th century, the village of Belfast was apparently experiencing a series of unfortunate events that made it seem as though the little town were cursed: "An outbreak of distemper struck cats and dogs, a black plague struck the cows, Barbara's neighbor came down with an unknown disease, and the town church caught fire for no apparent reason. Barbara, a maker of aromatic potions and remedies, was blamed for all the sudden calamities."[15]

Barbara was tried as a witch and sentenced to death by stoning; somehow a strange chain of events led to a stone that was aimed at Barbara connecting with the forehead of the town clerk, and Barbara fled the scene. Local legend states that as Barbara was pursued by the angry throng of townsfolk, she frantically ran along the High Point rocks—finally slipping on the wet stones and tumbling to her death in the chilly Atlantic. Perhaps her ghost, reportedly still seen wandering along the High Point rocks, haunts the slippery shoreline in hope of one day clearing her name.

How to find it: High Point is a rocky cliff overlooking the ocean just off US 1 in Belfast. To access US 1, which runs along the Maine coastline, take I-295 to exit 28 onto US 1. About 90 miles along US 1 will be High Point and the town of Belfast.

Joshua L. Chamberlain House (Brunswick)

Built in the 1820s as a private residence for Joshua Chamberlain— the Civil War hero of Little Round Top at Gettysburg, governor of Maine, and eventual president of Bowdoin College—and his family, the house is now a museum with seasonal guided tours. Many visitors taking the tour complain about hip pain when they enter the house; perhaps not coincidentally, Chamberlain was shot in the hip during the Civil War, dying many years later from the lingering effects of his injury. Numerous photographs taken in the house by visitors reportedly yield ghostly orbs as well as phantom faces in many of the building's glass surfaces.[16]

How to find it: The Joshua L. Chamberlain House, located at 226 Maine Street in Brunswick., is owned by the Pejepscot Historical Society. Guided tours of the museum are offered during the summer and autumn, Tuesday through Saturday on the hour from 10 to 4. From I-295, take exit 28 eastbound onto US 1. Stay straight on

Pleasant Street, and then take a right onto Maine Street. For more information call 207-729-6606 or visit the Pejepscot Historical Society's Web site at community.curtislibrary.com/pejepscot.htm.

Marshall Point Lighthouse (Port Clyde)

The picturesque Marshall Point Light—perhaps best recognized today as the lighthouse at which Tom Hanks ends his cross-country run in *Forrest Gump*—is reputedly home to the ghost of a 12-year-old boy. A grim local legend states that a boy named Ben Bennett was chased around the light by a group of angry bootleggers who beheaded him with a machete once they caught him.[17] The source of this legend—as well as the presumptive motivations of the bloodthirsty seagoing bootleggers—remains unknown.

How to find it: The Marshall Point lighthouse—attached by a white bridge to the keeper's house, which is now a museum—is located at the southernmost tip of Port Clyde. The grounds and the Marshall Point Light Museum are open to the public, but the lighthouse itself is not. Take Atlantic Highway (US 1) to River Road (ME 131 south). Where ME 131 intersects with Seal Harbor Road (ME 73), continue straight onto St. George Road, which remains ME 131. At Tenant's Harbor, turn right onto Main Street and then left onto Port Clyde Road (still ME 131). For more information, contact the Marshall Point Lighthouse Museum at P.O. Box 247, Port Clyde, ME 04855, or call 207-372-6450.

Owl's Head Lighthouse (Owl's Head)

According to Susan Smitten, Owl's Head Light is home to an amazing story about a young couple, Richard Ingraham and Lydia Dyer, who were shipwrecked in winter near the lighthouse and then frozen in a solid block of ice. It is doubtful that either of Owl's Head's reputed ghostly residents—a short, stout man who reportedly leaves size 10 boot prints in the mud around the lighthouse and a "little lady," both of whom have been seen by many visitors —are Ingraham or Dyer: When a rescue party found the couple, they were brought to the lighthouse, where the keeper chipped them out like a sculptor and warmed the bodies. To everybody's surprise, the couple was still alive and went on to have a family, leading long, full lives.[18]

How to find it: The comparatively small Owl's Head Light is at the entrance to Rockland Harbor, in Owls Head Light State Park, Owl's Head. From US 1 in Maine, take a right at the termination of US 1 onto South Main Street (ME 73). South Main Street will become Ingraham Street. After about a mile, turn left onto North Shore Drive; then take another left onto Main Street and yet another left onto Lighthouse Road. Owls Head Light State Park is open to the public, but the lighthouse itself and the keeper's house are not. For more information, call 207-941-4014.

Pemaquid Point Lighthouse (Bristol)

Yet another Maine lighthouse built to curtail the alarming number of shipwrecks that had been occurring on the surrounding shores, the picturesque Pemaquid Point Light has become best known for the streaks of granite running down its white sides and only slightly less known for the mournful cries of unseen sufferers that are reportedly heard near the lighthouse after dark. The apparition of a red-haired lady wearing a shawl—believed by locals to be the wife or lover of one of the many sailors killed in shipwrecks off Pemaquid Point—is sometimes witnessed standing near the lighthouse's fireplace. The lighthouse is also home to a Fisherman's Museum in what used to be the lighthouse keeper's quarters.

How to find it: The Pemaquid Point Lighthouse and Fisherman's Museum are open to the public. From I-295, take exit 28 for US 1, which intersects with ME 130. Take ME 130 south to Bristol for about 14.5 miles. The route leads to the parking lot at Pemaquid Point. There is a small fee to access the parking lot for the lighthouse and museum. For more information, call the Fishermen's Museum at 207-677-2494.

kennebec valley

Strand Cinema (Skowhegan)

According to author Thomas A. Verde, "renovating an old building is one of the surest ways to anger and agitate spiritual entities."[19] Many of the sites in this volume will certainly attest to this concept —perhaps none as emphatically as the old Skowhegan Cinema. A classic example of the 1920s movie house, the cinema was purchased by Bob and Joanne Perry in 1972. Their plan was to keep the theater largely as it was for first-run movies but convert the upstairs into an apartment. If the purported disturbances that occurred during the renovation are any indication, it's fair to assume that some unseen entity didn't much care for this plan.

While working on the wiring, Bob Perry received an electrical shock despite the fact that the building's power had been turned off by the power company. When an electrician was called to investigate, he too received a massive shock though the the power was still cut off. As if those events weren't disconcerting enough, the Perrys also had a large stack of firewood piled in a back room of the theater, and one day Bob entered the room to find the logs laid out on the floor end to end so they covered the entire area.

Many of Verde's reports of the incidents at Skowhegan Cinema came from interviews with psychic Leslie Bugbee, whom the Perrys had called in to investigate the disturbances. One such incident stands out as being particularly mischievous:

> During the renovation, Joanne [Perry] had an unopened can of wood stain in the middle of the floor. A friend dropped by, and Joanne went downstairs to greet her. When the two went back up to the apartment, they saw a roll of masking tape lift up and roll across the floor at them. It stopped at their feet; then they looked up and saw the wall.[20]

Sure enough, the can of wood stain, which was still sealed when Joanne had left the room, had apparently opened itself up and thrown its contents in a grand splatter across the wall.

Although the more malicious of the Skowhegan Cinema's incidents occurred while the Perrys were renovating the upstairs portion of the building, the theater itself hasn't been without its unexplainable disturbances. For example, a group of rowdy moviegoers had been acting up during a showing—one of the *Halloween* movies, no less—when a large chunk of plaster dislodged itself from the balcony above their heads and crashed to the floor right in front of the disorderly group.[21]

How to find it: Skowhegan Cinema is now Strand Cinemas at 19 Court Street in Skowhegan. From I-95, take exit 150 onto Weeks Road westbound. Go right onto Higgins Road, then left onto Canaan Road (US 2). Canaan Road will become Water Road just before it intersects with ME 150. Take a right onto North Avenue (ME 150), a left onto Winter Street, and then another left onto Court Street. For more information or movie show times, call 207-474-3451.

western maine mountains

Norway Mill (Norway)

At the old Route 302 mill—in operation since the turn of the 20th century—tools are said to move themselves around when nobody is looking, breakers and machine switches turn themselves on and off although nobody is anywhere near them, and the apparition of an old man wearing early 1900s coveralls has reportedly been seen by many of the mills' employees—often by multiple workers at the same time—sauntering along one of the catwalks above the churning machinery. It is said that the ghost is one of the mill's early workers, who stumbled and fell off the catwalk into the machinery below.[22]

How to find it: The old Norway Mill is located along Mill Hill Road in Norway. From I-95, take exit 63, and make a right onto Shaker Road (ME 26). Follow ME 26 about 17 miles to the intersection of ME 26 and ME 118, taking a left onto ME 118. Go left onto Harrison

Road (ME 117), then right onto Sodom Road, which will be come Mill Hill Road.

University of Maine (Farmington)

If the various stories are true, the University of Maine at Farmington campus might very well be one of the most haunted colleges in New England. Reports abound of unexplained noises and strange occurrences in dormitory buildings all over campus, and one of the campus's academic buildings is even said to be home to the spirit of an international celebrity.

In the late 1970s the Mallett Hall dormitory experienced a series of disturbances that speculation linked to a former female student's untimely death from an automobile accident. Reportedly the disturbances started with footfalls coming from empty rooms and hallways and from an attic that proved empty on investigation. Eventually this progressed to more extreme disturbances that focused on a single dorm room housing two girls: They were repeatedly awakened in the middle of the night by loud bangs as if someone were lifting one of the room's heavy desks and then suddenly dropping it. Plus the room's rocking chair would begin rocking back and forth, apparently of its own volition. One night one of the female students in the room even claims to have heard the sound of someone whispering her name from the above bunk, despite the fact that nobody had been in the room with her.[23]

Standing next to Mallett Hall is Purington Hall, another dormitory building in which sounds have reportedly emanated from empty rooms. For decades now, campus legend has stated that the building is haunted by the ghost of a former University of Maine housemother who had hung herself during the school's early years. Apparently, however, there is no evidence that the Farmington campus ever even had a housemother.[24]

The Nordica Auditorium is named after Farmington's own Lillian Norton—who changed her name to the more Italian-sounding "Nordica" when she began her successful career in opera—and it's also supposedly haunted, in this case by its namesake. Although the details of this purported haunting are vague, many psychics visiting the campus report having strongly felt the presence of the former opera star who had performed for "presidents, kings, and czars."[25]

How to find it: To access the Farmington campus of the University of Maine, take I-95 to exit 127 westbound onto Kennedy Memorial Drive (ME 137). At the intersection of ME 137, ME 8, and ME 225, stay straight on ME 225. Bear right on ME 27 into New Sharon, and then take a left onto US 2. Go right onto Farmington Falls Road, then right onto Main Street. To contact the University of Maine, call 207-581-1110, or visit the college's Web site at www.umaine.edu; to contact the Farmington campus, call 207-778-7210.

south coast maine

Boon Island Lighthouse (Boon Island)

Rhode Island has its haunted mansions, Connecticut has its haunted colonial inns, and Maine has its haunted lighthouses—and the Boon Island Light, according to reports, is no exception. Boon Island's name, according to local legend, came from a particularly nasty shipwreck from which only four men survived—and they considered their survival to be a boon from God. Following a series of shipwrecks—in one of which the survivors apparently resorted to cannibalism—in 1799 the original Boon Island Light was constructed. It has since been rebuilt over and over again as fierce storms repeatedly destroyed it.

Boon Island is reportedly home to a woman in white, who local legend states lived there with her husband, the lighthouse keeper. When her husband fell ill during a particularly fierce storm, the woman—knowing the importance of keeping the light blazing—climbed the many steps to light the beacon night after night after night. When someone from shore eventually traveled to Boon Island to check on the couple, the husband was dead and the wife had apparently gone mad. Since then, a spectral woman in white has been witnessed walking both in the tower and along the rocks below.

Susan Smitten, in her *Ghost Stories of New England*, tells of two U.S. Coast Guardsmen assigned to the lighthouse who one day went fishing and accidentally drifted too far offshore to make it back in time to light the beacon before nightfall. Finally making it back, they found—to their simultaneous relief and confusion—that someone (or some*thing*) had gone to the trouble of lighting the beacon for them.[26]

How to find it: The tall, slender, 133-foot Boon Island Light is on Boon Island, about 9 miles off the coast of York, 6 miles southeast of Cape Neddick. The lighthouse can be seen distantly from Cape Neddick and Long Sands Beach in York. To access the York-area beaches, from I-95 take exit 7, and bear right at the traffic lights onto US 1. At the top of the hill, head left onto ME 1A, which offers access to a number of York-area beaches. To access Long Sands Beach specifically, drive 1 mile on ME 1A; once you come to a monument, bear left. Take a right onto Long Sands Road, which you will follow to a stop sign, and then go left onto Long Beach Avenue. Long Sands Beach will be on your right-hand side. Currently, the Boon Island Lighthouse is not open to the public, but the Isles of Shoals Steamship Company out of Portsmouth, New Hampshire, offers occasional lighthouse cruises with views of the Boon Island Light. Call 800-441-4620 or 603-431-5500, or see their Web site at www.islesofshoals.com for more information.

Cape Neddick Lighthouse (Cape Neddick)

Also called the Nubble Light in reference to the rocky island on which it resides, the Cape Neddick Lighthouse is a relatively famous beacon that has "probably appeared on more postcards and calendars than any other New England lighthouse."[27] The Cape Neddick Light was built in 1879 following a number of shipwrecks on the rocks surrounding the entrance to the York River, the most notable among them being the crash of the *Isadore* in which all who were aboard perished. Local legend states that a phantom ship—possibly the *Isadore*—has been seen from the shores near the Cape Neddick Light and that a former lighthouse keeper still haunts Nubble Island and "brings peace to those in distress."[28]

The Cape Neddick Light, the most-photographed lighthouse in America, is purportedly a great spot to see the phantom ship *Isadore*.

How to find it: The picturesque Cape Neddick Lighthouse is on Nubble Island at the entrance to the York River. From I-95, take exit 7 and bear right at the traffic lights onto US 1. At the top of the hill, bear left onto ME 1A. After driving 1 mile on ME 1A, you will come to a monument; bear left. Take a right onto Long Sands Road, which you will follow to a stop sign. Go left onto Long Beach Avenue (MA 1A) and follow the shoreline. Watch for a right turn onto Nubble Road. Take Nubble Road for approximately 1 mile to Sohier Park. There you can park for free and view the Cape Neddick Lighthouse. Nubble Island and the lighthouse itself—just a few yards from the rocky mainland—are off-limits. For more information, contact The Friends of Nubble Light, 186 York Street, York, ME 03909.

Captain Lord Mansion (Kennebunkport)

Now a lavish and ornately decorated bed & breakfast, the Captain Lord Mansion in Kennebunkport was built in 1815 by the wildly successful shipbuilder Nathaniel Lord. Although Nathaniel had the misfortune to pass away the very year that his labor of love was completed, the Federal-style mansion housed generations of his family up until the house was purchased a man named Jim Thromulous in 1972.

Thromulous hired a number of decorators and contract workers to refurbish the house, many of whom would come away from the project with the impression that the Lord Mansion was far from an ordinary home. As the refinishing process began, the house was reportedly permeated with the overpowering stench of rotting fish,[29] a sensation not been experienced by any of the home's owner before or since. While some of the workers were willing to write off the strange odor as an unexplainable anomaly, none of those present for the disturbances in the mansion's "music room" was quite as flippant.

The Captain Lord Mansion's music room is a large, open room used for baptisms, weddings, and wakes. Considering the intense emotions inherent in such life-changing events, perhaps the notion that the mansion's unexplained disturbances have centered around the music room should not come as a surprise. Over the fireplace in the room hangs a portrait of Sally Clark-Buckland, a fifth-generation descendant of Nathaniel Lord. A contract worker named Tom Glassman comments in Thomas Verde's *Maine Ghosts & Legends* that the portrait bothered everyone working in the mansion, and it was one of those paintings where "the eyes would follow you wherever you walked."[30] It was in front of this portrait that Glassman claims to have met and had a conversation with a man who, after claiming that Buckland was his aunt, disappeared into thin air.

The most bizarre and inexplicable occurrence during the refurbishing process also took place within the music room. In front of several witnesses, the portrait of Buckland supposedly started to glow while strange lights started shooting from the portrait and

The Captain Lord Mansion's music room, where most of the building's otherworldly disturbances have been reported.

around the room and the lights and radio turned on and off on their own. The owner of a local occult shop told Glassman, who was until then skeptical of paranormal phenomenon, that an angry spirit—possibly Buckland herself—was upset at the alterations being done and was attempting to chase the workers out of the house; moreover, it was the same ghost that finally drove Lord's descendants to sell the mansion.[31] Disturbances continued throughout the renovation process—footfalls were heard walking down empty hallways and even *through* walls—and on an eventful winter night, during a raging winter storm, several witnesses claimed to see a disembodied light float across a room and through a solid wall.[32] The reasons for the disturbances remain unclear, but perhaps these startling events are what caused Thromulous to resell the property again in 1978, before the restoration was even finished.

Interestingly—and unlike some of Connecticut's and Rhode

Island's haunted mansions—the Captain Lord Mansion makes no mention of the house's haunted history on the inn's official Web site or on many of the Internet travel guides. Web sites covering paranormal phenomenon, however, claim that guests staying in the inn's Lincoln Suite (so named after one of Nathaniel Lord's boats; each of the Lord Mansion's bedrooms is named after a ship that Lord had built) have witnessed the apparition of a woman—widely believed to be the Nathaniel's wife's spirit—floating across the room.[33] Some stories even have a guest waking in the middle of the night to see a young woman sitting in the Lincoln Suite's rocking chair, which then rose off the ground and floated across the room with the young woman aging into an old hag as the chair moved.[34] Interestingly, the Lincoln Suite was originally known as the Wisteria Room; the word *wisteria* (although a type of plant) allegedly means "remembrance of the dead."[35]

How to find it: The Captain Lord Mansion bed & breakfast stands at 6 Pleasant Street in Kennebunkport. Take I-95 to exit 25, ME 35 south. Follow ME 35, which will merge with ME 9A, until it intersects with ME 9. Take a left onto ME 9 east, which will bring you over a drawbridge. Go right onto Ocean Avenue and then left onto Green Street. The Lord Mansion is located two blocks down on the left, on the corner of Pleasant Street. For reservations or other information call 800-522-3141, e-mail innkeeper@captainlord.com, or visit the Captain Lord Mansion's official Web site at www.captain lord.com.

City Theater (Biddeford)

The City Theater—a venue once known as the Biddeford Opera House—is the home of several strange, unexplained, recurring phenomena that have been startling theatrical cast and crew members since the early 20th century. According to the theater's many, many witnesses over the years, strange lights move along walls, ladders shake and shudder as if an unseen person is climbing their rungs, overhead light fixtures sway back and forth as if invisible hands are pushing them like a swing, and single piano notes sometimes ring through the theater, emanating from a visibly empty stage.

Considering that a female form has been said to appear in dressing-room mirrors and a male form has been seen standing in the locked balconies, most consider the City Theater to be haunted by at least two distinct spirits. According to Susan Smitten's *Ghost Stories of New England*, these spirits might very well be a Mr. Murphy[36]—the theater's manager and projectionist during the 1940s and 1950s—and Eva Green, an actress who reportedly passed away from heart failure at the opera house on Halloween night in 1904 following a particularly exhausting performance.[37] Locals attribute events that involve the crew and their props—such as the aforementioned shaking ladder—to Mr. Murphy, and events that involve the actual onstage performances—such as the curtains or light fixtures swaying in time to the onstage music—to Miss Green.

How to find it: The City Theater is located at 205 Main Street, Biddeford. Traveling south on I-95, take exit 36 to the ramp for US 1 south. US 1 will become Main Street; stay straight on Main Street (do not bear right onto US 1). Head over the Saco River Bridge and into Biddeford. About ½ mile on your left is the City Theater. Traveling north on I-95, take exit 32. Go left at the traffic lights onto ME 111, continuing through several additional lights. At a five-way intersection, bear left onto US 1 north. Turn right at the second light onto Main Street. After about ½ mile, City Theater will be on your right. For more information on the theater, contact City Theater Associates, P.O. Box 993, 205 Main Street, Biddeford, ME 04005. Call 207-282-0842, or visit City Theater's Web site at www.citytheater.org.

Harbor Watch Inn (Kennebunkport)

The property that is now home to the Harbor Watch Inn and its two connected restaurants has been used for various purposes through the years, including a cemetery and three different houses—but to-day nobody quite seems to know the identity of the elderly woman who allegedly haunts this Kennebunkport inn. Even if the apparition of an old woman hadn't been visible to multiple guests and hotel staff in room number 1, the ghost's mannerisms would almost certainly imply the presence of an elderly woman: the hotel's heat has been known to turn back up by itself after a staff member turns it down, and room number 1's rocking chair has reportedly moved itself over to the window on multiple occasions.[38]

How to find it: The Harbor Watch Inn is located at 60 Ocean Avenue in Kennebunkport. From I-95, take exit 25 southbound onto ME 35. Continue on ME 35 until it intersects with ME 9. Go left onto ME 9, and then go right onto Ocean Avenue. For more information or to make reservations, call 207-967-3358 or 800-695-8284, or visit the inn's Web site at www.harborwatchinn.com.

Kennebunk Inn (Kennebunk)

The Kennebunk Inn, which has existed in one form or another since 1799, was a quiet tavern inn with no history of paranormal activity—until 1978. That year Arthur and Angela LeBlanc purchased the property and began renovating, remodeling, and modernizing the building. As with so many other old buildings covered in this volume, the sudden changes to the long-existing Kennebunk Inn seemed to have awakened a presence that has felt the need to make its existence known.

It was in 1978 that a waitress named Patty emerged from the newly reopened Kennebunk Inn's cellar and announced to the staff that the tavern had a ghost and its name was Cyrus. When asked how in the world she would know this, Patty insisted that the name just came to her; the one thing she was certain of, however, was that the building was haunted.

Sure enough, strange things began to happen in the cellar—boxes would tip over for no apparent reason and other unexplained events. After a while, these occurrences spread from the cellar to the rest of the tavern and eventually to the inn's rooms upstairs. Dudley, a popular bartender at the inn, would be randomly struck from behind by wooden mugs that had been hanging on the

The Kennebunk Inn, whose cellar is said to be home to a mischievous ghost known as Cyrus.

wall yet inexplicably launched themselves and flew several feet before making contact with Dudley's torso. Another incident involved a waitress who had just finished talking about how she didn't believe the inn's ghost stories—and a glass goblet she had been carrying on a tray launched itself sideways and smashed against an adjacent wall. One hotel guest complained that his room's door kept opening itself over and over again in the middle of the night despite the fact that he kept closing and locking it, and many other guests have reported unexplainable experiences. Throughout the Kennebunk Inn's past 30 years, most of the paranormal activity seems to center around the cellar, the bar area, the kitchen, and guest rooms 7 and 11.

Eventually a local newspaper ran a story about the Kennebunk Inn and its mischievous ghost, "Cyrus." When a woman named Priscilla Perkins Kenney read the article, she knew instinctively that the spirit the newspaper had mentioned had to have been her father, one-time Kennebunk Inn night watchman *Silas* Perkins. Silas, who was also a fairly successful poet, loved the Kennebunk Inn. He passed away in one of the tavern's rooms of a heart attack at age 72 in 1952.[39] Although there is little definitive evidence of a connection between the historical Silas Perkins and the inn's ghost thought to be named Cyrus, Thomas A. Verde's *Maine Ghosts & Legends* seems to imply that the owners and staff of the Kennebunk Inn generally accept that their mischievous but friendly ghost is none other than Silas himself.

How to find it: The Kennebunk Inn is located at 45 Main Street, Kennebunk. From I-95, take exit 25 to ME 35 south. Go right onto Main Street at the first set of stoplights; the Kennebunk Inn is located three blocks down on the right. For reservations or information call 207-985-3351, e-mail info@thekennebunkinn.com, or visit the Kennebunk Inn's Web site at www.thekennebunkinn.com.

Nonantum Resort (Kennebunkport)

The (comparatively) large and luxurious Nonantum Resort has been host to a variety of strange incidents over the years—so much so that the 117-room hotel's paranormal phenomena seem almost like a "greatest hits" compilation of various unexplained occurrences that have been reported at New England's other reputedly haunted inns and bed & breakfasts. Phantom footfalls have been heard, lights have turned themselves on, and doors have unlatched, opened, and closed on their own. Cleaning staff have reported that they've turned around to find that furniture they had moved just moments earlier while cleaning a room or a hallway had repositioned itself in a completely different location. Dinner plates have allegedly rotated completely around without human assistance. Breathing and coughing noises have emanated from empty rooms. One guest even alarmingly reported that his room was shaking[40]—he thought that an earthquake had hit coastal Maine (which would be a rarity, to say the least). Needless to say, no other guest or staff member felt any shaking that night; if there had been an earthquake, it was localized entirely within the confines of the guest in question's room. Considering the seemingly random and

The Nonantum Resort in Kennebunkport claims quite a variety of disturbing paranormal phenomena.

varied nature of the disturbances experienced at the Nonantum Resort, it should come as little surprise that there is yet to be an accepted theory on the origin of the hotel's presumptive ghosts.

How to find it: The Nonantum Resort is a Victorian hotel located at 95 Ocean Avenue, Kennebunkport. From I-95, take exit 25 southbound onto ME 35. Continue on ME 35 until it intersects with ME 9. Go left onto ME 9, and then take a right onto Ocean Avenue. For more information or to make reservations call 207-967-4050 or 800-552-5651, e-mail the innkeepers at stay@nonantumresort.com, or visit the resort's Web site at www.nonantumresort.com.

Old Village Inn (Ogunquit)

Built in the mid-1800s, the Old Village Inn is certainly old enough to have had its share of interesting owners and guests—although exactly why some of them may still be staying at the inn in a different form is a mystery. Still, according to reports, one unseen resident at the Old Village Inn treats the 19th-century building like home. Although lights in other rooms of the Old Village Inn have been known to turn themselves on and off, the inn's room 2 seems to be at the center of the paranormal phenomena in the seven-guestroom building. After closing down the inn and turning off all the lights for the night, staff and managers have discovered that the lights and television in room 2 had mysteriously turned themselves back on. It is also in this room that guests have claimed to feel strange gusts of wind rush by them.[41] The origin of the Old Village Inn's apparent ghost(s) and why room 2 has been chosen as its or their home are both unknowns.

How to find it: The Old Village Inn bed & breakfast is located in the center of Ogunqiut at 250 Main Street. From I-95, take exit 19 onto ME 109 eastbound. Go right on US 1, which will become Main Street in Ogunquit. For more information or for reservations call 207-646-7088, or visit their Web site at www.theoldvillageinn.com.

Tides Inn By-The-Sea (Kennebunkport)

If the eyewitness testimony is reliable, it appears that the Tides Inn's original owner-proprietor has stayed on past her earthly tenure to keep an eye on her little Kennebunkport bed & breakfast. Originally known as the New Belvedere Inn, the Tides Inn By-The-Sea was built in 1899 for Emma Foss. In the early 20th century, Emma played hostess to such esteemed guests as Theodore Roosevelt and Sir Arthur Conan Doyle, but her tenure as the inn's proprietor would come to an untimely end when financial trouble forced her to sell the building to an employee of hers, one Mr. Allen, with whom she supposedly had bad blood.[42]

In recent years a variety of disturbances have been reported at the Tides Inn; when the current owners took control of the inn, the smoke detector outside room 25—Emma's room—would sound for no apparent reason, often in the dead of night. According to Mark Jasper's *Haunted Inns of New England,* the inn's most frequent disturbances seem to happen to "uptight men" and men named Allen.[43] Such guests have claimed to have experienced paranormal phenomena ranging from waking to find an apparition of an old woman matching Emma Foss's description standing over them to waking to find bruises up and down their legs, as if they had been beaten while they slept.

How to find it: The Tides Inn-By-The-Sea is located at 252 Kings Highway on Goose Rocks Beach in Kennebunkport. From I-95, take exit 32 eastbound onto ME 111. Bear right onto West Street, following West Street until it intersects with ME 9. Take a right onto Pool Street (ME 9), then a left onto New Biddeford Road. Go right onto Kings Highway, which runs along the coast. For more information or to make reservations call 207-967-3757, e-mail the innkeepers at info@tidesinnbythesea.com, or visit the inn's Web site at www.tides innbythesea.com.

Waldo Emerson Inn (Kennebunk)

The Waldo Emerson Inn, built by the great-uncle of the writer Ralph Waldo Emerson in 1753, once experienced a disturbing series of paranormal phenomena—loud noises would erupt from nowhere, household objects would launch themselves straight across the room, and there were even rumors of a demonic possession—that resulted in seven Catholic priests performing exorcisms for seven straight days and nights during the 1920s.[44] Nowadays the inn still reports the occasional unexplainable event—such as lights that turn themselves on and off—but nothing so alarming to warrant another exorcism. Indeed, the most troubling occurrence at the inn nowadays seems to be the footfalls that are sometimes heard on winter nights moving from the closet underneath the main stairway, up the stairs, and then back down the stairs again.[45]

The charming-looking Waldo Emerson Inn in Kennebunk has, in fact, experienced multiple exorcisms to rid the inn of disturbing events.

How to find it: The Waldo Emerson Inn, located at 108 Summer Street, holds the honor of being the oldest home in Kennebunk. From I-95 north, take exit 25 to ME 35. Turn left at the first traffic light, and then take a quick right onto Summer Street (ME 35). The inn is on the left, next to Kennebunk's famous "Wedding Cake House." For more information or to make reservations, call 207-985-4250 or 877-521-8776, or visit the inn's Web site at www.waldo emersoninn.com.

Wood Island Lighthouse (Biddeford Pool)

At the mouth of the Saco River is Maine's oldest remaining lighthouse, the 47-foot-tall Wood Island Light. The lighthouse has been home to at least one unfortunate event: after renting out his extra dwelling to a young man named Hobbs, lighthouse keeper Frederick Milliken was murdered by his inebriated tenant, who was then so grief stricken that he took his own life. Now, objects have a tendency to move on their own, and lights turn themselves on and off. Lighthouse keepers in recent years have affectionately named their ghost Fred.

How to find it: The Wood Island light sits on Wood Island at the entrance of the Saco River in Biddeford Pool. The island is accessible only by boat, and the lighthouse and grounds are not open to the public except through tours given by the Friends of Wood Island Lighthouse, which itself is a chapter of the American Lighthouse Foundation. For more information, contact The Friends of Wood Island Lighthouse, P.O. Box 26, Biddeford Pool, ME 04006, or email Brad@woodislandlighthouse.org.

part two
ghosts of
the green mountains:
haunted vermont

The Elmwood Cemetery is supposedly home to a phantom gravedigger who wanders the graveyard by night.

Vermont might be well known as a quiet and peaceful wooded haven of simple New England living, but life among the rolling Green Mountains is not without its surprises, as several of the entries in this chapter prove. Charming covered bridges and bed & breakfasts and rural cemeteries often contain storied histories that may betray their otherwise peaceful façade; this hidden Vermont history presents itself to the world of the living in the form of spectral apparitions and things that go bump in the night—not to mention an ancient sea monster—known as Champ or Champy—that many believe resides in Lake Champlain.

Perhaps the best-known example of Vermont's paranormal history is that of the Eddy brothers, William and Horatio, who would conduct "materialization séances"[46] for hundreds of captivated guests in their Chittenden farmhouse throughout the 1870s. The Eddy brothers' conjuring reportedly produced dozens of apparitions in period dress, and spiritualism enthusiasts would come from all over the world to witness the spectacle in utter astonishment. When Horatio and William Eddy were growing up, it was said that unseen hands used to rock their cradles—and that was just the beginning of the brothers' contact with the other side. Their father quickly discovered the financial opportunities of having such "gifted" children and toured with them throughout the country, putting them into a trance to have them contact the dead.[47] Unfortunately for the young boys, to prove the act's legitimacy, their father also allegedly committed acts that today would have him arrested for child abuse: while the boys were in a trance, the father would place hot coals in their hands and pour boiling water over their arms (the brothers, according to legend, never even flinched), and then pour hot wax over their mouths to prove that they weren't throwing their voices.

The Eddy brothers apparently inherited their father's entrepreneurial spirit, for by the time they took control of the family's home in 1874, they had begun to charge guests for their séances—10 dollars per person—and the guests were encouraged to thoroughly investigate the house to try to uncover any trickery. As far as anybody knows, not a single skeptic ever proved that the Eddy brothers were anything but authentic mediums. Their house is now a private residence that has been moved from its original location to grant it anonymity—which is why it isn't listed in this chapter as one of Vermont's public haunted places. Worry not, though, Green Mountain travelers: plenty of haunted locations are dotted along the Vermont countryside to keep a ghost hunter busy for weeks.

NORTH CENTRAL VERMONT AND THE CHAMPLAIN VALLEY

Brigham Academy (Bakersfield)

It is said that the sounds of someone playing basketball have been heard from outside the Brigham Academy gym, even in the middle of the night when the building has been empty. Multiple witnesses state that they have seen a stationary basketball begin rolling itself across the level playing floor. (Throughout the rest of the building, too, there have been reports of furniture rearranging itself and of formerly locked doors swinging wide open.) Who this phantom player might be and why he is still at the school remains a complete mystery; there is no official record of any student ever dying on the court, so perhaps the ghost is a former student who has returned to relive his best days.

How to find it: The Brigham Academy in Bakersfield is listed as a historic site by the state of Vermont. From I-89, take exit 19 onto St. Albans Street, and then go right onto Fairfax Road (VT 104 north). Take your first right onto Fairfield Hill Road (VT 36 east), which intersects with VT 108. Go left onto North Main Street (VT 108 north); Academy Road and the school itself will be on the left.

Elmwood Cemetery (Northfield)

The graveyard near St. John's Roman Catholic Church in Northfield is said to be home to a phantom gravedigger who has appeared late at night and with an otherworldly glow about him. Witnesses have also reported various other unexplained disturbances in the graveyard, such as shadowy apparitions who disappear into thin air and statues that turn their heads to stare at intruders.

How to find it: Elmwood Cemetery is located in Northfield, bordered by Cemetery Street, Vine Street, North Street, and Cross Street in Northfield. From I-89, take exit 5 onto VT 64 westbound. Go right onto VT 12 into Northfield; Vine Street will be a left-hand turn.

Gold Brook Bridge (Stowe)

Built in 1844, which makes it one of the oldest covered bridges in the country, the 50-foot-long Gold Brook Bridge, known to in-the-know locals as both Stowe Hollow Bridge and Emily's Bridge, has a history of unexplained phenomena dating back over 150 years. Over time, people have reportedly seen strange glowing lights, anthropomorphic mists, and handprints appearing on moisture-covered car windows. If you discuss the bridge with locals, they would advise you to stay away once the sun goes down: Gold Brook Bridge is reputedly the eternal home of one of the nastier spirits to be found in this volume. Local legend states that, following orders from parents who forbade them to marry, a young woman named Emily and her lover had planned on meeting at the bridge to elope one fateful night sometime in the middle of the 19th century. When her would-be fiancé didn't turn up by dawn, Emily, in a fit of anger and remorse, hanged herself from one of the bridge's rafters. If the many numerous stories of travelers' unpleasant encounters on the bridge are any indication, Emily is still feeling vindictive and frequently takes out her anger on just about anybody or anything passing through.

There have been many incidences of animals and cars being clawed while traveling through the Gold Brook Bridge, resulting in lines of flesh being pulled from animal hide and paint scraped right off metal body panels. It seems as though every book that mentions the Gold Brook Bridge has a different incident to relate; Joseph Citro's *Passing Strange* tells of a man who saw a female form circle his car and try furiously to force open his locked doors.[48] Perhaps the most disturbing "Emily encounter" can be found in

The Gold Brook Bridge in Stowe, also known as Emily's Bridge for an apparent suicide there, is reputed to be home to a vindictive, vengeful spirit.

Susan Smitten's *Ghost Stories of New England*. It relates how Kristy Aucoin mistakenly thought she would attempt to reason with Emily. The resulting incident caused Kristy to report her experience to the International Ghost Hunter's Society:

> Feeling that Emily needed help in moving on, Kristy tried to contact the ghost. Using techniques she'd only ever read about, she attempted to reach Emily by talking to her and asking questions. "I asked her why she remained here. What could possibly anchor someone here so long?"
>
> The response surprised Kristy. "A pain slowly settled into the back of my neck, while a pressure on the front made it difficult to breathe," she wrote in her report of the event. "The pain was excruciating, unbelievable." As the pain worsened, Kristy heard a roar reminiscent of a seashell echo. She tried to stop the "attack" but it persisted, so she ran for her car, barely

able to see from the pain in her head and neck. Once safely in her vehicle, Kristy says the pain stopped.[49]

It is clear from Kristy's experience that Emily is not a spirit to be trifled—or reasoned—with. What is notable about all the reported "attacks" is that the traveler is apparently safe as long as they remained in their car with the doors locked. If there is any truth to the reports of strips of paint scratched off a car's bodywork, however, it might be a good idea to steer clear of the bridge if you're driving a shiny new Porsche or Corvette. And if you listen to the locals, it might be a good idea to steer clear of the bridge *altogether* once the sun has dipped below the horizon.

How to find it: The Gold Brook Bridge in Stowe is a lovely, picturesque covered bridge—the type that New England is widely known for. From I-89, take exit 10 onto VT 100. Go right onto Gold Brook Road, and then bear left, continuing on Gold Brook Road. Take a left onto Covered Bridge Road.

The Ice House Restaurant (Burlington)

The first structure erected on the property that now houses the Ice House Restaurant was the home of John Winan, a shipbuilder who specialized in steamboats. Fire destroyed the 1808 home in 1868, and the property was converted to an "ice house"—essentially a factory that supplied big chunks of ice taken from Lake Champlain to businesses and residences in the Burlington area during the era before refrigeration. That same building is now a unique and popular restaurant. However, the ghosts of the building's past apparently live on into the present, for there have been reports of "dragging" noises—as if an unseen presence were dragging a huge slab of ice across the floor—and several witnesses (including a relative of paranormal investigator Thomas D'Agostino) have claimed to see the apparition of an old woman swinging a bell within the walls of the former ice factory.[50]

How to find it: The Ice House Restaurant is located at 171 Battery Street. From I-89, take exit 14 onto US 2 westbound. US 2 becomes

The Ice House Restaurant in Burlington serves up unnerving sounds from the cellar along with its meals.

Burlington's Main Street. Take a left on Battery Street. For more information, call 802-864-1800.

Merchant's Bank (Burlington)

Now a branch of Vermont's own local Merchant's Bank, the small brick building on College Street used to be the office of an attorney, who kept his practice into old age. It is said that the apparition of an old man—presumably the attorney—sitting alone in what is now the bank's employees' lounge but was apparently once the man's office—occasionally startles bank employees. And then the apparition disappears into thin air.

How to find it: The Burlington branch of Merchant's Bank is located at 164 College Street in Burlington. From I-89, take exit 14 westbound onto US 2. US 2 becomes Burlington's Main Street; go right onto St. Paul Street, then right again onto College Street. For more information about this particular branch, call 802-865-1898, or visit the bank's Web site at www.mbvt.com.

Old Stagecoach Inn (Waterbury)

Built in 1826 as a travelers' depot and later used as a stagecoach stop, the Federal-style Old Stagecoach Inn—listed on the National Register of Historic Places—was remodeled in 1890 as a Victorian-style tavern. The woman responsible for the inn's current appearance was Margaret Spencer, an eccentric socialite who was said to not only smoke cigarettes when it was still considered a cultural faux pas but also chew tobacco. Her bad habits were well-documented, and there are rumors that she involved her teenage daughter in bootlegging activities. There were even accusations that she was responsible for her husband's death—Albert Spencer died in 1907 in London, and some claimed that Margaret poisoned his soup. Needless to say, Mrs. Spencer was not very popular within her circle of New England elite.

Around 1948 the inn was sold to a man named C. B. Norton, who converted the old house into an inn. Guests soon began to report sightings of an apparition of a woman wearing a white shawl in the hotel's room 2, which used to be Mrs. Spencer's bedroom. Not only did the inn's phantom resident match the physical description of Margaret Spencer, the timing would have been about right—the former owner died in 1947 at the age of 98. Other strange occurrences have also been reported at the inn—rocking chairs have been said to move of their own volition, and the current innkeeper was once startled to find out that guests had been checked in without his knowledge; the description of the woman staffing the front desk matched that of—you guessed it—Margaret Spencer.[51]

How to find it: The Old Stagecoach Inn is located at 18 North Main Street (US 2) in Waterbury. From I-89, take exit 10 westbound onto VT 100. Then go left onto US 2. For more information call

802-244-5056 or 800-262-2206, mail the innkeepers at lodging@ oldstagecoach.com, or visit the inn's official Web site at www.old stagecoach.com.

Shard Villa (Salisbury)

Considering that the Shard Villa is now a retirement community, the concept of death is one that is an unfortunate consequence of daily life there. That such a place is allegedly haunted would probably come as no surprise to most; that its ghost is said to be that of the home's original 19th-century owner—a lawyer fancifully named Columbus Smith—might come as a bit more of a surprise.

The mansion was built in 1872 and earned its name due to the case for which Smith was best known: he had been hired to get back the money of a woman named Mary Francis Shard, which was apparently being held by the British royal family. The process called for Smith to sail to England several times over the course of 14 years; the case was so stressful, local legend states, that it turned Smith's hair and beard prematurely gray.

The lack of pigmentation in the lawyer's hair was far from the most trying misfortune of his life, however—the man had two children who both died tragically young (it is known that a son passed away at 14 from a neurological disease; the cause of the other child's passing is unknown). Perhaps the greatest traumatic event to a parent is having a child's life end before their own, and Smith's ordeal was doubled. It was said that his physical and mental health deteriorated rapidly following the untimely death of his children. According to Joseph Citro's *Green Mountain Ghosts, Ghouls & Unsolved Mysteries*, the children's former tutor once visited the mansion to check up on Columbus and recollected that the mansion's owner had "lost his health and reason"; at one point the tutor was awakened by "a curious animal roar from the lips of the stricken man."[52]

Columbus Smith might have been losing his mind and body, but despite his terrible loss, he remained a kindly, giving man. He even willed that his old home be converted into a rest home for the elderly upon his passing. His instructions were implemented, and since then, strange sights and sounds have apparently become commonplace at the mansion: items disappear and then randomly reappear in unlikely locations; lights and shadows are seen where they shouldn't be; the sound of a baby crying has been heard although it can't be tracked down; and on one occasion the director of the rest home, a woman named Peggy Rocque was surprised to find that one of the upstairs bathtubs had apparently filled itself—even though nobody had been able to turn the rusty faucet handle for years.[53] Moreover, many staff members have claimed to see the apparition of a man with gray hair and a gray beard roaming the halls and then evaporating into thin air.

How to find it: Shard Villa retirement home is at 1177 Shard Villa Road in Salisbury. From I-89, take exit 3 onto VT 107 westbound. Go right onto VT 100 into Hancock, and then go right again onto VT 125. Take VT 125 through East Middlebury, and go left on Halladay Road not long after VT 125 and VT 7 merge. Go left on Farmingdale, then a quick right onto Shard Villa Road. For more information, call 802-352-4369.

University of Vermont (Burlington)

Not one, not two, but *seven* of the University of Vermont's buildings are said to be haunted. Considered by many to be a "public Ivy"—a term popularized by the book *Public Ivys* by Richard Moll—it is one of the few public colleges and universities that essentially compete with the private Ivy League schools in terms of quality of education and staff. UVM (shorthand for its Latin name, *Universitas Viridis Montis*) has three buildings ("Grasse Mount," the Federal-style mansion that now houses the University Development and Alumni Relations offices; Continuing Education; and Admissions) where strange noises such as doors opening and closing and phantom footsteps are a commonly reported phenomenon. Plus Converse Hall has a ghost that reportedly likes to flick lights on and off and has been known to mischievously clack the keys on typewriters and computer keyboards. Similarly, the building that is now UVM's public relations office used to be the private practice of a

UVM's Converse Hall looks every bit the haunted dormitory.

physician named Dr. Booth; whenever the lights there flicker on and off or a strange noise is heard, it is apparently common for those in the building to half-jokingly blame Dr. Booth.[54]

In a building known as The Bittersweet, which houses UVM's Department of Environmental Studies, the apparition of a woman wearing a turn-of-the-20th-century bell-shaped skirt and odd, up-swept hair has been reported numerous times by different individuals.[55] But it is the campus Counseling and Testing Center that seems to generate the most reports of ghostly activity: there have been reports of doors opening and the sound of footfalls moving through the doorway, although nobody is there; a janitor has reported that an unseen foot kicked his mop bucket down the hall-way; and tenured professors have claimed to see the apparition of an elderly man with a bulbous nose.[56] The spirit of this building is presumed to be that of a former sea captain named Jacobs, who was the house's original owner.

How to find it: The University of Vermont is located at 85 South Prospect Street in Burlington. From I-89, take exit 14, going right from the off-ramp onto Williston Road (VT 2), which will become Main Street. The UVM campus will become visible almost immediately. For more information, call 802-656-3131, or visit the school's official Web site at www.uvm.edu.

northeast kingdom

Hayden House (Albany)

William Hayden Jr. built his stately brick mansion on Vermont's Route 14, just outside Albany, hoping that the grand house— allegedly complete with a ballroom suspended by a spring floor— would be enjoyed by generations of his descendants. Unfortunately, within three generations the Hayden line had petered out, with members of the family reportedly succumbing to strange and inexplicable illnesses one after another.

Local lore states that the Hayden family had been afflicted by a curse, put on William Hayden Sr. by his mother-in-law, Mercie Dale. According to legend, William Sr. borrowed a large sum of money from his wife's mother to ostensibly fund the family business; instead, he squandered the money on his hard-partying lifestyle, then refused to pay Mercie back. The woman's health declined—some even believe that Hayden poisoned her to tie up loose ends—and she supposedly cursed Hayden on her deathbed, stating that the entire family line would perish within three generations.[57]

It is said that people often see strange lights bobbing around outside the mansion. Joseph Citro, in *The Vermont Ghost Guide*, elaborates that William Jr. was said to have used illegal Chinese laborers to work for him building railroads, and many of these illegal workers are buried at the back of the Hayden family property. Citro speculates that the lights that so many people claim to witness might very well be the ghostly lanterns of these perished railway workers.[58] It is also said that people have heard orchestral music coming from the Hayden house when it has supposedly been empty; perhaps the mansion's ghosts are reliving the good times they had at William Jr.'s lavish ballroom parties?

How to find it: The Hayden House, a brick Greek-Revival mansion listed on the National Register of Historic Places, is located on VT 14 just outside Albany. From I-91, take exit 26 eastbound onto VT 58. Follow VT 58 for about 2.5 miles to the intersection of VT 58 and VT 14. Take a left onto VT 14 south. VT 14 will take you through Albany; the Hayden mansion is south of Albany, slightly obscured by trees, just past Bailey Hazen Road on the right. As the Hayden House is still a private residence, trespassing is prohibited.

Inwood Manor (Barnet)

At this charming 32-room inn, strange sights began to welcome unsuspecting guests following an extensive renovation. The apparition of a little girl has reportedly been seen on the cellar steps, and the apparition of a woman in a striped 19th-century dress has been spotted floating up the inn's main staircase.[59] Local legend states that the phantom inhabitants are a mother and daughter who drowned in the nearby Connecticut River.

How to find it: Inwood Manor is located on Lower Waterford Road in Barnet. From I-93, take exit 44 onto St. Johnsbury Road (NH 18 and NH 135) westbound. Where the road splits into NH 18 and NH 135, bear right onto Franconia Road (NH 18) and cross the Connecticut River. Go left onto Lower Waterford Road. As of the publication of this volume, the inn was closed for renovations, and information on a possible reopening date was unavailable, as was current contact information. If you want to visit this location, please be respectful of private property; the building might have changed hands and might not be open to the public.

SOUTHERN AND CENTRAL VERMONT

Barrows House (Dorset)

This large 1784 Federal-style home built for the Dorset church's pastor is now the Barrows House, an inn boasting many amenities. If the stories are true, the Barrows House also boasts an unseen spirit that chooses to make its presence known through inexplicable and often anachronistic noises.

As readers of this volume surely realize by now, the sound of footfalls echoing down vacant hallways is a fairly common, though no less unsettling, occurrence in an allegedly haunted locale. The Barrows House has had its share of mysterious footfalls, but also heard in the elegant Dorset hotel has been the sound of chairs being dragged across the ballroom floor; not only was the ballroom empty of any living human presence at the time of the disturbance, but the once-hardwood ballroom floor is now carpeted.[60] According to Mark Jasper's *Haunted Inns of New England,* Barrows House staff members have expressed a belief that at least some of the inn's unexplained phenomena can be linked to a past guest named Mr. Darrell, an eccentric, Bentley-driving older gentleman who used to stay at Barrows House at the same time every year before passing away.[61]

How to find it: Barrows House is located at 3156 Warner Memorial Highway (VT 30) in Dorset. From US 7, take a left onto Depot Street (VT 30), which will become the Warner Memorial Highway. For more information or to make reservations, call 802-867-4455 or 800-639-1620, or visit the Barrows House Web site at www.barrows house.com.

Bowman House (Cuttingsville)

John P. Bowman made a fortune out of tanning—the process by which animal hide is converted into leather—and built a beautiful, stately mansion for his family on Route 103. Sadly, not long after, he also had to build a mausoleum across the street—his first daughter died as an infant, and then his wife and another daughter passed away within seven moths of each other, all of them, from all accounts, from natural causes. The building's namesake has been immortalized on the property by a mournful-looking statue of Bowman holding a wreath and his top hat while he despairingly locks the mausoleum door.

Today, although the mansion remains privately owned, it is open to the public for tours. Apparently, though, the current owners refuse to stay overnight in their gorgeous house! According to reports, the apparition of a woman in 19th-century garb makes startlingly regular appearances at the Bowman House—especially at night—and objects in the mansion's rooms have been known to move around without the aid of a living human hand. The most famous such incident occurred within view of several witnesses who were taking a tour of the mansion: a little girl being dragged along on the tour stuck her tongue out at a woman's portrait hanging in one of the mansion's halls; immediately, the painting flung itself off the wall at the child. Apparently whatever haunts the Bowman House simply will not tolerate a misbehaving child's insubordination.[62] The current owners apparently embrace the unexplained events that have occurred at the Bowman House, for the grounds now boast their very own haunted bookstore.

How to find it: The Bowman House and Laurel Glen Mausoleum are located on Rockingham Hill Road off VT 103 in Cuttingsville. From I-91, take exit 6 onto Rockingham Road (VT 103) westbound. After traveling 30 miles on VT 103, take a left onto Rockingham Hill Road. The Bowman House and Laurel Glen Mausoleum will be about a quarter mile down Rockingham Hill Road. For more information, contact the Preservation Trust of Vermont at 802-658-6647.

Dorset Inn (Dorset)

It only makes sense that the nation's oldest continually run place of lodging—which has been in business since 1796—would have a ghost or two, but the Dorset Inn is unique in that its alleged ghost seems to reveal itself only a little bit at a time. The apparition, taken as a whole, is said to be a man with "dark puffy hair"[63] wearing a gray jacket—what might be a Civil War Confederate uniform—who is often seen as a torso with no head or legs or a head with no torso. The staff has long reported cold spots in various places in the inn, including its attached restaurant and tavern, plus strange noises have been said to emanate from room 32 when it's vacant, and the same room's door has been found locked even when it was intentionally left unlocked.[64]

How to find it: The Dorset Inn on the Green is located at 8 Church Street in Dorset. From US 7, take a left onto Depot Street (VT 11), and stay straight on Bonnet Street (VT 30). Follow VT 30 into Dorset; Church Street will be on the left. For more information, call 802-867-5500, or visit the inn's Web site at www.dorsetinn.com.

Lake Bomoseen (Castleton)

The strange apparition that has been reported coasting along the waters of Castleton's Lake Bomoseen is one of peaceful disquiet. An empty phantom rowboat has been seen by a number of visitors to Bomoseen State Park; some have even attempted to approach the boat, which vanishes before they can get close. Local legend states that some time in the early 19th century, a group of three slate workers from West Bomoseen were rowing across the lake to a tavern on the eastern shore when they disappeared without a trace. It is the image of this boat that, when the conditions are right (some claim a full moon is necessary), can be seen floating along to this day.[65]

How to find it: Lake Bomoseen is in Bomoseen State Park, the entrance for which is at 1422 West Castleton Road in Castleton. The park is open to the public from Memorial Day through Labor Day. From I-87 or I-89, take the exit for VT 4 (I-87: exit 19, VT 254 east to VT 4; I-89: exit 1 to VT 4 west). From VT 4, turn onto VT 30 traveling northbound; Lake Bomoseen runs alongside the western edge of VT 30. To access the state park, keep traveling north along VT 30 until reaching Hortina Road, a left-hand turn. Follow Hortina Road past three ponds on the left side of the road, and go left onto Black Pond Road, which leads into entry points for both Half-Moon State

Park and Bomoseen State Park. The Bomoseen State Park office is located at 22 Cedar Mountain Road, Fair Haven; for more information, call 802-265-4242, or visit www.vtstateparks.com/htm/bomoseen.cfm.

Southern Vermont College (Bennington)

A scenic mountainside college campus that offers breathtaking views of Vermont's Green Mountains, Southern Vermont College is a liberal arts school that prides itself on building connections between students and the community. It also appears that the picturesque school continues to have strong connections to whoever might have lived on the campus grounds in the past.

Southern Vermont College's main campus building is a palatial-looking mansion that was once the residence of Edward Everett, an esteemed 18th-century politician who also served as president of Harvard. Over the years many SVC students and staff members have reported witnessing lights turn themselves on or off in locked rooms and locked doors and windows open on their own.[66] Apparitions have also been seen—a woman and a child walking hand in hand along the banks of the campus's Upper Pond[67] and a woman in white who roams the mansion as well as the nearby grounds. Many speculate that this often-viewed woman in white might be Everett's second wife,[68] but—as is the case with so many college and university hauntings—there seems to be little to no hard evidence to support this claim.

How to find it: Southern Vermont College is nestled on the western outskirts of Bennington at 982 Mansion Drive. From VT 7, turn onto West Main Street (VT 9), also known as the Molly Stark Trail, westbound. The seventh left-hand turn will be a major intersection with Monument Avenue; take this left, and travel down Monument Avenue southbound until you come to Mansion Drive, which will be the second right. Mansion Drive is a long, sweeping road that leads to Southern Vermont College's main campus. For more information about the school, call 802-442-5427, or visit the college's Web site at www.svc.edu.

The peaceful-looking Saint Michael's Church in Brattleboro reportedly hosts the restless spirit of an organist.

St. Michael's Church (Brattleboro)

Local legend states that a large tomb sat on the grounds at St. Michael's Church. The tomb held the corpse of the church's original organist—a man so respected that the church's parishioners were said to have buried his beloved organ with him. Sure enough, in time locals began to claim to hear the sound of organ music echoing throughout the night. According to Joseph Citro's *Green Mountain Ghosts, Ghouls & Unsolved Mysteries,* the legend also states that the phantom organ playing got worse and worse as time went on, to the point where the "music" had been reduced to one prolonged note. On opening the tomb to investigate, parishioners found to their horror the rats had eaten most of the organist's fingers.[69]

How to find it: St. Michael's Roman Catholic Church is located at 47 Walnut Street in Brattleboro. It isn't immediately clear if the tomb of local legend is somewhere on the property or within the church itself. From I-91, take exit 2 eastbound onto Western Avenue (VT 9), which will become High Street. Go left onto Main Street and then right onto Walnut Street, which is on the banks of the Connecticut River.

Sumner's Falls (Hartland)

Before Hartland was settled by the Europeans of the colonial era and became a thriving logging and milling community, Sumner's Falls—also known as Hartland Rapids—was a popular and well-fished Abenaki camping and hunting ground on the Connecticut River. It was so cherished by these Native Americans that it appears some tribesmen opted to never leave. Strange sights are often seen by locals, hikers, and campers in the Sumner's Falls region: mysterious canoes being paddled by one or two shadowy figures appear out of the fog, then disappear just as suddenly; campsites are spotted from across the Connecticut River, but the phantom campsites are mysteriously absent when any curious party crosses to investigate.

How to find it: Sumner's Falls is a short section—about 2 miles long—of white water on the Connecticut River on the Vermont/New Hampshire border in Hartland. From I-91, take exit 9 onto US 5 northbound. US 5 runs along the banks of the Connecticut River after crossing I-91.

The White House Inn (Wilmington)

Now a cozy country inn with a magnificent view of the rolling Green Mountains, the White House of Wilmington was once a sprawling Victorian mansion belonging to the family of lumber and paper baron Martin Brown. "An elegant reminder of a former era," writes Susan Smitten, "it features formal gardens, 14 fireplaces, and two terraces supported by soaring pillars. . . . The house even once had an indoor bowling alley and a nine-hole golf course."[70] Like so many other expansive mansions in this edition, the White House Inn has had its share of paranormal phenomena, much of it surrounding inn employees and patrons who happen to share the same surname as the mansion's original owners!

Brown's family lived in the White House of Wilmington for a time, but he then moved his family's permanent residence to Boston; the home was used as the family retreat until Brown himself died in 1965, at which point it was sold to Bob Gringold, who renovated the mansion into the inn that it is today. About 10 years after the White House Inn opened for business, a housekeeper—whose last name was Brown—complained to Gringold of closet doors slamming shut in a number of the rooms as she was attempting to clean. A few years later, a guest named Clara Brown claimed that the night before, she awoke to discover an elderly woman sitting in the room's rocking chair. While Clara was attempting to make sense of the scene, the old woman spoke: "My dear, I don't mind your being here, but I think one Mrs. Brown is enough, and you should really go."[71] The old woman then vanished, but the chair continued to rock back and forth for several moments afterward.

Quite a few years later, another incident took place in a different room—but involving the very same rocking chair that held the apparition seen by Clara Brown. A family had been staying in a pair

A spectral old woman has been said to watch over sleeping guests at the White House Inn in Wilmington.

of adjoining rooms. In the middle of the night, the children came running into the parents' room, yelling that an old woman was in their room. When the parents went to investigate, the room was empty—but the chair was rocking back and forth.

Besides these isolated incidents—and an inexplicable cold spot in the pantry—reports of strange activity have been somewhat few and far between. There are the usual reports of unexplained footfalls, but apparently a visitor's chances of seeing the apparition of an old woman are rare—unless, perhaps, the visitor's last name just happens to be Brown.

How to find it: The White House Inn is located at 179 Route 9 East (VT 9), just outside Wilmington. Take I-91 to exit 2, and go right onto VT 9 westbound. After traveling for about 18 miles, the inn will be at the junction of VT 9 and VT 100. For information and reservations call 802-464-2135 or 866-774-2135, e-mail info@whitehouse inn.com, or visit the inn's Web site at www.whitehouseinn.com.

White River Bridge (Hartford)

"Energy can't be destroyed," asserts former U.S. Department of Defense weapons researcher and current paranormal expert Stephen Marshall, "That's a basic rule of science. But energy can be transformed."[72] This is the hypothesis by which Marshall, a physicist by training, bases his forays into the spirit world. He claims it would be an "unscientific statement" to state that there are no such things as ghosts; people are seeing *something*—whether it be the spirits of the once living, an impression on the fabric of time being played back like a recording, or simply a hallucination on the part of the witness. If one follows Marshall's logic, to say that there's simply no such thing as ghosts would be akin to abandoning the scientific method of inquiry and experimentation.

It is this belief that the existence of ghosts *can* be studied that led to Marshall's investigation of Vermont's White River Bridge, which was the scene of a horrific train wreck that left more than 30 dead in 1887. At 2 AM on a fateful February morning, the Hartford Railway's *Montreal Express* was behind schedule and attempting to make up time on its way north when several of its aftmost cars toppled off the bridge and into the icy river below. Since then there have been several reports of the apparitions of a conductor and a boy, both dressed in 19th-century attire, who appear to be so solid that witnesses don't realize what they've seen until after the duo disappears into thin air. Sure enough, after visiting various supposedly haunted sites in New England, Marshall finally found success at the White River Bridge using thermal heat imaging to spot ghosts. As evidenced by the existence of cold spots in so many purportedly haunted locations, the ghosts displayed in Marshall's thermal imaging appear as an area colder in temperature than the surrounding area; such imaging results often clearly depict the outline of a human body.[73]

The apparition of the White River Bridge's young boy, according to Susan Smitten's *Ghost Stories of New England*, belongs to one Joe McCabe, who helplessly watched his father die in the *Montreal Express* wreck. Since the boy survived the wreck, one has to wonder why his ghost—appearing as a child—would appear at the crash site. Marshall posits that McCabe's emotional attachment to the site caused his spirit to return to that place and time "to honor his father's memory";[74] the popular hypothesis among many paranormal investigators that people and events can leave an impression on a place and then be replayed like a hologram when the conditions are right also might apply to the apparitions at the White River Bridge. Whatever it is that people are seeing there, you can be sure that Stephen Marshall is investigating the science behind *why* people are seeing what they're seeing.

How to find it: The White River Bridge in Hartford is on Bridge Street, near where the White River runs into the Connecticut River. From I-91, take exit 12 onto Bugbee Street eastbound. Go right onto Hartford Avenue (US 5), left onto Maple Street (VT 14), and then right onto Bridge Street.

PART THREE
A TRADITION OF APPARITIONS:
HAUNTED NEW HAMPSHIRE

Ghostly machinery is said to still be heard operating
at the Cocheco Mill in Dover.

New Hampshire is a state filled with ghost stories, to be sure, but it is also a state filled with strange legends and tall tales. Consider, for example, the legend of "Ocean-Born Mary": On July 28, 1720, *The Wolf*, a ship headed for Londonderry, New Hampshire, was boarded by the pirate ship of the feared Don Pedro. As the pirate and his bloodthirsty men prepared to loot the ship and burn it where it floated, Don Pedro noticed that a pair of Scottish emigrants, James and Elizabeth Fulton, were cradling their newborn daughter in terror. Something must have melted in Don Pedro's heart, for he declared that if the couple were to name their child after his mother, Maria, he would spare the lives of all aboard the vessel. The young couple complied.

Years later, as a widow with four children of her own, Mary was sought out by Don Pedro, and the two fell in love. Depending on who you ask, Don Pedro was later either killed in a duel or hanged by the authorities who caught him after he had been on the lam for years, but "Ocean-Born" Mary lived to the ripe old age of 94, passing away in 1814. Legend states that she still haunts the house in Henniker that she shared with the formerly fierce pirate Don Pedro and that she watches over and protects any person who lives in the house, even going so far as to extinguish inferno-level house fires: Sometime during the 1960s, then-owner of the house, David Russell, accidentally dropped a kerosene heater, and the old timber quickly became engulfed in flames. As Russell watched the fire grow, the flames were suddenly and abruptly extinguished; legend attributes this unexplained incident to the providence of Mary's spirit.

As interesting as the legend might be, there are several plot holes in the story. For example, Mary Fulton married a man named James Wallace, who died when he was 81. Some suggest that James Wallace actually *was* Don Pedro, who had changed his name to conceal his identity, but that doesn't explain why storytellers would contend that Don Pedro sought Mary out *after* her young husband had passed away. Perhaps most damning to the story is the fact that Mary did not live in Henniker until she was in her 70s, when she moved in with her son William. The house that has been labeled "the Haunted Ocean-Born Mary House" actually belonged to another of her sons, Roger Wallace; Mary, despite supposedly haunting the house, never actually lived there. Still, the witnesses to the Ocean-Born Mary legend have been many; who's to say that people aren't seeing Mary's apparition in her son's former home? Such are the mysteries of the unknown.

However entertaining the tale of Ocean-Born Mary might be, the following New Hampshire ghost stories seem far more plausible.

Great North Woods and White Mountains

Beal House Inn and Restaurant (Littleton)

A charming, cozy hotel that was built in 1833 as a farmhouse, the Beal House Inn and Restaurant is named after the woman who founded the current establishment exactly 100 years after the house was built. Over the past several decades, many of the inn's guests and staff have reported being awakened by heavy footfalls and the slamming of doors without being able to find any evidence of a living human cause. There have also been reports of individuals hearing voices while they were alone and even being touched by unseen hands in various rooms throughout the inn.

How to find it: The Beal House Inn and Restaurant is located at 2 West Main Street in Littleton. From I-93, take exit 41, turning right after the exit ramp. The inn is located at the intersection of NH 302 and NH 18. For more information or to make reservations, call 603-444-2661, or visit their Web site at www.bnblist.com/nh/bealhouse.

Mount Moosilauke (Benton)

Hikers and other visitors to Benton's Mount Moosilauke woods have reported seeing a shadowy form dart in between the trees; when they take a closer look, there is nobody to be found. Local lore states that the shadowy form might be Dr. Thomas Benton, an early-19th-century physician—descended from the town's earliest settlers, for whom the town was named—who was said to have lost his mind and gone into seclusion.

Thomas D'Agostino recounts the strange and twisted legend of Dr. Benton in his *Haunted New Hampshire*:

> [Benton] returned to his hometown a full fledged Doctor of Medicine. All was well. He even became engaged and sought a bright future for himself and his fiancée. Plans, however, were short lived. According to accounts, his fiancée died of typhoid fever, and in his despair, Thomas retreated from his practice to a mountain cabin that he had built for seclusion. . . .[75]

That was pretty much the last of Dr. Benton that residents of the area would see—at least in his earthly form. But it wasn't long before strange occurrences began happening both in Benton and nearby Woodstock. Livestock would disappear or be found mutilated, and eventually people began to vanish. Apparently many in the surrounding communities thought that Dr. Benton might have had a hand in these mysterious occurrences. It seems that in the doctor's possession was a trunk that contained the results of the experiments of his mentor, a professor at Benton's medical school. It has been said that the life's work of this professor—and, eventually, of the reclusive Dr. Benton—was the quest for eternal life and that Benton was using the livestock and citizens of nearby towns to carry out his twisted experiments:

> Fear began to fill the townsfolk. Experimenting on animals was one thing, but humans? Word got out that the babies from nearby towns were disappearing—kidnapped while they slept. It was concluded that Benton was stealing the toddlers for his experiments on immortality. The once friendly and amorous doctor was now the devil's concubine, using the blood of the young and innocent for his elusive serum.[76]

The legend goes on to state that one day Benton snatched a young girl out of her yard in broad daylight, and a posse was assembled to track him down; when they caught up with him, he began dangling the girl over a cliff. They pleaded with him to let her go, and let go of her he did—right over the cliff. As the posse attempted to rescue the girl, Benton escaped and was never seen again.

Today, people see the dark shadow of *something* darting between the trees of the dark New Hampshire wood surrounding Mount Moosilauke; some claim that this dark shadow is the spirit of Dr. Benton, still restless and roaming the forest, searching for his next victim so that he might carry on his experiments. Others claim that Benton might very well have succeeded in his experiments, achieving the long-sought secret of eternal youth—and the shadow roaming the forest is none other than Benton himself, still eluding capture.

How to find it: Scenic Mount Moosilauke is located in the forests between North Woodstock and Benton. The frequently hiked trails, which lead directly to the mountain's summit, are best accessed from Ravine Road. From I-93, take exit 32 onto NH 112 West. Go left onto NH 118. Ravine Road will be a right-hand turn after about 7 miles. Parking is available near the trail entrance on the right side of the road, near the Ravine Lodge.

Mount Washington (Coos County)

To the Native Americans who lived near New Hampshire's Presidential Mountain range before the arrival of European settlers, Mount Washington was known as *Agiocochook*, which translates to "Home of the Great Spirit." Perhaps it shouldn't be surprising, then, that Mount Washington is thought by many to be the abode of a mysterious force that has come to be known as "the Presence."

What the Presence might be is hard to put into words. It does ghostly things like knock on doors, project voices from unseen mouths, tramp footfalls from unseen feet, and rearrange objects in the Mount Washington Observatory. Apparently, witnesses have even seen solid objects suspended in midair right in front of their eyes. According to Joseph A. Citro's *Passing Strange*, "Those who

Photo courtesy of Dale Ewa Gelfand

Native Americans called Mount Washington the "Home of the Great Spirit," but today, many say it is home to a mischievous spirit known as the Presence.

have had a run-in with it somehow know intuitively that it is not a ghost."[77] Some who have encountered the mysterious being claim that it looks like an earthbound cloud but doesn't move the way a cloud would. Yet the Presence isn't thought to be anything living or even anything made of physical matter. It just *is*.

Citro posits that "different people experience [the Presence] in different ways, so everyone has their pet theories to explain it."[78] Some have only heard voices, laughter, or footfalls, yet some have felt a physical push knock them off balance. Some witnesses insist that the Presence is a benign (if a bit mischievous) spirit, yet others maintain that the Presence might be to blame for any number of Mount Washington's many mishaps—since 1888, an average of two people a year have died on New Hampshire's highest mountain.[79] Some even believe that the Presence was the cause for 1967's

Skyline Switch railway accident: at the junction the switch was always left in the "straight" position for the train to continue forward, but on the fateful day of September 17, 1967, something unseen pushed the switch out of position and caused the disaster, which killed eight passengers and injured many more.

Not man or animal or even ghost, the Presence might very well be a Great Spirit. Whether it is benign or malicious, we may never know—but it is telling that the Native Americans who named the mountain were said to have kept their distance.

How to find it: Mount Washington, part of the Presidential Range, is the highest point in the Northeast United States. From I-93, take exit 40 to NH 302 eastbound. Mount Washington itself is pretty difficult to miss, but the entrance is considered to be Base Road, off Route 302. For more information on the mountain, visit www.mount washington.com. For information on the Mount Washington Observatory, visit www.mountwashington.org.

Sugar Hill Inn (Sugar Hill)

Its breathtaking views of the Presidential Range and easy access to some of the best skiing in the Northeast notwithstanding, the Sugar Hill Inn began life simply as the sturdy, well-built 1789 farmhouse of the Oakes family, one of the first families to settle in the Franconia region. In 1929 the house became the Caramat Inn, a change that—much to the good fortune of the Richardson family who had purchased the property—coincided perfectly with the nearby inception of America's very first ski instruction school.[80] Nowadays the apparition of a man in the building's kitchen has been seen by multiple guests and staff members, and it is well known within the community that what appeared to be an elderly couple once walked through a solid wall in plain view of numerous witnesses.

How to find it: The Sugar Hill Inn is located on NH 117 in Sugar Hill. From I-93, take exit 38 onto NH 116 northbound; then bear right onto NH 18 through the town of Franconia. Go left onto

NH 117; the Sugar Hill Inn will be on the right-hand side about ½ mile up the road. For more information or to make reservations call 603-823-5621, e-mail info@sugarhillinn.com, or visit their Web site at www.sugarhillinn.com.

Stark Road Cemetery (Conway)

Travelers heading down Conway's Stark Road have reported seeing strange, glowing mists and "ghost lights"—floating, glowing orbs—hovering over the tiny plot of gravestones in the small community cemetery. Seeing that the graves belong mostly to the eponymous Stark family, local lore has it that the strange lights are their spirits keeping watch over the family plot.

How to find it: The Stark Road Cemetery is about 2 miles down Stark Road, between Eaton Road (NH 153) and East Main Street (NH 302 and NH 113), in Conway. From I-93, take exit 40 onto Main Street (NH 302), and go right onto Stark Road.

Toll Hill (Eaton Center)

The ghost of a white horse is said to roam the fields near his former farm, where local legend states that he was accidentally left out during a blizzard—due to his white coat and the storm's fury, the horse was neither seen nor heard trying to gain entry back into his barn. His body was discovered by his guilt- and grief-stricken owner at the gates of the barn a few mornings after the storm had passed.

How to find it: Toll Hill is a grassy plain on the aptly named Horseleg Hill Road. From I-93, take exit 32 onto NH 112; then turn right (southbound) onto NH 153. Travel approximately 10 miles on NH 153, and Horseleg Hill Road will be a left-hand turn.

DARTMOUTH AND THE LAKES REGION

Alton Town Hall (Alton)

During the 1920s, a town selectman named Arthur Twombly would use the spacious third floor of Alton's town hall building to host gala events, including band performances and ballroom dances. It is said that the same space is today haunted by the ghosts of past revelers—and some of the building's unexplained activity might be the doings of the spirit of Mr. Twombly himself.

Constructed in 1894, the brick-faced Alton Town Hall is prominent and unmistakable due to its 85-foot clock tower. Even though the town hall's clock has functioned without a problem since its construction, reports indicate that somebody still feels the need to check up on it now and then, for ghostly footfalls have apparently been heard ascending the empty stairwell on multiple occasions. The most frequent site of disturbances, however, is undoubtedly the third floor—the site of Mr. Twombly's social events—where phantom voices have often been heard, and the chairs have even been known to rearrange themselves as if in preparation for an upcoming gathering.[81]

How to find it: The imposing Alton Town Hall stands at 1 Monument Square (Main Street) in Alton. Take I-93 to exit 20 onto US 3 toward Laconia. Take NH 11A onto NH 11 southbound. Alton's town hall with its grand clock tower is fairly hard to miss. To contact the Alton Town Hall, send a letter to P.O. Box 659, Alton, NH 02809.

Bow Lake (Strafford)

Cries of distress, moans, and otherworldly screams are said to accompany strange lights after dark in the woods and around the shore of Bow Lake in southeastern New Hampshire. Nobody is quite sure what the cause of the disturbances is, but some say that the strange lights can be so bright that it's like the sun had risen over the lake in the wee hours of the morning.

How to find it: Bow Lake is on the border of Northwood and Strafford in southeastern New Hampshire. From I-93, take exit 14 onto NH 9 eastbound. Go left onto Bow Lake Road, which runs along Bow Lake.

Dartmouth College (Hanover)

One of the country's oldest and most prestigious private colleges, Dartmouth is similar in this way to a number of other New England institutions—and also in that it is said to be haunted. In particular, the Alpha Theta fraternity house has had a number of reports of unexplained apparitions roaming the building before disappearing into thin air. As is the case with so many supposedly haunted New England private colleges, students and alumni are surprisingly tight-lipped about the paranormal goings-on at their places of higher learning (see the entries in this volume about Yale University and Trinity College). Therefore, specific details about the Alpha Theta house's haunting are difficult to come by, although rumors abound. Local legend states that many decades ago, the frat house's boiler exploded, taking with it the house as well as several fraternity members and their girlfriends. This tale seems to be an inflated version of a true, tragic event: in the winter of 1934, gas leaking out of the furnace poisoned all the fraternity brothers and their girlfriends as they slept. Although a new Alpha Theta house was built on the property, the ghosts have apparently decided to stick around—rumors that the building was haunted began to circulate very soon following the tragedy.

How to find it: Dartmouth College is a private Ivy League college located in Hanover in western New Hampshire. From I-91, take exit 13 onto West Wheelock Street. The campus will be immediately visible. For more information about the school, call 603-646-1110, e-mail the school at contact@dartmouth.edu, or visit the school's official Web site at www.dartmouth.edu. For more information on the Alpha Theta fraternity at Dartmouth, e-mail alpha.theta@dartmouth.edu, or go to www.dartmouth.edu/~atheta/.

Kimball Castle (Gilford)

Kimball Castle was built in 1897 after railroad magnate Benjamin Kimball visited the German countryside and was inspired by the sprawling, Gothic estates that he saw on the Rhine River. The castle stayed within the family until 1960, when his son's wife died and willed it to the Mary Mitchell Humane Society and the Alvord Wildlife Sanctuary. Unfortunately these organizations didn't know quite what to do with the property, and it fell into a state of gross disrepair over the decades; sadly, looters and vandals took everything of value out of the castle. Perhaps it is this state of neglect that has awakened the home's spirits—presumably members of the Kimball family—for the apparition of a woman has been reportedly seen roaming the grounds, and the lights in Mrs. Kimball's old sewing rooms are said to turn themselves on and off. Many visitors may soon be able to experience these happenings themselves because the property was recently purchased by David and Mary Jodoin, who plan on opening the castle to the public as a toured museum once major renovations are completed.[82]

How to find it: Kimball Castle sits atop Lockes Hill Road in Gilford. From I-93, take exit 20 onto NH 11 eastbound toward Lanconia and Gilford. Go right onto Lake Shore Road, staying on NH 11. Turn right again on Lockes Hill Road.

Raccoon Mountain Road (Center Ossipee)

Phantom horses seem to like the New Hampshire countryside, as evidenced by the white steed in Eaton Center and this spectral steed, as well. Many travelers on Center Ossipee's Raccoon Mountain Road have claimed to have seen the apparition of a horse that suddenly appears, either following them or standing in the trail before them, only to have the horse disappear as suddenly as it appeared. Some travelers have even claimed that they thought the horse was real until they tried to pet it and their hand passed right through the animal.[83] Local lore states that the horse belonged to a rider who fell into a nearby ravine and perished, and the horse was never recovered.

How to find it: Raccoon Mountain Road in Center Ossipee is located near Ossipee Lake, just beyond the Moultonville Mill Pond Bridge. From I-93, take exit 23 onto NH 104 eastbound. Turn onto

NH 25 east toward Moultonborough and Moultonville. Just past the intersection of NH 25 and NH 16, take a left onto Raccoon Mountain Road. The phantom horse has been reported galloping up and down the entire length of the road.

merrimack valley

Country Tavern (Nashua)

The charming and inviting Country Tavern was built as a private residence in 1741. When the restaurant opened its doors for business in 1982, the very first meal served there ended up on the floor—unseen hands reportedly sent the plate flying off the table right in front of the stunned customers.[84] Since then those unseen hands have smashed glasses against walls, dumped salad dressing on the floor, turned the radio and lights on and off unexpectedly, and tampered with waitress's hairstyles—while they are trying to serve guests. Paranormal researcher Christopher Balzano relates that one night, a Country Tavern guest went out to the back parking lot to have a cigarette. As he stood there smoking, he noticed that the dining room's door swung open and closed at least a dozen times although nobody seemed to be anywhere near it, let alone walking through it. Asking the staff about the phenomenon, he was told that the dining room was not in use on that particular night.[85]

Speculation is that the ghost of one Elizabeth Ford, the building's original tenant, is not happy that her former home is now open to the public. And given her tragic story, it's hardly surprising that her spirit would be a restless one—even if she weren't annoyed at having her home invaded by strangers. She married a wealthy sea captain, who built her the beautiful home that today houses the Country Tavern. When the sea captain returned to Nashua after a 10-month voyage, however, he was shocked and dismayed to find that his beloved bride had just given birth.[86] After doing the math and realizing that there was no possible way that he could be the child's father, Elizabeth's husband went into a rage and murdered both mother and child, then quickly fled. Aside from the physical phenomena taking place in the restaurant, the apparition of a woman with light hair wearing a flowing, white gown has also been reported throughout the Country Tavern's years in operation. That this woman in white matches the physical description of Elizabeth Ford certainly comes as no surprise to anybody. In fact, the Country Tavern's Web site not only proudly announces that their establishment's haunting has been covered by *Hard Copy* and *Unsolved Mysteries,* it also attributes the building's paranormal activity to Elizabeth's ghost, and the restaurant's menu proudly relates the site's ghostly history.

How to find it: The Country Tavern is located at 452 Amherst Street in Nashua. From US 3, take exit 6 onto Amherst Street (NH 101) westbound. For more information, call 603-889-5871, or visit the restaurant's Web site at www.countrytavern.org.

Devil's Den (Auburn)

The "ghost lights" of Mine Hill's "Devil's Den" have perplexed and fascinated New Hampshire hikers and sightseers for centuries. Simply stated, ghosts lights are balls of energy—similar to the orbs often caught on film via spirit photography but visible to the naked eye—that appear seemingly from nowhere and dance and dart through the ether, eventually disappearing as suddenly as they had appeared. Also called will-o-the-wisp and *ignus fatuus,* among other names throughout history, ghost lights have classically been written off as either marsh gas or ball lightning by scientists. Those more spiritualistically inclined, however, might be more apt to believe that ghost lights are physical representations of a spirit's energy. Some even think that ghost lights are our glimpse of an afterlife funeral procession, the lights being ghostly candles being carried through the woods. Whatever the cause of the ghost lights that have been seen wandering the woods of Mine Hill, the phenomenon remains as fascinating as it is unexplainable.

How to find it: The Devil's Den is located in the woods of Mile Hill in and around Auburn. The woods are most easily accessed off Bunker Hill Road; from NH 101, take exit 1 southbound onto

NH 128, Manchester Road. Continue on NH 128 for approximately 2 miles, and then turn left onto Bunker Hill Road.

Gilson Road Cemetery (Nashua)

Gibson Road Cemetery, a small and tranquil plot of grave markers in southern New Hampshire, has gained some notoriety among the paranormal community for being an exceptionally active site of unexplained goings-on. Many, many witnesses have claimed to hear voices flitting around the gravestones even when they've been alone in the cemetery; numerous photographs taken at the graveyard have been developed showing shadowy forms, misty figures, and glowing orbs; and some people have even claimed to see the apparition of a black, hooded figure standing by the cemetery's farthest wall. The New England Ghost Project (www.neghost project.com), Ghost Quest (www.ghostquest.org), and Thomas D'Agostino [87] have all investigated the Gilson Road Cemetery, and each and every investigation has produced some degree of what is claimed to be a ghost photograph or an electronic voice phenomenon (EVP) recording.

How to find it: The Gilson Road Cemetery is located on Gilson Road in Nashua, near the Massachusetts border. From US 3, take exit 5W onto West Hollis Street (NH 111). Go left onto Country Side Drive, then left again onto Gilson Road. The cemetery is less than ½ mile down Gilson Road.

Griffin Memorial School (Litchfield)

A small, quiet little school nestled in the rural community of Litchfield, Griffin Memorial School is reportedly home to a series of unexplained, recurring events, such as voices that whisper down empty halls and desks that rearrange themselves into strange patterns within empty classrooms. Also reportedly seen in and around the school is the apparition of a little boy running around, seemingly playfully. A local legend holds that a young boy accidentally hanged himself on a fence that surrounds the nearby ballfield,[88] and speculation among believers in the paranormal is that it's this boy's ghost who has been sighted and is responsible for the strange goings-on that have been witnessed by maintenance crews within the school after hours.

How to find it: The Griffin Memorial School is located at 229 Charles Bancroft Highway (NH 3A) in Litchfield. From the Everett Turnpike (US 3), take exit 5 onto NH 111, and cross the Merrimack River. Take a left onto Webster Street, which will merge with NH 3A after about a mile. The school is 6 miles farther on NH 3A. For more information, call the Griffin Memorial School at 603-424-5931.

Indian Rock Road (Nashua)

A disproportionately large number of black skid marks adorn the asphalt on Indian Rock Road near the Boire Field Airport. Perhaps there are simply a lot of muscle car aficionados in the region who like to light up their rear tires in a display of horsepower-driven machismo, but the local legend surrounding this road is that the apparition of a little boy often runs out into the road in front of speeding cars, forcing the drivers to swerve or brake frantically to avoid hitting him. On investigation, those who claimed to have seen the phantom boy report, there is nobody to be found. Some locals claim that the boy lived nearby and chased a ball out into the road before being cut down by a hit-and-run driver, yet others claim that the boy's family lived nearby, and they were all murdered in a botched robbery—the child shot in the back as he tried to escape across the road.

How to find it: Indian Rock Road is located near Daniel Webster College and the Boire Field Airport in Nashua. From US 3, take exit 7W onto Amherst Street (NH 101A). Go left onto Charron Avenue; after traveling about 1,000 feet, take a right onto Pine Hill Road. After about a half a mile, take another right onto Indian Rock Road.

New Hampshire State Hospital (Concord)

Once called the Asylum for the Insane, the New Hampshire State Hospital is a well-known and well-respected mental health care facility located in Concord. Being a hospital that has been host to numerous troubled souls over the years, perhaps it shouldn't come as a surprise that many of the hospital's former residents have apparently stayed on long after their earthbound tenure has ended. Over the years many employees have reported such disturbances such footfalls echoing down empty corridors, elevators traveling to floors without being summoned, and stacks of paperwork being pushed off desks.

How to find it: The New Hampshire State Hospital is a publicly funded mental health care facility located at 36 Clinton Street in Concord. From I-93, take exit 14 onto Bridge Street. Turn left at the second light onto Main Street, and then turn right onto Pleasant Street after passing the Capitol Building. From Pleasant Street, bear left onto South Street, and then bear right onto Clinton Street. After passing the Concord courthouse, the New Hampshire State Hospital will be on the right. Due to the nature of treatment at the New Hampshire State Hospital, the building is considered private property; trespassing is not recommended. For more information, call 603-271-5300 or 800-852-3345, extension 5300; or visit the hospital's Web site at www.dhhs.state.nh.us/DHHS/NHH/default.htm.

Pine Hill Cemetery (Hollis)

A collection of nearly ancient grave markers, the Pine Hill Cemetery is known to many locals as "Blood Cemetery" due to the large number of interred members of the Blood family who reside there. Local legend states that Abel Blood and a number of his Blood relations (sorry, I couldn't resist) still walk the cemetery at night, restless and without peace for one reason or another. Many even claim that this restlessness is due to the fact that the entire family was murdered—even though anybody taking the time to read the dates on the grave makers would see that the Blood family passed on at lengthy intervals from one another, a number of them leading long lives into their 70s. It is also said that if one walks through the Pine Hill Cemetery at night, sometimes the hand on Abel Blood's gravestone, which is eternally pointing up toward heaven,

The hand marking Abel Blood's headstone in the Pine Hill Cemetery in Hollis is said to turn itself around to point to the earth.

actually turns around to point down at the ground—or, perhaps, toward hell.[89]

How to find it: The Pine Hill Cemetery is located on Nartoff Road in Hollis. From US 3, take exit 6 onto Broad Street (NH 130) west-bound. Nartoff Road will be a right-hand turn off Broad Street. The cemetery is located near the intersection of Nartoff Road and Pine Hill Road.

River Road (Manchester)

Manchester's River Road is home to a bizarre local legend about a phantom jogger with white hair and red running shorts who mate-rializes and runs a distance, ignoring any people who approach him and try to talk to him. According to reports, numerous wit-nesses have gathered to see the incredible spectacle for them-selves, but sources disagree on when the phantom jogger actually appears—Shadowlands, the online haunted-places index, claims that the ghost jogger appears every Halloween night at 1:45 AM,[90] whereas Thomas D'Agostino's *Haunted New Hampshire* claims that the jogger appears simply at "about 2:00 AM."[91] Witnesses who have claimed to see the phantom jogger say that one can hear the jogger's footfalls, but he leaves no imprint on the ground, even if there is freshly fallen snow.

How to find it: River Road in Manchester is located alongside Stark Park near the Merrimack River. From I-293, take exit 6 onto Front Street. Go right onto Amoskeag Road, and cross the Merrimack River. Take a left onto Elm Street (US 3), and take another left onto River Road. River Road runs approximately 3 miles along the Merrimack River, and the phantom jogger has reportedly been seen getting in his workout all along the road's length.

Siam Orchid Restaurant (Concord)

This popular Thai eatery in downtown Concord has become as well known within the community for its well-documented unexplained disturbances as it has for its delicious meals. It seems that employees and patrons alike have reported hearing voices speak to them, only to find . . . nothing when they turn around to see who is addressing them. It has also become fairly commonplace for cups and glasses to slide independently across tables at the Siam Orchid, often in the middle of busy lunch and dinner rushes. And residents of the building's upstairs apartments have apparently reported hearing loud noises emanating from the restaurant—of the type that might accompany heavy furniture being moved around—during the middle of the night, when the restaurant was empty and securely locked. Although the disturbances at the Siam Orchid have been documented in books (such as Thomas D'Agostino's *Haunted New Hampshire* [92]) and various Web sites, no explanation is given for the restaurant's apparent haunting. The identities of the alleged spirits at the restaurant remain a mystery—nonetheless, many guests and employees have been experiencing something very out of the ordinary.

How to find it: The Siam Orchid Restaurant is located at 158 Main Street in Concord, New Hampshire. From I-93, take exit 14 onto Loudon Road (NH 9). The restaurant is on the corner of Loudon Road and Main Street. Call 603-228-1529 or 603-228-3633, or visit their Web site at www.siamorchid.net.

Tío Juan's Margaritas Mexican Restaurant & Watering Hole (Concord)

The successful and popular chain of Margaritas restaurants—which has locations all over the Northeast—had its origins in Concord, New Hampshire, when a businessman named John Pelletier transformed a steakhouse into Tío Juan's Mexican Restaurant & Watering Hole in the 1980s. Before becoming Tío Juan's the building was Concord's original courthouse, police station, and jail. It's the building's role as a jailhouse, locals reckon, that is the source of the restaurant's recurring paranormal phenomena: plates, glasses, and chairs move by themselves—the last of these often while patrons are sitting on them!—voices are heard emanating from empty spaces, and occasionally guests' alcoholic beverages disappear right out of their glasses.

When the Concord jailhouse was converted into a restaurant in the 1970s, the owners opted to design the restaurant around the building's structure rather than to attempt a costly and time-consuming renovation. The results are an idiosyncratic and unique dining experience that includes the host greeting restaurant guests from what used to be the courthouse witness stand and a special seating area of "dining cells"—formerly the jail cells, now converted into dining areas that have been colorfully painted with Mexican-themed murals. Whether the establishment's former status as a jailhouse has any connection with the building's current alleged spirit—who has been affectionately dubbed "George" by the restaurant staff[93]—the restaurant has attracted many patrons who might otherwise be indifferent toward Mexican food.

How to find it: The original Tío Juan's Margaritas Mexican Restaurant & Watering Hole in Concord stands at 1 Bicentennial

Square, which becomes Warren Street at the end of the block. From I-93, take exit 14 to Loudon Road (NH 9). Go left onto Main Street, and then make the first left onto Bicentennial Square/ Warren Street. Call the Concord location at 603-224-2821 or visit the chain's Web site at www.margs.com.

Vale End Cemetery (Wilton)

There appears a moral attached to the local legends that surround the Vale End Cemetery, for it would seem that a lack of respect for the dead has produced the graveyard's various alleged ghosts. Two apparitions have been reportedly seen by many witnesses through the years—an old man and a younger woman. Local legend states that a young man had his deceased bride's grave marker moved, but left the body in its resting place; the ghost of the young woman is actually the bride, and the ghost of the old man is her father, searching for the grave marker so that he can pay his respects. The Vale End Cemetery is also home to a column of blue mist that seems to rise from the shared grave of Mary Ritter and Mary Spaulding; apparently a man who was married to both women at different times had the bright idea to bury them both under the same headstone since they were both named Mary. If the reports of blue mist are true, it seems as though one or both of the Marys didn't approve of this idea.[94] Several paranormal investigators have visited the site and stated that their visits have produced convincing ghost photographs and EVP recordings. A group that calls itself TrueGhost has posted a picture on their Web site, www.trueghost.com, taken by team member Shane Sirois, that depicts a blue mist floating in front of the picture's frame.[95]

How to find it: The Vale End Cemetery is located on the Isaac Frye Highway in Wilton. It is open to the public during the day but closes nightly from 7 PM to 7 AM. (There have been unfortunate incidents of vandalism at the graveyard, so please be respectful of this and every other location listed in this volume.) From US 3, take exit 7W onto Amherst Street (NH 101A). NH 101A will become

Milford Road, then Nashua Street, then Elm Street. Just after NH 101A merges with NH 101, bear right onto Wilton Road (NH 31), which will become Forest Road. Take a left onto the Burton Highway, then another left onto the Isaac Frye Highway. The cemetery will be on the left, about 1,000 feet past the intersection with Putnam Hill Road.

Windham Restaurant (Windham)

Built in 1812 as a private residence for the Dinsmore family, what is now the Windham Restaurant has existed as an eatery for most of the 20th century, although the building's ownership and culinary specialty has changed numerous times over that span. Nowadays the Windham Restaurant offers fine dining in an inviting, casual atmosphere. The sign that hangs over the door reads FOOD AND SPIRITS, and, as the restaurant's own Web site suggests, the "spirits" offered by the eatery might be "truer than you think"[96] for there have been reports over many years of unexplained yet mischievous phenomena at the Windham Restaurant as well as the building's previous incarnations as Thai and French establishments. According to the restaurant's Web site, "Sometimes, when the staff would come in early in the morning they would find the chairs on the second floor turned around facing the window like someone was watching a parade. The place settings would also be moved so the forks and knives were crossed like an X."[97] The Web site also describes a pair of events that occurred involving empty boxes that were wrapped as holiday decorations—the boxes were found stacked like towers and then later suspended in midair over the stairway.

Paranormal researcher Ron Kolek, the lead investigator for the New England Ghost Project, claims that while he was present, a waitress's necklace fell off her neck and onto the ground; the woman then began to cry out of frustration—it was far from the first time that such an event had occurred.[98] It is also a common occurrence, according to reports, to see plates or wine glasses fly off shelves and shatter onto the floor. It isn't clear who the Windham

Restaurant's phantom prankster might be, but several sources claim that at least three apparitions have been seen in the building: a little boy, a little girl, and a man wearing a blue suit. The man in the blue suit—playfully nicknamed "Jacob" by the staff—has caused the most consternation at the restaurant. One of the building's current owners, a woman named Loula, saw a man wearing a blue suit fall down the main stairs; when she rushed to help him, the man vanished.

The New England Ghost Project has investigated the Windham Restaurant, and the trip has produced what they claim to be very convincing ghost photographs as well as some startlingly eerie EVP recordings. Their findings can be seen at the NEGP Web site: www.neghostproject.com/casefiles/windhamrest.htm.

How to find it: The Windham Restaurant is located at 59 Range Road in Windham. From I-93, take exit 3 onto Indian Rock Road (NH 111), and turn right to travel westbound. Take a right onto Range Road (NH 111A).

new Hampshire seacoast

Cocheco Mill (Dover)

A collection of small businesses occupy the site of what was once the Cocheco Mills, a riverfront Dover property that's also home to many unexplainable sights and sounds that might very well be linked to the mill's past tragedies and misfortunes. Unfair and dangerous business practices marked the building's early days, with many female workers forced to labor obscenely long hours for very little pay during the 19th-century era predating labor unions. Many of these women were said to have fallen victim to the dangerous machinery used to refine the mill's cotton crop. But the mill's greatest single misfortune was undoubtedly the massive fire of January 26, 1907, in which at least four people lost their lives.[99]

Although the mill buildings currently house a variety of separate businesses, the site's connection to the past is apparently strong if the nature of its reported paranormal phenomena is credible. Passersby have been said to regularly witness lights emanating from presumably locked buildings, including the mill's basement, which has been closed up for years, and voices as well as the sound of industrial machinery have been said to echo throughout the buildings' empty corridors long past closing.

How to find it: The former Cocheco Mills site is located on the Cochecho River (the misspelling of the company's name was a result of a clerical error at the company's inception[100]), at 1 Washington Center in Dover, New Hampshire. From I-95, take exit 5 to Spaulding Turnpike (NH 16) westbound. From NH 16, take exit 8 to NH 9 east. The mill buildings take up an entire block bordered by Washington Street, Main Street, and Central Avenue.

John Paul Jones House (Portsmouth)

Now a historic museum that conducts occasional seasonal tours, the John Paul Jones House was built by Gregory Purcell and his young wife, Sarah, in 1758. When her husband passed away, Sarah decided to turn the stately, handsome home into an inn to generate some income. The building's name is derived from the fact that American Revolutionary naval hero John Paul Jones stayed in the inn numerous times while he was in New Hampshire—and there is even some speculation that he and Sarah Purcell were carrying on a sustained affair. The house changed hands a number of times before it was purchased by the Portsmouth Historical Society and made into the town's first museum. Throughout the years, many witnesses have claimed to see the apparition of a woman's face staring out the front windows of the house, especially on days on which the building was closed to the public. Is the John Paul Jones House's wistful ghost that of Sarah Purcell, staring out the window and hoping for her lover to return for another stay at her inn? This seems like one of history's puzzles just begging for a formal paranormal investigation.

How to find it: The John Paul Jones House, located at 43 Middle Street in Portsmouth, is now both a museum and the home of the

Portsmouth Historical Society and is open to the public for tours on selected days. From I-95, take exit 7 onto Market Street eastbound. Go right on State Street (US 1); the John Paul Jones House is on the corner of State Street and Middle Street. For more information, visit the Portsmouth Historical Society's Web site at www .portsmouthhistory.org

Moulton Home (Hampton)

God have mercy! icy cold
Spectral hands her own enfold,
Drawing silently from them
Love's fiar gifts of gold and gem
"Waken! Save me!" still as death
At her side he slumbereth.

Ring and bracelet all are gone,
And that ice-cold hand withdrawn;
But she hears a murmur low,
Full of sweetness, full of woe,
Half a sigh and half a moan:
"Fear not! give the dead her own!"

—John Greenleaf Whitter, "The New Wife and the Old"

Strange legends revolve around the name Moulton in New Hampshire—so much so that John Greenleaf Whittier, the author of "Palatine" (see the entry on the Palatine Light in the Rhode Island chapter), wrote a poem about them. Considering the nature of these legends, it's no surprise that the mansion that bears the family name is said to have a ghost or two roaming the grounds. The Moulton home was built in 1763 by businessman, soldier, and state representative Jonathan Moulton [101] and his wife, Abigail. The man was allegedly a ruthless and cunning businessman, so much so that there were whispers of a deal with the devil. The rumor was that Moulton had sold his soul so that the devil would supply him with greater and greater wealth each month. Once a month, Moulton was said to leave an empty boot on the fireplace hearth, and Satan or one of his minions would climb down his chimney like a demented Santa Claus and fill the boot with gold ore. This legend was used to explain away Moulton's amazing accumulation of wealth as well as the fate of his original house; Thomas D'Agostino shares the legend in his book *Haunted New Hampshire*:

Old Moulton revered himself as a sharp dealer in business. It would seem that he thought he could con the curiosity out of a cat. When the devil went to fill his boot on the Ides of March in 1769, he found that no matter how much he put in, the leather would not load up. Satan pulled the boot from the hearth and found that not only was the sole cut out, it was placed over a hole cut in the floor so that the gold streamed into the cellar. The irate Lucifer immediately went into a hellish rage and burned the house to the ground.[102]

The attempt by Moulton to take advantage of the devil apparently cost him his deal, for after building a new home on the property in 1770 (there must be some kind of potential joke in the story about the destruction of Moulton's sole), Jonathan Moulton was broke.

It was around this time, local legend states, that Moulton brought another curse upon himself: as his wife was dying from smallpox, she made him vow not to remarry, or else she would come back and haunt him. Abigail died in September 1775; Moulton remarried within a year. Not only did Moulton break his vow to his beloved Abigail, he was said to have taken the expensive jewelry off her corpse before she was buried and given them to his new bride, Sarah, as a gift. According to the stories, it wasn't long before the couple was plagued with the sounds of doors slamming in the middle of the night, and several witnesses claimed to have seen Abigail, wearing her funeral gown, roaming around the home's grounds. It is even said that one night, as Jonathan and Sarah settled in for dinner, an unseen entity pulled the jewelry off Sarah's person and it floated out of the room, never to be seen again.[103]

After Moulton passed away in 1787, he was interred in a plot on the property, alongside Abigail's grave, and the house was sold to a family named Whipple. Although Jonathan was gone, apparently Abigail continued to haunt the old house, and an exorcism was eventually performed to rid the building of her spirit. Following the exorcism, the Whipples were said to have lived a quiet, ghost-free existence in the old house—until plans for a new railroad caused the house to be moved to a new plot of land in Hampton, and the railroad tracks were laid right on top of where Jonathan and Abigail were buried. Since then, Abigail's apparition has once again been reported in and around the old house, which today is the office of an insurance agent.

How to find it: The Moulton homestead, now a privately owned insurance office, stands at the corner of Drakeside Road and Lafayette Road (US 1) in Hampton. From I-95, take exit 2 onto NH 101 eastbound. Exit at Lafayette Road, after which one must pull a U-turn or turn around in a driveway to travel down Lafayette Road in the other direction. The house will be on the corner of Lafayette and Drakeside roads, on the right, just a few hundred feet from where NH 101 meets US 1.

The Rockingham Building (Portsmouth)

Built sometime in the late 18th century for Woodbury Langdon, the brother of former New Hampshire governor John Langdon, the Rockingham building—a large, stately brick edifice with green window boxes—practically towers over the surrounding small houses. In 1884 the building was converted into a hotel by beer brewer Frank Jones, and for many years the hotel was one of the most successful in New England, being considered "the most elegant and superbly furnished establishment . . . outside of Boston."[104] In 1973 the hotel was converted into apartments. Since then, the apparition of a woman wearing a white dress, who is said to be accompanied by an overwhelming odor of salty ocean air, has been reported roaming the building's halls by numerous tenants and visitors. Some say that the woman was a hotel guest who drowned in nearby Round Pond; still others claim that the apparition belongs to Woodbury Langdon's wife. Whoever the apparition might be, nobody seems quite sure what connection the scent of ocean air might have with the departed.

How to find it: The Rockingham—which now houses condos—is located at 401 State Street in Nashua. From US 3, take exit 7W onto Amherst Street (NH 101A). State Street will be a left-hand turn.

Sheafe Street Inn (Portsmouth)

If the reports are accurate, the small, unassuming Sheafe Street Inn is home to a ghost (or ghosts) with some very peculiar habits that apparently reflect some kind of personal moral code, for it has become commonplace for bottles of liquor brought by guests to their rooms to be inexplicably smashed, and culinary tools in the hotel's attached bakery have been said to put themselves away neatly while the cook's back is turned. What is especially curious about these behaviors is how they juxtapose with the alleged ghost's apparent hatred for sailors and women: examples abound of both types of people being shoved to the ground by an unseen force in and around the inn.[105] The spectral culprit might actually be two distinct entities, for the apparitions of both a horseman and a hunter have been reportedly seen within the building throughout the years.

How to find it: The Sheafe Street Inn is located at 3 Sheafe Street in Portsmouth. From I-95, take exit 7 onto Market Street eastbound. Go right on Market Street, then right again onto Sheafe Street. For more information, call 603-436-9104.

Sise Inn (Portsmouth)

What is now the Sise Inn began as a private residence, built for one Charles Treadwell in 1798. A family named Marsh took over the property sometime in the early 19th century, but the house got its permanent name when a merchant named John Sise married Lucy Marsh, and the couple moved into the Marsh estate. The building changed hands a number of times in the 20th century before becoming a place of lodging in 1986.

It appears that at least one of the Sise Inn's former residents has decided to dwell in the old house permanently and refuses to leave. The inn has been host to various unexplained phenomena over the years, most of which seems to center around room 204. For some reason, keys to room 204 are constantly misplaced and disappear without explanation. Sometimes the key to room 204 simply will not open the door's lock; at other times, the door to this room is found wide open even though it had been previously closed and locked.[106] There was also an incident that occurred involving the hotel's third-floor ice machine when the building was completely vacant except for the on-duty desk clerk, who heard the ice machine spitting out ice cubes. When she went upstairs to investigate, she found a trail of ice cubes leading to room 204, where a pile of the cubes was melting on the floor.[107]

Although the Sise Inn's disturbances most frequently occur in room 204, other incidents have been reported elsewhere in the hotel, many involving female guests and staff. Indeed, it would appear that the Sise Inn's resident ghost may have a taste for the young ladies, for female guests have reported feeling a physical presence lie down beside them in bed, and female staff members have felt hands touching them, as if someone were grabbing their hips or even, in some startling cases, trying to push them into a closet or a corner.[108]

How to find it: The elegant Sise Inn is located at 40 Court Street in Portsmouth. From I-95, take exit 7 onto Market Street eastbound. Go right onto Court Street just beyond where Market Street crosses US 1. For more information or to make reservations—request room 204 if you dare—call 603-433-1200 or 877-747-3466, e-mail the innkeepers at info@siseinn.com, or visit the inn's official Web site at www.siseinn.com.

Three Chimneys Inn and ffrost Sawyer Tavern (Durham)

Wealthy colonial entrepreneur Valentine Hill built his Durham house in 1649, and he built it well—it was apparently sturdy enough to withstand a barrage of Native American attacks in 1694 that left most neighboring dwellings in smoldering ruins.[109] The

The ghost of Hannah Sawyer is said to haunt the otherwise peaceful Three Chimneys Inn in Durham.

home went through several hands and underwent many changes before becoming the Three Chimneys Inn in 1998. Valentine Hill's son Nathaniel renovated and added to the house, subsequent descendants built a barn, and a graveyard was installed on the property. The early 1800s saw new owner George ffrost II renovate the house—which at that point could rightly be termed a mansion—into a Federal-style structure, and the ffrost family improved the property, including the addition of beautiful gardens. 1912 saw a new generation of ffrosts install a swimming pool and tennis courts.[110]

The Hill/ffrost house was not without its share of tragedy, however. A young girl named Hannah Sawyer, who was living in what is now the inn's guestroom number 6, was said to have committed suicide in her bedroom. A portrait of Hannah, her doe eyes glancing up from a book, still adorns the room; if the eyewitness reports of many of the Three Chimneys Inn's guest and staff are any indication, Hannah's spirit might very well adorn the building, as well. The inn has had the usual sort of unexplained phenomena common to colonial-era New England buildings: heavy footfalls echoing down empty corridors and emanating from vacant rooms (especially the guestrooms known as the Rafters and the Loft[111]), doors locking and unlocking themselves, rocking chairs swaying on their own, appliances and electrical devices turning themselves on and off, and the like—but the Three Chimneys Inn is truly remarkable for the apparition of Hannah Sawyer that has appeared before a number of witnesses over the past several decades. According to Thomas D'Agostino's *Haunted New Hampshire*, the apparition of a young girl, looking exactly like the portrait hanging in guestroom 6, has appeared on the stairway peering down on the guests and staff below. Investigating the inn for himself, D'Agostino captured what he believes to be a partial ghost photograph, as his attempt to photograph the portrait of Hannah Sawyer revealed what appears to be the translucent outline of a young woman standing in front of the portrait.

How to find it: The Federal-style Three Chimneys Inn, complete with an attached tavern known as ffrost Sawyer's, is located at 17 Newmarket Road in Durham. From I-95, take exit 4—the Spaulding Turnpike exit—onto NH 4 and NH 16 northbound. When NH 4 and NH 16 split, take NH 4 (Piscataqua Road) onto Dover Road South (NH 108). Go left onto Newmarket Street, and the Three Chimneys Inn will be on the left. For more information or to make reservations, call 888-399-9777, or visit their Web site at www.threechimneysinn.com.

part four
founding phantoms:
haunted
massachusetts

Guests at the imposing Hawthorne Hotel in Salem have reportedly
found themselves sharing accommodations with a lively—
though not living—being.

B oston. Cambridge. Salem. The names of these Massachusetts towns are practically synonymous with American history—and being among this country's oldest settlements, they are considered extremely haunted. Indeed, given the sheer number of supposedly haunted locations in northeast Massachusetts, the 50-mile radius around Boston might have one of the highest ghost concentrations in the United States. This region, along with the colonial homes turned into B&Bs on Cape Cod, might very well make Massachusetts the most haunted state in the country. The stories, I believe, will speak for themselves.

One story in particular represents a cautionary tale warning about the dangers of messing with inexplicable forces. The reported haunting of Charlesgate Hall in Boston's Kenmore Square is one that will send chills down the spine of anybody who has ever considered using a Ouija board to contact the spirits of the deceased. When you attempt to contact the spirits of the dead, the experts warn, it might be powerful, malignant forces that cross over, not a peaceful, loving spirit of the dear relative or friend you might be attempting to contact.

Northeast Region

Baker's Island Lighthouse (Baker's Island)

Maine doesn't hold a monopoly on haunted lighthouses, as the Baker's Island Light, the Boston Harbor Light, and several of the Cape Cod lighthouses prove. Baker's Island, which is 5 miles or so off the coast of Salem Harbor, is itself a fairly idiosyncratic place—the island, one of 15 northern Massachusetts islands known as the Miseries due to the inordinate number of shipwrecks suffered on their shores, is inhabited by a couple dozen vacationing families during the summer months but completely abandoned except for the lighthouse keeper during the winter. Baker Island remains electricity free, and all the homes on the island are illuminated by gaslight. Moreover, the island is said to be home to a number of paranormal inhabitants.

Ghosts apparently take up winter residence in many of the summer homes—it is said that many of the temporarily uninhabited homes have lights that turn themselves on in the dead of night; this apparently is also a frequent occurrence in the island's general store, both when the island is abandoned for the winter as well as in its more populous summer months. And a malicious-sounding entity is said to roam the island. Known as the Beast of Baker Island, this evil presence is reported to physically harass and pester island inhabitants, knocking them down in the dark like an unseen animal pouncing from the night shadows. Baker's Island is also home to a mischievous specter whose residence in the island's lighthouse is frequently made known to everybody on the island. Baker's Island's lighthouse is equipped with a loud foghorn that for years has sounded itself for no apparent reason in the middle of crystal-clear nights when the lighthouse keeper (and, indeed, everybody else on the island) had been fast asleep. Lighthouse keepers reported the apparent malfunction to the Coast Guard several times over the years, but repairmen could never find anything wrong with the foghorn.[112] It is a rare situation indeed when the most logical and rational explanation for a phenomenon happens to be a ghost with a mischievous sense of humor.

How to find it: Baker's Island is located in Salem Harbor, near Beverly, and is only accessible by boat. The lighthouse, which is closed to the general public, is located on the north end of Baker's Island and can be seen distantly from a number of area beaches, including Salem Willows Park and Winter Island in Salem, Chandler Hovey Park on Marblehead Neck, and Manchester-by-the-Sea's Boardman Avenue and Harbor Street area.[113]

Hawthorne Hotel (Salem)

Built in 1925 on the site of the original 1766 Salem Marine Society building, the Hawthorne Hotel is a six-story lodging house with 89 guestrooms, at least one of which is rumored to be haunted. According to Cheri Revai's *Haunted Massachusetts*, a guest once complained that he didn't like having to share a bathroom with an adjoining room and was annoyed to see the bathroom light on and hear the toilet flushing while he was in his room. His annoyance turned to alarm when he learned that his room, number 325, had sole access to the bathroom.[114]

The Hawthorne Hotel building is also still home to the Salem Marine Society, a benevolent society whose headquarters are on the Hawthorne's rooftop. It has been reported that the society's charts and furniture occasionally reorganize themselves. In addition, an antique ship's wheel has been said to rotate of its own accord.[115]

How to find it: The Hawthorne Hotel is located at 18 Washington Square West in Salem. From I-95, take exit 45 onto MA 128 north. Then take exit 26 onto Lowell Street east. Go left onto Essex Street, and then right onto Washington Street. Take a left onto New Derby Street (MA 1A north), which will lead directly into Washington Square. The Hawthorne Hotel will be on the right-hand side of MA 1A. For reservations or other information call 978-744-4080 or 800-729-7829, e-mail info@hawthornehotel.com, or visit the hotel's Web site at www.hawthornehotel.com.

House of the Seven Gables (Salem)

Built as the Turner-Ingersoll manor in 1668, New England's oldest existing mansion overlooks Salem's harbor. Now a museum open to the public, the mansion was the home of Susannah Ingersoll, Hawthorne's cousin, and has a rich history that makes its purported ghosts an unsurprising proposition. At one time a stop on the Underground Railroad, complete with hidden stairways and secret passages, the Turner-Ingersoll mansion and its history was also said to be the inspiration for Nathaniel Hawthorne's novel *The House of the Seven Gables*. The book largely deals with the concept of ancestral guilt[116]—the author's own great-grandfather was one of the leading antagonists of the infamous Salem Witch Trials—and implies that there might very well have been a curse placed on the land. Photographs of the Turner-Ingeroll house have been said to reveal spectral faces looking out from darkened windows,[117] and various apparitions that visitors have claimed to have witnessed

The Salem house that was Nathaniel Hawthorne's inspiration for his *House of the Seven Gables* is rumored to be the permanent residence of his cousin Susannah.

range from a spectral dressmaker to a young Victorian-era boy to slave children to Susannah Ingersoll herself.

How to find it: The House of the Seven Gables, also known as the Turner-Ingersoll Mansion, stands at 54 Turner Street in Salem. Nathaniel Hawthorne's own childhood home has been relocated from its original site a few blocks away and now stands as a supplemental museum on the Turner-Ingersoll property. From I-95, take exit 45 onto MA 128 north. Then take exit 26 onto Lowell Street east. Go left onto Essex Street and then right onto Washington Street. Take a left onto New Derby Street (MA 1A north), which will become Derby Street. Follow Derby Street into Salem's harbor area, and go right onto Turner Street and into the museum property. For more information or for tour reservations, call 978-744-0991, or visit the museum's Web site at www.7gables.org.

Joshua Ward House (Salem)

Originally built in the mid-1780s for wealthy sea captain Joshua Ward, this brick Federal-style mansion eventually became the final resting place for one of Salem's most infamous residents and now holds the distinction of being considered the town's most haunted house—and quite possibly one of the most haunted houses in New England. Sheriff George Corwin was one of the leading inquisitors of the Salem Witch Trial who was said to have been cursed by a man named Giles Corey—falsely accused of being a warlock and put to a ghastly death by being slowly crushed under the weight of one boulder after another placed on a board across his chest. Corwin died just five years later and was so detested at that point that he had to be buried in the basement of his home to keep his corpse from being desecrated.[118] Eventually Corwin's body was moved to a cemetery, and the Joshua Ward mansion was constructed on the property of Corwin's former home.

Today the Joshua Ward House is home to a prolific list of purported paranormal phenomena. In her book *Haunted Massachusetts*, Cheri Revai compiles a partial list:

> Stories abound about candles being melted, reshaped, and moved around; garbage cans being flipped upside down; alarms being set off by unknown sources; books, desks, and lamps being tossed around helter-skelter; and a persistent cold spot that fills an entire corner room. . . . [A] Polaroid photograph was taken that captured, quite unexpectedly, an apparition of a very spooky-looking woman, with matted and tousled black hair and a long black gown, who placed herself squarely between the photographer and his subject. . . . Another remarkable incident happened when a document that was about to be fetched from the closet came drifting out unassisted by human hands, unrolled itself, and laid itself out neatly before the eyes of two speechless men.[119]

Whether the interment of George Corwin—whose apparition has been reportedly spotted all over the Salem city limits through the years—had anything to do with the Joshua Ward House's reputation as a prodigiously haunted locale remains a mystery. What is

The most famous resident of the Stephen Daniels House in Salem is not its original owner but rather a phantom cat who's rumored to roam the inn's halls.

certain, however, is that the Ward House is a historically significant haunted house—George Washington once slept there (hence the home's former name of the Washington Inn)—with incredible ties to Salem's storied past.

How to find it: The Joshua Ward House stands at 148 Washington Street in Salem. From I-95, take exit 45 onto MA 128 north. Then take exit 26 onto Lowell Street east. Go left onto Essex Street and then right onto Washington Street.

Stephen Daniels House Inn (Salem)

Built in 1667 by a well-known sea captain named Stephen Daniels, this eponymous inn—the longest continuously run bed & breakfast in Salem—is tucked away on one of the quiet side streets in the city's bustling downtown area. The inn is a cozy place of lodging, and, if the accounts are accurate, it houses a few ghosts. Guests have reported witnessing the ghost of an old man as well as the specter of a woman tumbling down a flight of stairs. Perhaps the most often seen apparition at the Stephen Daniels Inn, however, is that of a black-and-gray-striped cat. The cat has been seen by so many that some frequent guests have been known to leave out a saucer of milk before going to bed.[120] According to accounts, the inn's current owner, Kay Gill, painted a portrait of a cat that bears a striking resemblance to the phantom feline that purportedly haunts the Stephen Daniels Inn. Now hanging in the Rose Room, this portrait was painted in 1953—a full 10 years before Kay bought the property.[121]

How to find it: The Stephen Daniels House Inn is located at 1 Daniels Street in Salem. From I-95, take exit 45 onto MA 128 north. Then take exit 26 onto Lowell Street East. Go left onto Essex Street and then right onto Washington Street. Take a left onto New Derby Street (MA 1A north), which will turn into Derby Street. Go left onto Hawthorne Street, then right onto Essex Street, and another right onto Daniels Street. For more information, or to make reservations, call 978-744-5709.

greater boston

Boston Public Garden

Nobody knows quite who the spirits are or why they haunt the Boston Public Garden, but for decades scores of witnesses claimed to have seen the apparitions of not one but two genteel women in 1930s-era dress roaming through the public park, established in 1837 by Horace Gray to be the country's first public botanical garden. The phantom urbanites are said to come from the direction of the Ritz-Carlton Hotel—indeed, some witnesses have claimed to see them actually emerge from the hotel's entrance—and they wander through the park, often smiling at passersby before they disappear into thin air.

How to find it: The Boston Public Garden is bordered by Boylston Street, Charles Street, Arlington Street, and Beacon Street between Boston's Back Bay and Downtown sections. From I-90, take exit 22, staying in the Prudential Center lane and merging onto Huntington Avenue. After about 2,000 feet, go right onto the Fenway and then right again onto Beacon Street. Travel just over 1 mile to access the garden.

Charlesgate Hall (Boston)

Built in 1901 as luxury apartments for the New England wealthy who preferred city life to country mansion living, Charlesgate Hall is a large, imposing structure squatting in the Back Bay section of Boston. Since its inception it has existed in several different incarnations—Boston University dorm building, private apartments, Emerson College dorm building, and now luxury condominiums. Nobody seems to know exactly why, but Charlesgate Hall has also garnered a reputation for being incredibly haunted throughout the years. The building was designed by the architect J. Pickering Putnam to be the defining structure of Boston's Kenmore Square, but several peculiar details of the building's design have left Bostonians scratching their heads for decades. For example, the building's east side is shaped like the letter C, meaning that you can see those apartments only if you're directly across the street. The top floor is also, strangely, not visible from the outside of the building. According to paranormal researcher Christopher Balzano, there have been rumors throughout the years that Putnam himself was an occultist and that Charlesgate Hall was "designed and built with the right materials to act as a magnet for the paranormal."[122]

Once B.U. began using the structure for student housing, stories began circulating about a suicide in the building. Soon reports began of alarm clocks going off at exactly 6:11 AM without anybody setting them. This clamor, along with many other stories, was linked to the purported on-campus suicide by the dorm residents. Holly Mascott Nadler, in her *Ghosts of Boston Town*, relates one such story:

On the sixth floor, three freshman girls moved into one of the rooms to find themselves accosted by the spirit world. The first to arrive decided to stake out the larger of the two closets, but when she placed her hand on the knob, she felt a sudden aversion to opening the door. She opted for the other closet. The second girl to enter the room also approached the larger closet, experienced the same unease, and suggested they leave it for the third roommate. Later, all three girls—presumably after the third had in turn rejected the off-putting closet—made a startling discovery: the year before, a student had hanged herself in the larger closet.[123]

On the same floor, in room 623, a male student reportedly woke up to the apparition of a man hovering over his bed; his screams woke the resident assistant, who barged in to witness the sight. The room was allegedly boarded up until B.U. sold the building in 1972.[124]

Local legend states that when Charlesgate Hall existed as an apartment complex between stints as a college dorm, it rented to a group of young people who were Wiccans, occultists, or Satanists, depending on whom you ask. This might just be rumor, but what is known with some degree of certainty is that the Ouija board enjoyed a kind of renaissance during the era in which Emerson College owned the building; there are several stories— on Web sites, in journals, and in books—in which Emerson students reported that they or peers were using Ouija boards while living at Charlesgate Hall. According to Holly Mascott Nadler, one student was using the board in 1988 when her father, an alleged psychic, called her; he knew somehow that she and her friends were using a Ouija board and begged her to stop. It seems that he felt she had opened a door, letting something dark through, and needed to figure out a way to close it.

Paranormal experts always warn against using Ouija boards or holding séances—especially by novices—claiming that when one opens doors without completely understanding the forces they're dealing with, what crosses over might not be welcome. It is too often the powerful, malignant spirits that will cross over, not the peaceful, loving spirits one might be attempting to contact. This seems to have been the case at Emerson. The stories escalated and some students even complained about being attacked by unseen forces; according to reports, Emerson actually banned the use of Ouija boards on campus due to these disturbances.[125] One such story, relayed by Cheri Revai in her book *Haunted Massachusetts*, particularly stands out as being a potential warning to anybody seriously considering the use of Ouija boards. It seems that an entity contacted via Ouija board by a group of friends had, for some reason, a vendetta against one of the group:

An entity with a grudge against a particular male student spelled out its hatred by repeating the young man's name obsessively and even saying the student "had to die." Several nights later, the student went to take a shower while his roommates foolishly continued to play with the board. When he noticed that the light in the bathroom was flickering, he reached up and screwed the bulb in tighter, fixing the problem. Then he stepped into the shower and was all soaped up when the lightbulb again started flickering. Unbeknownst to him, his friends had, at that very moment, received a message from an evil spirit that simply spelled out "H-A-H-A." They asked what was so funny, and it spelled out "A-C-D-C." Meanwhile, back in the bathroom, the male student thoughtlessly stepped out of the shower to tighten the bulb again, when he stopped short of doing it with a sickening realization: He was standing in a pool of water and would have been electrocuted.[126]

Indeed, stories like this from the 1980s and '90s abound, and the Emerson era of Charlesgate Hall's existence seems to be the zenith of the building's paranormal history. Apparitions—usually a man dressed all in black—were seen, and students would report feeling the physical presence of *something*: they would feel somebody unseen actually touch them or feel an unseen person climb onto the empty top bunk bed. One of the more startling tales sounds like something out of one of the *Poltergeist* movies:

Another young woman reported an incident involving a group of friends in a room of the Charlesgate wing known as the

Mansion. All of a sudden the door banged shut and the lights switched off. Unseen forces slammed the students about in the dark. When the lights turned back on, the terrified girls saw that the walls and ceiling were now gouged and scarred.[127]

If the frightening stories—and there are a heck of a lot of them—are true, it isn't immediately obvious whether the disturbances are a consequence of the building's peculiar construction, the occultists that had allegedly lived in the building, the students' monkeying around with Ouija boards, some unreported event in the building's past, or any combination of these factors. The number of reports centering around Charlesgate Hall that floated around the paranormal community in the late 1980s and into the 1990s, though—especially as the development of the Internet made the world a much smaller place—made it clear that something was not quite right there. In the synopsis of her record of Charlesgate Hall's paranormal disturbances, Holly Nadler writes that the '80s and '90s saw "glasses sliding across tables; room temperatures plunging 30 degrees; doors spontaneously shutting and locking; blankets plucked from sleeping students; students awakening far from their beds, on the floor, shivering with cold."[128]

If the disturbances at Charlesgate Hall continue, the current condo residents are quiet about it. Could it be that the building's more disturbing episodes were brought on entirely by young people dabbling with powers they didn't completely comprehend?

How to find it: Charlesgate Hall, located at 4 Charlesgate East in the Back Bay section of Boston, is now a condominium building. From I-90, take exit 22, staying in the Prudential Center lane and merging onto Huntington Avenue. Go left onto Dartmouth Avenue, then left again onto Commonwealth Avenue. Take a right onto Charlesgate East; Charlesgate Hall is on the corner of Charlesgate East and Beacon Street.

Colonial Inn (Concord)

Built in 1716 for former soldier and town physician Captain John Minot, what is now the Colonial Inn is a charming and elegant

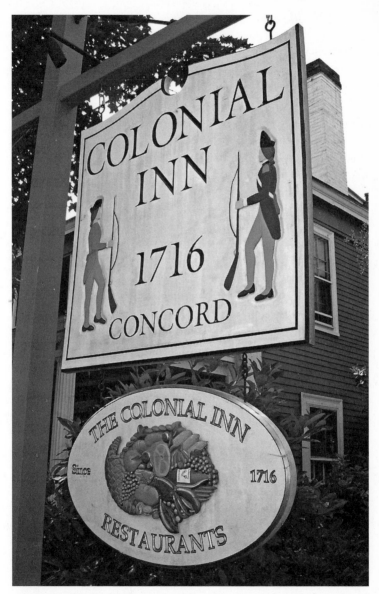

One of the oldest inns in Massachusetts, Concord's Colonial Inn may also have one of the most haunted guestrooms in the state.

hotel, surrounded by several artifacts of American colonial and literary history. The hotel's official Web site lists many of the historically significant politicians and famous celebrities who have stayed at the inn (names as various as Franklin D. Roosevelt, J. P. Morgan, John Wayne, Shirley Temple, Steve Martin, Kurt Russell, Goldie Hawn, Ally Sheedy, Joe Perry, Arnold Palmer, Faye Dunaway, Dan Quayle, Glenn Close, Bruce Springsteen, and Queen Noor of Jordan adorn the guest list[129]) and Henry David Thoreau's family once lived in the home. But it also states that "the ghost who sometimes visits room 24 has never left a name."[130] The Web site includes a testimonial from a bride who claims to have been visited by the apparition of a woman while she and her groom were staying in room 24 on their honeymoon. And although Cheri Revai's *Haunted Massachusetts* states that the hotel's other rooms had been considered "ghost-free,"[131] the Colonial Inn's Web site suggests that there have been additional inexplicable incidents in other parts of the hotel recently, although it doesn't go into detail about what these incidents have been.

How to find it: The Colonial Inn, on Concord's town common at 48 Monument Square, is so named due to the historical significance of many of its structures. From I-95, take exit 30B onto MA 2A west. Stay on MA 2A west, and bear right onto Lexington Road, which will lead directly into the center of Concord. Continue straight through the rotary, and the Colonial Inn will be directly ahead on Monument Square. For more information or to make reservations, call 978-293-3056 or 866-728-4545, e-mail colonial @concordscolonialinn.com, or visit the inn's Web site at www .concordscolonialinn.com.

Harvard University (Cambridge)

You would think that one of the most prestigious schools in the entire country would have scores of ghosts of intellectuals and philosophers roaming its grounds—and it may. But the ghosts best known to the Cambridge campus are those of textile workers seeking entry into the university's Thayer Hall, which used to be a textile mill.[132] The apparitions reportedly materialize occasionally at night, and they enter Thayer Hall through doors that no longer exist, apparently walking straight through the building's thick, brick walls. There is no historical record of any kind of disaster in which several mill employees might have died on the job, so the haunting of Thayer Hall may very well lend credence to the popular theory of many paranormal researchers that a large number of reported hauntings are actually imprints on the fabric of space and time that are played back like a hologram recording when the conditions are just right. Of course, there is always the possibility that the former mill employees loved their jobs so much that they yearn to return to work even in the afterlife. Either way, the puzzling phantoms of Thayer Hall continue to confound Harvard's scholars and students alike.

How to find it: Harvard University, one of the country's premier Ivy League universities, is located in the Boston suburb of Cambridge. Thayer Hall is on Cambridge Street, between Massachusetts Avenue and Quincy Street. From I-90, take exit 18 onto Cambridge Street in Boston, which becomes River Street after crossing the Charles River into Cambridge. Bear left onto Prospect Street, and then go left again onto Cambridge Street (a completely different road than the Cambridge Street in Boston).

Lesley University (Cambridge)

A small but respected liberal arts college, Lesley University reportedly has phantom footfalls that echo down the hallways of its classroom building on Avon Hill. It's also reported that objects in this building—textbooks, desks, chairs, and the like—have been known to move around while the building is empty, sometimes even relocating from one room to another.

How to find it: Lesley University is on Everett Street in Cambridge, Massachusetts. From I-90, take exit 18 onto Cambridge Street in Boston, which becomes River Street after crossing the Charles River into Cambridge. Bear left onto Prospect Street, and then take another left onto Cambridge Street (a completely different road than the Cambridge Street in Boston). Go right onto Massachusetts Avenue, then right again onto Everett Street just beyond Harvard's campus.

Longfellow's Wayside Inn (Sudbury)

A large inn originally built in 1702 by one David Howe, the Wayside Inn was once owned by Henry Ford, was written about by Henry Wadsworth Longfellow (*Tales of a Wayside Inn*), and is one of the focal locations for a mysterious and anonymous New England tradition known as the Secret Drawer Society (SDS). On the surface, the Wayside Inn seems like any other large, privately owned B&B, but its storied past and unique reputation truly set it apart from just about any other place of lodging in the Northeast.

Simply stated, the Secret Drawer Society is less a formal organization than a kind of informal written tradition, a means by which travelers anonymously share with others their tales and memories. Author Mark Jasper details his introduction to the SDS in his book *Haunted Inns of New England*:

> Guests leave notes for other guests to read; some even hide bits of treasure, leaving maps and clues to their whereabouts. The tradition was started back in the early 1900s and continues to this day. The SDS is really more than just leaving notes on bits of paper. It's about sharing memories. I spent over an hour examining notes written by newlyweds, grandparents, small children, and people from all over the world. It was hard not to become emotional as people I'd never met suddenly came to life, sharing their joy and wonderful memories about their stay. The more I read, the more I was overcome by feelings of intense warmth.[133]

Many pieces of furniture in the Wayside Inn contain hidden compartments where guests have hidden away letters detailing any information that these travelers deemed important enough to pass on. Many of Wayside's SDS letters describe guests' encounters with the inn's resident ghost, one Jerusha Howe, "the Belle of

Sudbury." Local legend states that Jerusha's English lover had gone away to sea, promising to marry her when he returned. The years went by, but the man never returned—he simply vanished off the face of the Earth, either by choice or by mishap—and Jerusha slowly lapsed into seclusion, becoming a recluse by the age of 40.

Practically every part of the Wayside Inn has experienced some kind of paranormal phenomenon—from whispers coming from nowhere to the phantom aroma of citrus perfume (reportedly Jerusha's preferred scent) to footfalls echoing down empty corridors—but the most active rooms in the inn are said to be numbers 9 and 10. Needless to say, some of the Wayside Inn's more startling encounters have been recorded via SDS and relayed by Mark Jasper. For example:

> 11/18/89 6:15 PM
> What was that noise??? Why did the lights go out??? The sound of drums, fife, cannons and we thought we were in the middle of a re-make of a Revolutionary War movie. . . .[134]

Perhaps the *most* startling tale to come from the inn was related to Jasper by a CPA from Virginia who was in Sudbury for a business meeting in late April 1998. He presumably didn't know about the SDS tradition, or else he surely would have hidden a note at the inn itself, but he still felt compelled to share his experiences:

> At 4:50 AM I was awakened by what felt like fingernails scratching at the bottom of my right foot. It was a one-time scratch that started at . . . my [heel] and continued in the direction of my toes. I immediately woke up and found myself lying on my left side with my legs slightly bent. At the same instant, I felt pressure against my back as if someone had curled up against my back and inserted their knees under mine. I attempted to roll over but couldn't because of the tremendous pressure that was holding me in place. I tried to speak, but found my jaw was in a frozen stage. I felt as though someone was right up against my back trembling uncontrollably. I then clearly heard a young woman's voice whisper in my ear, "I am very cold . . . you are very seductive . . . (followed by garbled words) . . . Peter."

Almost immediately, I felt release of the grasp I was under and was able to roll over. The room was dark, and I did not see anyone present. I then turned the lights on and searched the room but found no one. My doors and windows were locked from the inside.[135]

It is impossible to know for sure what really happened to the CPA from Virginia; if the experience wasn't a dream and was truly an encounter with the supernatural, it wouldn't be difficult to imagine that the confused, reclusive spirit of Jerusha Howe is still yearning for the embrace of her lost lover, an Englishman who very well might have been named Peter.

How to find it: The historic Longfellow's Wayside Inn is located at 72 Wayside Inn Road in Sudbury. From I-95 north, take exit 26 onto MA 20 west. Stay on MA 20 for 11 miles, and then turn right at the large green sign for Wayside Inn Road. The inn will be ¼ mile down on your right, with parking on the left. For information or to make reservations, call 978-443-1776 or 800-339-1776, or visit the Wayside Inn's Web site at www.wayside.org.

Omni Parker House Hotel (Boston)

Two well-known events in Massachusetts history are referred to as the "Boston Massacre." The later one involves the collapse of the Red Sox at the hands of the Yankees going into the 1978 playoffs (a pain finally alleviated by the dominance of the hometown team in the early 21st century); the first one was the slaughter of five Bostonians at the hands of British troops who were trying to avoid a riot in March 1770. It is near this site that entrepreneur Harvey Parker built a massive 550-room hotel—which he named the Parker House Hotel, after himself—in the mid-19th century.

The site may have been imprinted with tragedy, but that didn't stop the hotel from amassing an impressive list of celebrities and politicians from making what is now the Omni Parker Hotel their home away from home in Boston. Ulysses S. Grant, Franklin D. Roosevelt, John F. Kennedy (who proposed to Jacqueline Bouvier in the hotel and held his bachelor party there), and Bill Clinton adorn the guest list; amazingly, Malcolm X, Ho Chi Minh, and Emeril Lagasse are among the former employees! A pair of rival ghosts from the other Boston massacre—Babe Ruth and Ted Williams—were said to frequent the hotel's restaurant. The Parker House also played a great role in literary history—Charles Dickens used to stay at the Parker while visiting the United States, and it was at the Parker House that a group of literary legends—including Henry Wadsworth Longfellow, Ralph Waldo Emerson, Henry David Thoreau, and Nathaniel Hawthorne—formed a group known as the Boston Saturday Club, which met the fourth Saturday of every month. The Parker House has also been the site of numerous culinary inventions, among them Boston cream pie and the Parker House roll.

For years, all over the hotel, guests have reported hearing strange noises—such as voices from nowhere and footsteps coming from empty hallways—that can't be explained. The apparition of a dark, presumably male form wearing a top hat has been reportedly seen on almost every floor of the hotel through the decades. The third floor specifically has had a large number of reported disturbances. One of the hotel's elevators apparently likes to stop on that floor without anybody pushing the call button. In room 303, where a traveling businessman allegedly had a heart attack and died, guests have reported hearing coarse laughter, smelling the overwhelming odor of whiskey, and, on a couple of occasions, the contents of the room's wastepaper basket reportedly spontaneously combusted.[136] Perhaps the most frequently recurring ghost of the Omni Parker House was that of Harvey Parker, who reportedly appeared at the foot of "his" guests' beds stating, "I've come to check on your accommodations. Do you have everything you require?"[137] According to the hotel's Web site, however, Harvey's ghost has not been seen in a couple of decades.

How to find it: The historic Omni Parker House is located at 60 School Street, on the corner of School and Tremont. From I-90, take exit 22, staying in the Prudential Center lane and merging onto Huntington Avenue. Go right onto Tremont Street, then the first left onto School Street. For more information or to make reservations, call 617-227-8600 or visit the Omni Hotels chain Web site at www.omnihotels.com.

westeRN RegioN

Bash Bish Falls (Mount Washington)

According to local legend, visitors to Bash Bish Falls in Mount Washington State Forest have reported hearing the sweet sound of a woman's voice join the rhythmic sounds of the waterfall—the highest in Massachusetts—and have on occasion seen the falling water take on the shape of a woman's face or figure. According to *Haunted Massachusetts,* the waterfall's ghostly presence is reputed to be that of its Mohican namesake, a woman named Bash Bish who was wrongly sentenced to death for adultery. As Bash Bish was about to be cast over the falls in a canoe, an aura of light was said to envelop her, and her head was suddenly surrounded by white butterflies. Bash Bish reputedly then took her fate into her own hands and jumped into the turbulent waters below; legend has it that her body was never found.[138]

How to find it: From the MassPike (I-90), take exit 2 in Lee. Follow MA 102 west for 4.7 miles to Stockbridge. Turn left and take US 7 south for 7.7 miles through Great Barrington. Go right on MA 23 west for 4.9 miles to South Egremont. Turn left onto MA 41 south, and then take an immediate right onto Mount Washington Road; continue for 7.5 miles (becomes East Street). Turn right onto Cross Road then right onto West Street, and continue for 1 mile. Turn left onto Falls Road and follow for 1.5 miles to the parking lot and trailhead on the left. Coming from New York, take NY 22 to Copake Falls and look for NY 344 east (into Taconic State Park). NY 344 becomes Falls Road. Parking lot and trailhead are 2 miles on the right. For more information call 413-528-0330, or visit www.mass.gov/dcr/parks/western/bash.htm.

Houghton Mansion (North Adams)

Now a Masonic lodge in this town nestled deep within the Berkshire Mountains, the Houghton Mansion was the happy home of the Albert C. Houghton family—that is until a tragic automobile accident changed the fate of the family (and the house) forever. Albert, his daughter, Mary, family friend Sybil Hutton, and chauffeur John Widders were driving the Houghtons' Pierce-Arrow along a Berkshire mountain road one summer day in 1911 when Widders was forced to navigate around a roadside work crew. Something went terribly wrong, and the edge of the road collapsed underneath the car, sending it tumbling down a cliff. Widders and Albert Houghton survived with minor injuries; Sybil and Mary were not so lucky. Perhaps blaming himself for the deaths of two innocent souls, John Widders committed suicide on the mansion grounds not long after the accident.

Following Albert Houghton's death, the house was willed to the Masons, who certainly didn't know that there were ghosts included in the package. There have been numerous reports over the years of a girl's voice echoing down the hall, even though the building is empty of anyone other than the witness. Lights have been known to turn themselves on and off, and many pictures taken at the house have revealed what appear to be ghostly orbs floating throughout the building.[139]

How to find it: The Houghton mansion—now the North Adams Masonic Temple, with guided tours scheduled on occasion—is located at 172 Church Street in the Berkshire County town of North Adams. From the MassPike (I-90), take exit 1, going right off the exit onto Old Stockbridge Road (MA 102). Follow MA 102 until it intersects with US 7; take a left onto US 7, northbound. Stay on US 7 for about 25 miles, and then bear right onto Main Street (MA 2) in Williamstown. Follow MA 2 for 4½ miles into North Adams. Church Street will be a right-hand turn off of MA 2. For more information, call 413-663-3486, or visit the lodge's Web site at http://houghton-mansion.tripod.com.

Quabbin Reservoir (Belchertown)

Underneath what is now the Quabbin Reservoir—which covers 39 square miles, is 18 miles long, has 181 miles of shoreline, and holds 412 billion gallons of water—lie the remains of what were once the Massachusetts towns of Prescott, Enfield, Dana, and Greenwich. The inhabitants of these towns were relocated, including those who had been interred within the local cemeteries—except for Native American burial grounds, which were respected as sacred ground[140] by the state of Massachusetts. Today, reports of ghost lights hovering over the water—apparently interpreted by some as being UFOs—are somewhat commonplace, and people have even reported seeing animal life around the reservoir that normally wouldn't reside anywhere near central Massachusetts—such as crocodiles and mountain lions.[141]

How to find it: The Quabbin Reservoir, fed by the Swift and Ware rivers, is a very large public water supply—one of the largest man-made water supplies in the country, in fact—and state park, complete with various hiking and mountain biking trails, located in Belchertown. To best access the state park area located around the reservoir, take the MassPike (I-90) exit 8 onto Ware Street (MA 32), northbound. Take a left onto Main Street, MA 9 west, which will become Belchertown Road and eventually Ware Road. The main entrance to the park is located at 485 Ware Road. For more information, call 413-323-7221, or visit the Massachusetts State Parks Web site for Quabbin Reservoir at www.mass.gov/dcr/parks/central/quabbin.htm.

Route 44 (Rehoboth and Seekonk)

One of the most often-reported phantom hitchhikers in the United States is Massachusetts's own red-headed wanderer, a large-framed (over 6 feet tall and broad shouldered) man with red hair and a red beard, dressed in flannel shirt and jeans like a lumberjack or woodsman. The red-headed hitchhiker has appeared to people in a number of ways: Sometimes he appears at the side of the road. Sometimes he appears right in front of a car and disappears just as the car is about to hit him. Sometimes he disappears as he reaches for a car's door handle. Sometimes he enters the car and rides for a while—actually conversing with the driver. Sometimes, when he accepts a ride, the driver has car trouble right after he disappears, and his final message to the driver is sardonic laughter.

How to find it: The red-headed hitchhiker has reportedly appeared to drivers traveling along MA 44 near the Seekonk and Rehoboth town line.

central and southeast regions

Bird Island Lighthouse (Marion)

Pirate Captain Billy Moore's wife had an addiction to tobacco that would prove fatal—although not for the reason that one might expect. When Moore and his wife took control of the Bird Island Light sometime in the late 1820s, Moore decided to initiate a "no tobacco" rule, much to his wife's chagrin. She would often beg for the substance from travelers, despite her husband's assertions that it had given her a "consumptive cough."[142] The psychological control that Moore exercised over his wife was apparently symptomatic of abusive behavior—citizens of nearby Marion would often comment that the woman looked as if she had been beaten, coming into town sporting ugly bruises and even the occasional black eye.

One morning in February 1832, a distress flag was seen flying over the Bird Island Lighthouse. The help that arrived discovered Mrs. Moore dead, a victim of what Mr. Moore asserted was tuberculosis, and she was duly buried on the beach. But when Marion townsfolk raised suspicions about the couple's domestic disputes, Billy Moore disappeared forever. Since then, subsequent Bird Island lighthouse keepers reported that in the dead of night an old woman would knock on their door and then reach out an arm toward them as if she was desperately grasping for something. The keeper's house was demolished when the light was deactivated in 1933 (it was eventually relit in 1997), but passersby still occasionally report seeing the apparition of an old woman either walking the beach or walking across the icy water to Bird Island with a corncob pipe sticking out of her mouth.[143]

How to find it: The Bird Island Light is located just outside Marion, at the entrance to Sippican Harbor in Buzzard's Bay. Closed to the public, the lighthouse is best viewed by boat. For more information, write the Bird Island Lighthouse Preservation Society, 2 Spring Street, Marion, MA 02738, or call 508-748-0550.

Lizzie Borden Bed & Breakfast (Fall River)

The grisly events of August 4, 1892, overshadow the comparatively innocuous paranormal activity that has reportedly taken place at the small inn named for Fall River's most notorious citizen. But said unexplained phenomena only serve to amplify the Lizzie Borden Bed & Breakfast's popularity as an unconventional tourist attraction.

On August 11, 1892, Lizzie Borden was arrested for the murders of her father and stepmother, who a week before had been hacked to death with an ax or hatchet within the confines of their cozy New England house. Lizzie and her sister, Emma, were apparently living in an unhappy home; shortly before the murders, a local druggist refused to sell prussic acid—a very poisonous substance similar to cyanide—to Lizzie, who claimed she needed it to clean a sealskin coat, and Lizzie's parents felt ill around the same time. Many in Fall River speculated that Lizzie—and possibly her sister as well—were attempting to poison Mr. Borden and his second wife.

On the morning of August 4, 1892, Lizzie yelled to the maid that somebody had murdered her father. Her stepmother's body was found in an upstairs bedroom shortly thereafter. The woman had sustained 18 or 19 blows from the murder weapon, and the man had been the victim of 10 or 11 gashes. Although Lizzie Borden's testimony was uneven and her behavior inside the courtroom was suspect, she was acquitted of the murders due to a lack of concrete evidence: no murder weapon or bloody clothes were ever found. The jury concluded that considering Lizzie had shouted up to the maid just minutes after her father's murder had apparently occurred, Lizzie would not have had time to dispose of a murder weapon and clean off or change her clothes. Several different theories have been put forth as to what really happened within the Borden home that morning—including that the girls' uncle had committed the crime, that their father also had an illegitimate son who committed the act, and that Lizzie committed the crimes in an unconscious state similar to sleepwalking—but the murders remain a notorious mystery, with Lizzie Borden being the only true suspect.

Despite the macabre events that have occurred within the house, the reputed ghosts inhabiting the Lizzie Borden Bed & Breakfast are apparently playful and mischievous at worst. Guests and staff have reported hearing furniture moving around on empty floors, the sounds of voices coming from empty rooms, and the sounds of cats meowing—even though the building's only cats are the stuffed black cats that adorn many of the inn's rooms. In a few isolated incidents, guests have reported seeing the apparition of a gray-haired woman in Victorian-era dress who seems to be performing daily household chores—such as dusting or making the bed—before disappearing before their eyes. Only one reported paranormal incident at the bed & breakfast stands out as being truly troubling: not long after the inn opened for business, a housekeeper was putting away linens in one of the guestrooms when she turned around to see the apparition of a corpse, hacked up and bloodied, lying on the room's bed. The housekeeper fled the premises, never to return.[144]

How to find it: The Lizzie Borden Bed & Breakfast and Museum is located at 230 Second Street in Fall River. From I-195, take exit 7 onto MA 81 south. Go right onto Rodman Street, then right again at the next light onto Second Street. The Lizzie Borden Bed & Breakfast and Museum is on the right just after St. Mary's Cathedral. For information about daily tours or to make reservations, call 508-675-7333, or visit the inn's Web site at www.lizzie-borden.com.

Minot's Ledge Lighthouse (Offshore of Cohasset and Scituate)

About a mile off the coast of Cohasset is an area of the Atlantic Ocean that the Quonahassitis tribe believed to be the underwater home of a demonic presence that would attack any seafaring vessel that ventured too near.[145] Today we know that the Quonahassitis's aquatic demon is actually an equally evil granite ledge that rises maliciously from the ocean floor, waiting to punch holes in the hull of any unsuspecting ship. As the number of shipwrecks on what came to be known as Minot's Ledge rose with the increase in sea traffic during the middle of the 19th century, it became clear that some kind of lighthouse would be necessary to warn ships of the danger lying dormant not far underneath the surface of the Atlantic's turbulent waters.

Taking over three years to construct, the original Minot's Ledge Light rose 114 feet from the dangerous ledge underneath, a complex of girders and pillars that made the light look more like an offshore oil rig than the traditional image of a New England lighthouse. Minot's Ledge Light began operation in 1850 and immediately garnered a reputation for being unsafe. During storms, Atlantic waves almost as tall as the lighthouse itself would crash down on the structure, and during the winter the doors and locks would freeze shut, trapping inhabitants inside—or, much more dangerously, outside.

According to Susan Smitten, tragedy befell the original Minot's Ledge Light in April 1851. On the morning of April 11, the lighthouse keeper went ashore, leaving two assistants named Joseph Antoine and Joseph Wilson behind to man the light. Not long after the keeper went ashore, a fierce storm swept through Massachusetts, bringing high winds and torrential downpours for days on end. On April 16, Cohasset residents were awakened in the middle of the night by the incessant ringing of the Minot's Ledge Light's fog bell. It continued to toll, keeping the shoreline residents awake all night. By the time daybreak arrived and a party was sent to investigate, the lighthouse was gone—demolished by the storm and completely swept into the depths of the Atlantic.[146]

In 1860 a second light was constructed on Minot's Ledge. This one faced the same dangers and difficulties of the first—huge waves crashing down, freezing doors and locks—but this lighthouse was sturdier, made out of durable granite, and still stands today. But echoes of the first lighthouse linger in the form of apparent paranormal phenomena. During the 17 years that the lighthouse was manned before being completely automated, keepers would report strange knocking sounds in the lighthouse, and the fog bell would sound by itself apparently for no reason. Since the lighthouse became automated in 1977, boaters sailing near the light have reported that two men appeared to be hanging off the side of the lighthouse, clinging for dear life onto what look like girders—even though the current lighthouse is made of concrete, and therefore has no need for support girders. Could this be yet another case of "ghosts" actually representing an image imprinted on the fabric of space and time and "played back" like a recording when the conditions are right? An interesting side note has one of the men screaming in a foreign tongue. Joseph Antoine's native language was Portuguese.

How to find it: Minot's Ledge Light rises from the Atlantic Ocean like a relic from some sunken, underwater city. The nearest towns are Cohasset and Scituate, but the lighthouse is best viewed by boat. It is fully automated and closed to the public.

Spider Gates Cemetery (Leicester)
Also known as Quaker Cemetery and Friends Cemetery, Spider Gates is so named because of the pair of menacing-looking arachnids that adorn the graveyard's wire-work front gate. As with so many New England cemeteries, Spider Gates is said to be haunted; if the local legends are true, however, ghosts might very well be one of the Leicester graveyard's more innocuous phenomena. For years, it has been said that strange voices and blood-curdling screams could be heard emanating from within the graveyard's perimeter after dark. It is also said that the region is, like Connecticut's Dudleytown, a biological dead zone—an area in which animal life tends not to thrive.

Spider Gates has also supposedly been the site of multiple suicides by hanging from the same tree—aptly named "the hanging tree"—although such deaths have never been reported by the media and remain purely speculative. One such story has a young couple out for a drive when they encounter car trouble near Spider Gates. The young man goes for help and never comes back; police later find his lifeless body swaying from the branches of the hanging tree.[147] Equally dubious are the claims that the cemetery is the home to ritualistic Satanic and cult practices; the graveyard has been regularly patrolled by police for some time now, and the graveyard's only trespassers tend to be teenaged thrill seekers looking for a scare. Spider Gates' most fantastical legend, however, is undoubtedly the rumor that if one walks along the walls of the cemetery in a particular order, a portal to another dimension will open for the would-be traveler[148] as if he is a character from a *Legend of Zelda* video game. Where this last legend originated remains a mystery—to date, nobody has stepped forward to claim that they have traveled into another dimension after unlocking the puzzle of Spider Gates cemetery's magical walls.

How to find it: The Quaker Cemetery, better known as Spider Gates, is located along Manville Road in Leicester, near Worcester Regional Airport. From I-290, take exit 11 and go left onto Cambridge Street. Then take a left onto Main Street (MA 9). Go right onto Chapel Street, and then bear left onto Manville Road. The Quaker Cemetery will be a couple hundred feet up.

cape cod and the islands

Barley Neck Inn (East Orleans)

The Barley Neck Inn was built as a two-story Greek-Revival home in 1857 by sea captain Isaac Doane and his wife, Mary. The inn was subsequently added to by various owners through the years and now includes two restaurants, as well. Over the past few years, several staff members and guests have reported that windows and doors they had securely closed and locked were later found wide open, and lights would often turn on and off by their own volition. Staff members have also reported an invasive aroma of sweet-smelling perfume that seems to come from nowhere. Perhaps most curious, however, is the phenomenon that led to a "no trays" policy at the inn's Joe's Beach Road Bar and Grille—apparently the Barley Neck Inn's mischievous resident ghost had a propensity for knocking the drink trays out of the hands of unsuspecting waiters and waitresses.[149]

How to find it: The Barley Neck Inn stands at 5 Beach Road in the rural community of East Orleans, on the "elbow" of Cape Cod. From I-495, stay on the highway until it terminates and becomes MA 25. At the intersection of MA 25 and MA 6, take a left onto MA 6, then a right onto the Sagamore Bridge. After crossing the Sagamore Bridge, stay straight on MA 6, and follow this route into Orleans. After MA 6 exit 12, at the Orleans Rotary, stay right and join MA 6A; continue on MA 6A to the second traffic light, and take a right onto Main Street. At Nauset Beach, Route 6A will fork off onto Beach Road and Barley Neck Road, alongside Meeting House Pond. For more information, call 508-255-0212, or visit the inn's Web site at www.barleyneck.com.

Barnstable House (Barnstable)

Although it is now used as an office building, stories about the former Barnstable House restaurant still circulate amongst locals and those who regularly vacation on the Cape. It was a place in which strange, unexplainable things tended to happen, including glasses flying off the bar or a table and smashing against the wall. But the most infamous tale involving the circa-1716 structure involves a fire in the building back in the 1970s. According to reports, firefighters responded to the call and discovered within the building a woman wearing a long, flowing dress; when the fire reached her floor, she floated out the window and down to the ground, where she promptly vanished into thin air. Other reports claim that one of the firefighters talked to the woman, and when he looked down he noticed that she had no feet—she had been floating the whole time that he was talking to her.[150]

Local legend states that the building's original owner was a sea captain named John Paine who moved the building to Barnstable from Scituate sometime in the early 18th century. When he moved the house, he installed a well in the basement that tapped an underground stream running underneath the structure; it was in this well that his daughter Lucy drowned when he was away on a trip. It is also rumored that a man named Edmund Howes hung himself from a tree on the Barnstable House property. Perhaps these stories explain some of the inn's strange events and sightings. In 2007 a paranormal group called the New England Society of Paranormal Investigators (NESPI) visited the old house and conducted their own research; their investigation yielded a number of very startling electronic voice phenomenon (EVP) recordings.

How to find it: The Barnstable House, which now houses offices, is located on the Old King's Highway (MA 6A) in Barnstable on Cape Cod. From I-495, stay on the highway until it terminates and becomes MA 25. At the intersection of MA 25 and MA 6, take a left onto MA 6, then a right onto the Sagamore Bridge. After crossing the Sagamore Bridge, stay straight on Route 6, and follow this route farther up the Cape. Take a left onto North Dennis Road in Dennis, which will become South Yarmouth Road, and then bear right onto the Old King's Highway (MA 6A). The EVP recordings made at the Barnstable House are available at the NESPI Web site: www.nespi.net.

Beechwood Inn (Barnstable)

Located roughly at Cape Cod's northernmost shore, the Beech-wood Inn is a quaint and picturesque Victorian-style bed & break-fast that was built in 1853 as a private residence and later became Cap'n Grey's Smorgasboard Inn. The inn has garnered an impressive reputation for being among the Cape's very best his-torical lodging places, but it has also earned a reputation for its mischievous but friendly prank-playing ghost.

Over the past half century the last three owners of the inn have experienced inexplicable pranks. Famous ghost hunter Hans Holzer first investigated the inn in the mid-1960s, after receiving an invitation from the inn's owner, Lennart Svennson, who had experi-enced a number of disturbances. By the time that Mr. Holzer actu-ally got to Cape Cod for an in-person visit in 1967, however, the inn (at that point still called Cap'n Grey's Smorgasboard Inn) had changed hands. The new owner, a Hyannis attorney named Jack Furman, was happy to cooperate with Mr. Holzer's investigation as he, too, had already experienced a number of strange phenomena in his short tenure as the inn's proprietor:

> There has been on one occasion an umbrella mysteriously stuck into the stairwell in an open position. . . . On another oc-casion when the inn was closed in the evening early, my man-ager returned to find the front door bolted from *the inside*, which appeared strange since no one was in the building. At another time, my chef observed that the heating plant went off at 2:30 [AM], and the serviceman, whom I called the next day, found that a fuse was removed from the fuse box. At 2:30 in the morning, obviously, no one that we know of was up and around to do this. In addition, noises during the night have been heard by occupants of the inn.[151]

The inn's current owners, Ken and Debbie Traugot, have ex-perienced the exact same brand of mischievous behavior since purchasing the property in 1994: lightbulbs have mysteriously un-screwed themselves, a motorized skylight opens and closes on its own accord, and room doors have continued to deadbolt themselves from the inside.[152] Although Hans Holzer's investigations of the inn suggested that the building's spirits might have been remnants from the eponymous Captain Grey's slave-trading days—and there might even be bodies buried on the premises[153]—the Traugots feel that their ghost is a friendly female spirit who means no harm and who, apparently, only enjoys having a little fun at the owners' expense once in a while.

How to find it: The Beechwood Inn is located at 2839 Main Street (US 6A) in Barnstable on Cape Cod. From I-195, take exit 22A to MA 25 west. MA 25 will end at the intersection with MA 6, becoming MA 28 just before the Bourne Bridge. After the bridge, take a left onto the Old King's Highway (MA 6A). Stay on MA 6A, which will eventually become Main Street. The inn will be on the left. For more information or to make reservations, call 508-362-6618 or 800-609-6618, or visit the inn's Web site at www.beechwood inn.com.

Bramble Inn and Restaurant (Brewster)

The Bramble Inn Cape Cod bed & breakfast also happens to be one of two allegedly haunted inns to have been owned by the same couple (see the Pepper House Inn in this chapter). Built in 1861—and created by joining two smaller buildings together—the Bramble Inn was purchased by Cliff and Ruth Manchester in 1985, and it wasn't long before they noticed what seemed to be an ominous feeling in one of the inn's guest rooms. Although details aren't readily forthcoming, many guests have complained about the foreboding feeling received when they have entered that specific room, and it has so frightened chambermaids that they have reportedly refused to clean it.[154]

How to find it: The Bramble Inn and Restaurant is located at 2019 Main Street (MA 6A) in Brewster on Cape Cod. Take I-495 until the highway terminates and becomes MA 25. At the intersection of MA 25 and MA 6, stay straight over the Bourne Bridge onto MA 28 (General MacArthur Boulevard); then take a left at MA 6A, which runs along the northern shore of Cape Cod Bay. For more information, call 508-896-7644, or visit the inn's Web site at www.bramble inn.com.

Crocker Tavern Bed & Breakfast (Barnstable)

The Federal-style house was built in 1734 and converted into a tavern by Cornelius Crocker in 1754. Several important meetings took place here during the Revolutionary War.[155] The last of the Crocker line to own the house were two sisters who willed it to the Society for Preservation of New England Antiquities in 1926. Today the Crocker Tavern Bed & Breakfast is a charming five-bedroom inn that reportedly stands more or less unchanged from the way it was in the 19th—and even going back to the 18th—century.

The centuries-old structure and furnishings aren't the only aspects of the Crocker Tavern Bed & Breakfast that connect the inn to its storied past, however. According to reports, the apparition of a woman has appeared to numerous guests and staff members, even more individuals have claimed to hear the sound of phantom footfalls walking down the hallway, and the inn's current owner, Jeff Carlson, has claimed that on more than one occasion he has been awakened in the middle of the night by a woman's voice pleading, "Help me! Help me!"[156] Speculation among locals is that the female spirit might very well be that of one of the two Crocker women who last inhabited the building.

How to find it: The Crocker Tavern Bed & Breakfast is located at 3095 Main Street in Barnstable on Cape Cod. Take I-495 until the highway terminates and becomes MA 25. At the intersection of MA 25 and MA 6, stay straight over the Bourne Bridge onto MA 28 (General MacArthur Boulevard); just after crossing the Cape Cod canal, go left onto MA 6A, which runs along the northern shore of Cape Cod Bay. For more information or to make reservations, call 508-362-5115, or visit the inn's Web site at www.crockertavern.com.

Fairbanks Inn (Provincetown)

The brick building now known as the Fairbanks Inn is literally as old as our country—it was built in 1776—and it reportedly holds a permanent reminder of the first men to fight and die for American freedom: the apparition of a colonial soldier has appeared to numerous witnesses within the structure. The inn was originally the home of Captain Eben Snow, and local lore states that the wood used to furnish the house was taken from the mast of captured or destroyed British ships, which might explain why the resident Minuteman has decided to stay.

How to find it: The Fairbanks Inn is located at 90 Bradford Street in Provincetown on the tip of Cape Cod. Take I-495 until the highway terminates and becomes MA 25. At the intersection of MA 25 and MA 6, go left onto MA 6 and right onto the Sagamore Bridge. After crossing the Sagamore Bridge, stay straight on MA 6 and follow this route up the length of Cape Cod. Once MA 6 enters Provincetown, take a left onto Conwell Street, and then a right onto Bradford Street (MA 6A). For more information or to make reservations call 800-324-7265, email info@fairbanksinn.com, or visit the inn's Web site at www.fairbanksinn.com.

High Toss Pizza and Café (Wellfleet)

A building that was brought over sometime around 1750 from the now-submerged island of Billingsgate—which had been located just to the south of Wellfleet—what is now the High Toss Pizza and Café has undergone numerous incarnations through the years. But one thing that hasn't changed is the mischievous nature of its alleged ghost. Employees have claimed to hear somebody call their name from another room or the sound of glass shattering or the sound of someone working in the kitchen, only to find the rooms empty on investigation.[157] Nobody is quite sure who High Toss Pizza's ghost might have been when still among the living—a former resident of Billingsgate or simply a recent pizza aficionado—but one thing is for certain: the restaurant's playful ghost continues to make life interesting for staff and guests alike.

How to find it: High Toss Pizza and Café restaurant is located at 50 Main Street in Wellfleet on Cape Cod. Take I-495 until the highway terminates and becomes MA 25. At the intersection of MA 25 and MA 6, go left onto MA 6, then right onto the Sagamore

Bridge. After crossing the Sagamore Bridge, stay straight on MA 6, and follow this route up the Cape to Wellfleet. On entering Well-fleet, take a left onto Main Street. For more information, call 508-349-0005.

Inn at Duck Creeke (Wellfleet)

Nestled on a tidal marsh on the outer tip of Cape Cod is the Inn at Duck Creeke, a well-known bed & breakfast/tavern/seafood restaurant/occasional jazz club. Although the inn's paranormal activities haven't been widely publicized, they're becoming as well known within certain circles as Duck Creeke's more expected amenities—particularly for the sheer number and variety of different unexplained events that the owners, staff, and visitors have witnessed over the past several years. The Inn at Duck Creeke is actually a collection of different buildings, some of which date back to the 1700s and were moved to the property from different parts of the Cape. The main building was built in 1810 as a residence for a sea captain, and the property's tavern is one of the oldest still being run on Cape Cod.

Over the years this tavern has had many memorable nights of musical revelry, although some of the nights are memorable for more notorious reasons. Dan Gordon and Gary Joseph's book *Cape Encounters* claims that at least three people have died while on the Inn at Duck Creeke's property, two of them performers at the tavern:

> Many old-timers who have come into the bar share, "Yeah I was there on the night that the piano player died" or "I was here on the night that the guy hanged himself on the old locust tree out there" or "I was here the night the singer died."[158]

Perhaps these unfortunate incidents might explain some of the curious experiences that have occurred to some performers at the Inn at Duck Creeke's tavern. It has been reported that piano players have had their hair pulled while they are performing, that band members have been joined by the sound of a flute or even a phantom voice, and that witnesses in the crowd have seen an apparition walk onstage during a performance, then disappear into thin air.

For years the inn's owners, Bob Morrill and Judy Pihl, have dealt with the problem of finding doors open in the morning all over the inn's grounds even though they had been securely locked the night before. Many of the inn's staff and guests have also reported seeing apparitions, the most commonly recurring of which seems to be a short woman believed to be Eulalia Price, the inn's owner and manager for several decades following the 1930s. The spectral form of this woman has reportedly been seen in many different parts of the inn and tavern on many different occasions—she has even allegedly spoken to some witnesses, offering comfort to those who are troubled. The apparitions of two little girls, possibly twins, have also reportedly appeared to numerous guests.

The most startling event in the Inn at Duck Creeke's long and storied paranormal history occurred when the inn's owners and four friends decided to conduct a séance within the tavern, even though they knew next to nothing about contacting the dead. Most paranormal experts would tell novices that meddling in affairs they don't understand, especially those involving contacting the dead, is unwise—and following their unforgettable experience, Judy, Bob, and their friends would likely echo this advice. The séance encouraged a spiritual presence that resides within the building to come forward, at which point Judy was physically lifted out of her chair by an unseen force. *Cape Encounters* chronicles the remarkable experience:

> [Bob said,] "I looked at Judy, who was sitting next to me, and she was literally starting to come out of her chair. Her chair was tilting back and she was coming up."
>
> "At first, I felt cold and felt like I was being pushed down," explained Judy. "Later I felt as if someone was literally pulling me back, and I said 'Stop!' because it felt very physical. . . ."
>
> Afterward, Eugene told them that at the moment Judy was rising out of her chair, there was a woman in the room behind

her. Karen peeked and saw a number of figures coming from the older part of the house and moving toward the group.[159]

Needless to say, the group stopped the séance at that point; it is troubling to think what would have happened if they hadn't, considering the "number of figures" that were advancing on the group like zombies in a horror movie. Although they can't explain how or why, the group also claims that they lost time during the séance, a phenomenon that is more common with alleged UFO sightings and abductions than paranormal episodes. When they looked at the clock, expecting it to be around 10 PM, to their astonishment it was over three hours later.

It should be remembered that this alarming encounter allegedly occurred as a consequence of the group having invited spirits into their world via a séance—something definitely best left to only the most experienced paranormal experts. Judy and Bob insist that their usual ghost encounters tend to be "more subtle than frightening"[160] and stress that they are comfortable with their ghosts. Such encounters certainly haven't negatively affected the inn's business, as it continues to be a remarkably popular and beloved spot to dine and lodge.

How to find it: The Inn at Duck Creeke is located at 70 Main Street in Wellfleet on Cape Cod. Take I-495, and stay on the highway until it terminates and becomes MA 25. At the intersection of MA 25 and MA 6, take a left onto MA 6, then a right onto the Sagamore Bridge. After crossing the Sagamore Bridge, stay straight on MA 6, and follow this route up the length of Cape Cod. On entering Wellfleet, take a left onto Main Street. For more information or to make reservations, call 508-349-9333, or visit the inn's Web site at www.innatduckcreeke.com.

Old Yarmouth Inn (Yarmouth Port)

The Old Yarmouth Inn bed & breakfast has actually existed as such since 1869—the inn's current owners, Arpad Voros and Sheila Fitzgerald, proudly display a guest book dating back to that year.

The B&B and its attached tavern are also reportedly home to a mischievous ghost that likes to turn on appliances when nobody is looking and send wineglasses and ashtrays flying off tables. According to Mark Jasper's *Haunted Inns of New England,* the alleged ghost's exploits tend to be of the prankish variety; the only truly troubling paranormal occurrence was an incident in which a "groaning howling sound" began to emanate from inside the tavern's wall, and then "the walls and windows began shaking and rattling."[161]

How to find it: The Old Yarmouth Inn, which is on the Register of Historic Places, is located at 223 Main Street (MA 6A) in Yarmouthport on Cape Cod. Take I-495 until the highway terminates and becomes MA 25. At the intersection of MA 25 and MA 6, take a left onto MA 6, then a right onto the Sagamore Bridge. After crossing the Sagamore Bridge, stay straight on MA 6, and follow this route up the length of Cape Cod. Take a left on Willow Street, then a right onto Main Street. For more information or to make reservations, call 508-362-9962, or visit the inn's Web site at www.old yarmouthinn.com.

Orleans Inn (Orleans)

Once a hangout for the disreputable gangsters of the Irish mafia in the 1940s and '50s, what is now the Orleans Inn was built in 1872 by Aaron Snow II—a descendant of an original *Mayflower* family. Although the Orleans Inn has its ties to some of America's earliest European settlers, it was its role as a rowdy gangland hangout—complete with a hidden, secret office where hordes of money was stashed away—that has probably contributed most directly to its reputation as a haunted locale. It was during this era that a bartender named Fred and a dishwasher named Paul both committed suicide in the building, and two prostitutes were murdered near the front door of the inn.[162]

Today, staff and guests claim to occasionally hear the faint sound of human conversation coming from empty rooms, doors that had been double or even triple locked are discovered wide

On the Cape Cod waterfront, the Orleans Inn may be home to ghostly reminders of the inn's more disreputable era.

open in the morning, and the dining room's tabletop candles have occasionally been known to mysteriously light of their own free will. The staff attributes these unexplainable events to Fred, the former bartender, and one of the murdered prostitutes. In his *Haunted Inns of New England*, Mark Jasper relates a story involving one of the Orleans Inn's former waitresses: One night after the inn's restaurant had closed, the waitress was getting ready to lock up the building and leave for the night: "She was alone at the time. As she was leaving, she playfully said, 'Good night, Fred,' referring to Fred the ghost. At that very moment, out of the darkness, a voice said, *'Goood nnnnight.'*"[163]

How to find it: The Orleans Inn stands at 3 Old County Road in Orleans on Cape Cod's ocean side. Take I-495 until the highway terminates and becomes MA 25. At the intersection of MA 25 and MA 6, take a left onto MA 6, then a right onto the Sagamore Bridge. After crossing the Sagamore Bridge, stay straight on MA 6, and follow this route into Orleans. At the Orleans Rotary, stay right and join MA 6A; travel on MA 6A for about ¼ mile, until it merges with MA 28. Follow MA 28 to the intersection with Old County Road. The Orleans Inn will be on the right, on the corner of the Cranberry Highway/Orleans Road (MA 28) and Old County Road. For more information or to make reservations, call 508-255-2222 or 800-863-3039, or visit the inn's Web site at www.orleansinn.com.

Penny House Inn (Eastham)

Originally a sea captain's home built way back in 1690, the Penny House Inn was lived in for a number of years by a family named Horton before it was converted into an inn. Occasionally staff and guests of the 12-room inn claim to see the apparition of a man who matches the description of one Isaiah Horton III, who used to live in the house.[164]

How to find it: The Penny House Inn is located at 4885 State Highway (MA 6) in Eastham on Cape Cod. Take I-495 until the highway terminates and becomes MA 25. At the intersection of MA 25 and MA 6, take a left onto MA 6, then a right onto the Sagamore Bridge. After crossing the Sagamore Bridge, stay straight on MA 6 and follow this route into Eastham. For more information or to make reservations call 508-255-6632 or 800-554-1751, e-mail Penny house@aol.com, or visit the inn's Web site at www.pennyhouse inn.com.

Pepper House Inn (Brewster)

The Pepper House Inn began life as an attractive, Federal Colonial home built by Captain Bangs Pepper in 1793. According to reports, a few guests have complained about feeling a "presence" in guest room number 5, and, according to Mark Jasper's *Haunted Inns of New England,* one couple experienced an incessant pounding on the door—as if someone were trying to get into the room—that continued throughout the night and frightened them so much that they were compelled to move a large piece of furniture to block the door.[165] Even though this episode may sound frightening, the reports of paranormal incidents are few and far between and are greatly outweighed by satisfied guests who have enjoyed every moment of their stay at the charming Pepper House Inn.

How to find it: The Pepper House Inn is located at 2062 Main Street (MA 6A) in Brewster on Cape Cod. Take I-495 until the highway terminates and becomes MA 25. At the intersection of MA 25 and MA 6, stay straight over the Bourne Bridge onto MA 28 (General MacArthur Boulevard); just after crossing the Cape Cod canal, go left at MA 6A, which runs along the northern shore of Cape Cod Bay. For more information or to make reservations, call 508-896-2062 or 888-896-2062, or visit the inn's Web site at www.pepper houseinn.com.

Simmons Homestead Inn (Hyannis Port)

The Simmons Homestead Inn, built by Savannah Simmons in 1820, is now a brightly decorated and inviting inn. Although many centuries-old Cape Cod inns have their own ghosts, the Simmons Homestead Inn is unique in that its ghost is that of a little girl who has purportedly conversed with the inn's living guests. Speculation and eyewitness accounts state that the inn's apparition is that of Susan Simmons, a member of the home's original family who drowned in the pond behind the house back in 1833. In recent years, this apparition has appeared to staff members and guests, one of whom claimed to have held a conversation with the ghost over several hours; according to this guest, the apparition said her name was Susan, which is amazing considering that the guest would have had no prior knowledge of the inn's history.[166]

How to find it: The Simmons Homestead Inn is located at 288 Scudder Avenue in Hyannis Port, Massachusetts. From I-495, stay on the highway until it terminates and becomes MA 25. At the intersection of MA 25 and MA 6, stay straight over the Bourne Bridge onto MA 28. Take a right onto Pitchers Way, which will become Scudder Avenue. For more information or to make reservations, call 508-778-4999 or 800-637-1649, or visit the inn's Web site at www.simmonshomesteadinn.com.

Village Green Inn (Falmouth)

If it seems like many of Cape Cod's elegant bed & breakfasts are home to some kind of paranormal phenomenon or another, consider that many of these inns are so cozy and inviting, it isn't surprising that former residents haven't wanted to leave. This might certainly be the case with Falmouth's Village Green Inn, a lovely place surrounded by a white picket fence, it was built in 1804. It seems that the Village Green Inn might be home to two distinct apparitions—a young woman with flowing black hair, believed to be the spirit of Sarah Dimmicks, the daughter of the home's original owners, who died at the age of 20—and an older gentleman with gray hair wearing a flannel shirt, believed to be the ghost of a Dr. Tripp, another former owner.

How to find it: The Village Green Inn is located at 40 Main Street in Falmouth on Cape Cod. Take I-495 until the highway terminates and becomes MA 25. At the intersection of MA 25 and MA 6, stay straight over the Bourne Bridge onto MA 28 (General MacArthur Boulevard). Follow MA 28 into Falmouth; just after MA 28 becomes Palmer Avenue, go right onto Hewans Street and right again onto Main Street. For more information or to make reservations, call 508-548-5621 or 800-237-1119.

Wildflower Inn (Falmouth)

The cheery and inviting Wildflower Inn is yet another old Cape Cod home converted into a highly successful bed & breakfast that seems to have retained a permanent resident. The alleged mischievous ghost of the Wildflower Inn apparently likes to rearrange items when nobody's looking—handymen and other workers have discovered their tools inexplicably reorganized, and the owner's elderly father intentionally leaves the billiard balls on top of the pool table in a specific order at night only to frequently find them scattered randomly along the table in the morning.[167] This ghost also purportedly appears to guests as a woman with long blond hair wearing a full-length dress in the Forget Me Not room.[168] But it is apparently very selective: there will be no sign of any activity for months at a time, and then the apparition will make itself known several nights in a row to the same guests.[169]

How to find it: The five-guestroom Wildflower Inn is located at 167 Palmer Avenue in Falmouth on Cape Cod. Take I-495 until the highway terminates and becomes MA 25. At the intersection of MA 25 and MA 6, stay straight over the Bourne Bridge onto MA 28 (General MacArthur Boulevard). Follow MA 28 into Falmouth; MA 28 eventually becomes Palmer Avenue. For more information call 508-548-9524, e-mail wldflr167@aol.com, or visit the inn's Web site at www.wildflower-inn.com.

part five
specters of steady habits:
HAUNTED
CONNECTICUT

The Church of Eternal Light in Bristol is said to be haunted by
the ghost of a woman who appears in the bell tower.

"When it comes to demon-infested states, Connecticut gets the prize," writes paranormal/folklore expert Joseph Citro in his book *Passing Strange*.[170] Besides the inordinate number of Connecticut locations that bear the Fallen One's name— "Satan's Ridge," "Devil's Den," "Devil's Hopyard," "Devil's Belt," "Devil's Meditation"—the quiet region of hilly suburbs that effectively represents the dividing line between Boston's "Red Sox Nation" and the Yankees' "Evil Empire" has also, troublingly, been the home to a few notable examples of ostensible demonic possession.

In 1974 an East Hartford man named Anthony Rossi sustained injury from what he attested was a demonically possessed Raggedy Ann doll. In 1981 demonic possession was the attempted defense for convicted murderer Arne Johnson. In 1986 a family in Southington, who had just moved into a new house (that had once been a funeral parlor), claimed that a demonic force had possessed their 15-year-old son. It would seem that the famous paranormal investigators Ed and Lorraine Warren—who are probably best known for their involvement in the Amityville, New York, poltergeist case made famous by *The Amityville Horror*—made a good career choice by calling Connecticut their home.

Besides these incidents of claimed possession, Connecticut is also home to many purported hauntings that don't appear to be the doings of what we conventionally refer to as "ghosts"—that is, the spirits of deceased human beings. A Sleepy Hollow–like headless horseman was once said to roam the area around Canton, poltergeist activity has been famously reported and investigated in Bridgeport and Stratford, a harbinger-of-death black dog is said to roam the woods of Meriden, local lore states that curses abound on Charles Island, and not one but *two* abandoned Connecticut settlements (Bara-Hack and Dudleytown) can be found. Rural Connecticut was even the setting for Tim Burton's 1988 film *Beetlejuice*, in which a recently deceased couple employs what can best be described as a somewhat demonic presence to rid their old house of its new inhabitants, to hilarious results.

Although the Nutmeg State could be said to have the greatest *variety* of paranormal activity of the New England states, Connecticut is not without its conventional ghosts, many of which call home the state's colonial-era taverns and inns. Indeed, Connecticut's storied links to American history help provide it with a paranormal pedigree that is rivaled by very few other areas in the United States.

Litchfield Hills and Western Connecticut

Bethel High School (Bethel)

A school that has been unfairly and cruelly dubbed "suicide high" by many cynical teens,[171] Bethel High School has had several reports of apparitions appearing within the second-floor hallways. Local lore states that at some point in the 1970s—different sources cite different years—a heartbroken young girl hung herself in the second-floor girls' bathroom. Since then, according to the legend, unsupervised backpacks left in the bathroom are later found ransacked and, some state, torn to shreds.

How to find it: Bethel High School, at 300 Whittlesey Drive, is part of the David W. Deakin Educational Park. From I-84, take exit 9 onto CT 25, turn left at Hawleyville Road, and take a right at Mount Pleasant Road (CT 6). Follow Route 6 for about 1½ miles, go left onto Old Hawleyville Road, right onto Plumtrees Road, and left again onto Whittlesey Road.

Dudleytown (Cornwall)

Nestled deep within the woods of Connecticut's quiet Litchfield Hills lie the remnants of an abandoned settlement—a settlement whose storied past has become one of the best-known paranormal legends in American folklore. Dudleytown—also known as Dudleyville and Owlsbury—has been the topic of numerous investigations, has inspired several fictional ghost stories, and has even been called (by *Ghostbusters* star and paranormal aficionado Dan Aykroyd[172]) "the most haunted place on Earth."[173]

Unfortunately, as is the case with many American legends, the story of Dudleytown has been retold and embellished throughout the years, the details varying wildly from one telling to another, to the point where it is difficult to ascertain the true history behind the legend. If you were to pick up three different guides to haunted locations in America, it's very likely that you'd read three diverse versions of the Dudleytown legend. One book—*The Legend of Dudleytown*, written by Reverend Gary P. Dudley, reputedly descended from the Dudley line—even insists that the Dudleytown "legend" is largely a fabrication, and the former settlement is hardly the haunted nexus of negative energy that it's claimed to be.

Because I grew up in Connecticut, the Dudleytown legend was one that I personally witnessed being passed enthusiastically by word of mouth from one would-be ghost hunter to another. In fact, when I was in high school, I made several visits to the so-called ghost town. This was in the days before a rash of visits by unfortunately irresponsible teens who—undoubtedly inspired by 1999's *The Blair Witch Project* movie—left campfires burning, left litter behind, and, in some cases, vandalized the property. These bad-apple incidents caused the property owners (a group known as Dark Entry, Incorporated) to close the site to outsiders and post no-trespassing signs. Recent visitors to Dudleytown have been arrested and fined for trespassing, so take heed.

The settlement of Dudleytown was founded by Thomas Grifis in 1739—however, even this fact is disputed. Although the land was purchased in 1739, it's doubtful that Grifis lived in the Cornwall area anytime before 1741.[174] One source even claims that Dudleytown was "first settled in 1738 by the William Dudley family,"[175] but this claim is not echoed in any other description of the town. By the late 1770s, the first of several unfortunate circumstances began to occur in the Dudleytown settlement—circumstances that paranormal investigators claim to be evidence of a Dudleytown curse.

According to at least three tellings of the Dudleytown legend, in the England of 1510 a man named Edmund Dudley was beheaded for his plot to overthrow King Henry VIII. Apparently decapitation wasn't punishment enough for Dudley's conspiracy against the king, for the legend states that Dudley's entire lineage had been cursed from that day forth, "to the effect that all Dudley family descendants from that point on would be surrounded by horror and death."[176] According to Gary P. Dudley's Web site, however, English history books prove that Edmund Dudley wasn't beheaded for conspiracy; rather, he was a scapegoat for the downturn of the English economy under King Henry VII.[177] This disparity between historical fact and "common knowledge" just goes to show that once the kernel of a story has been planted, if people want to believe it enough, it will continue to grow no matter what the truth may be.

Interestingly, although the "curse" is mentioned in nearly every depiction of the Dudleytown legend, the origin of the supposed curse is unknown. This curse was apparently transferred onto Thomas Grifis's land in 1748 when brothers Abiel, Barzillai, and Gideon (but no William!) Dudley moved onto the property. Although it is fact that the three Dudley brothers lived in Dudleytown, both Cheri Revai and Gary P. Dudley have called into question the brothers' connection to Edmund Dudley's lineage. Whether or not the supposed "Dudley curse" was the cause of all Dudleytown's woes (assuming, of course, that the Dudleys of Cornwall, Connecticut, are at all connected with the Dudleys of 16th-century England), it can't be denied that the small settlement experienced more than its fair share of misfortune over its short existence.

Dudleytown's bad-luck streak began in 1774, when an unknown illness struck the Adoniram Carter family. (Carter had purchased Abiel Dudley's home, and it is this connection that presumably links the unfortunate events of Dudleytown's history with the supposed curse.) Every member of Carter's immediate family died from the mysterious illness. Hoping to escape the same fate, Adoniram's brother, Nathaniel, fled to Binghamton, New York, with his wife and four children. But on the way to their new home, Nathaniel Carter's family was attacked by hostile Native Americans. Nathaniel, his wife, and his infant son were killed; his three other children were kidnapped and taken farther north.

Dudleytown's bad luck continued in 1804, when Sarah Fye was struck by lightning while standing on her front porch; her husband, Revolutionary War hero General Herman Swift, was said to have gone insane by the incident, "aimlessly wandering around the town, driven mad by his wife's cruel demise."[178] In 1872 Dudleytown resident Mary Cheney—who had married *New York Tribune* founder Horace Greeley—died mere days before her husband lost the U.S. presidential race.[179] Just a few years later, the children of John Patrick Brophy mysteriously disappeared, and his wife died of tuberculosis.[180] Shortly thereafter, the Brophy house burned to the ground, and John Patrick Brophy was never heard from again.

By the time the 20th century arrived, Dudleytown—like Bara-Hack across the state—was officially a ghost town, a completely abandoned settlement. That didn't deter New York physician Dr. William Clarke, who—apparently yearning to find an escape from the city—built a summer home in Dudleytown sometime between 1900 and 1920.[181] One weekend, Clarke left his wife alone at the home; when Clarke returned, his wife, who had apparently seen or experienced something terrifying, was "in a state of abject fear,"[182] and the encounter had caused her to go "completely insane."[183] The fate of Clarke's wife is still in debate—Elaine Kuzmeskus claims that Mrs. Clarke committed suicide two weeks later, and Cheri Revai claims that Mrs. Clarke had to be institutionalized for the rest of her life.

It seems that the fate of the Clarkes—the last family to live in Dudleytown—was the impetus that begat Dudleytown's reputation as a cursed place. In 1938 a book called *They Found a Way*[184] told the tale, and various media sources repeated it.

Throughout all these years, residents and visitors frequently reported seeing ghostly apparitions, black shapes emerging from trees and rocks, mysterious unidentified beasts roaming the forest, and the like. These sightings only enhanced Dudleytown's reputation as a cursed place. Ever the skeptic, Gary Dudley posits that all the ghosts seen over the years in Dudleytown might very well have been caused by one of the area's most abundant natural resources: rye: "If one is experienced in making bread, you are well aware that if rye is left for a while, it goes bad. The resulting [fungus] is almost a hallucinogen, [akin to LSD], and yes, it makes you SEE things, and it could also KILL you. Could that account for the supposed sightings of demons?"[185]

The existence of ergot-infected rye in Cornwall might represent a reasonable explanation for why a resident—William Clarke's wife, for example—would claim they had seen ghosts and demons, but it doesn't explain why visitors to the site had reported strange sightings up until Dudleytown's being closed to the public in the late 1990s. There are numerous reports of visitors photographing strange mists and globes, seeing strange animals stalking through the woods, hearing unnatural sounds in the area, and even just feeling some kind of negative energy on the plot of Cornwall ground known as Dudleytown.

Also to contend with is the fact that Dudleytown is what's known as a biological dead zone, an area where animals simply tend not to live. Although there are trees and plenty of owls (hence the name "Owlsbury") in the area, it does seem surprisingly still and quiet for a parcel of forest in rural Connecticut, an area that is normally teeming with chipmunks, squirrels, deer, bobcats, bears, and birds of all shapes and sizes. Is there a geographical reason for this anomaly? Does the lack of wildlife have something to do with the kind of vegetation growing in the area? Or do the animals—using the same keen instincts that allow them to correctly predict earthquakes—sense something about Dudleytown that causes them to stay away?

One of the most recurring themes for visitors to the ghost town is that of machinery not functioning properly. Both Dennis William Hauck and Ed and Lorraine Warren tell of television and movie crews who, like the investigators of the Bara-Hack settlement, could not get their equipment to work at all at the site. (According to Hauck's book, the film crew also witnessed a "black shape rising out of an old stone foundation. As they got closer, they all experienced trouble breathing, as if the life force were being sucked out of them."[186]) Doing search online results in numerous tales of visitors' cars not working once they returned to the Dark Entry Forest trail—a phenomenon I personally experienced. When I was in high school and felt the overwhelming desire, as many teens do, to scare myself silly, I and a group of my friends drove up to Dudleytown one late-summer evening. (This was, of course, before the area was closed to the public.) After stumbling around in the dark for some time, we finally found the abandoned settlement. It was eerily quiet—not even a cricket could be heard. We snapped some pictures and, already terrified by the fairly benign experience, returned to the cars to find that neither of them would start. If one of the cars hadn't turned over, we would have simply assumed that we had left the interior lights on by mistake and worn down the battery—but the fact that neither car would start was simply too strange. As these were the days before cell phones were normal accoutrements for American teens, we had no way to call for help. Afraid that our parents or the police would think that we were up to no good at night in the woods, we decided to roll our cars down what was then called Dark Entry Road and claim that we had experienced car trouble on the well-traveled Route 7. Once we got halfway down the hill, however, a friend of mine decided to try starting his car again. It fired right up. I tried mine. It also started immediately without a problem. Puzzled, we decided to head home for the night just in case our car trouble returned. I never experienced any trouble with that car again until its water pump failed over two years later. And when my friend developed his roll of film, there were white orbs in roughly a third of the photographs.

A few weeks after this experience, a different group of friends talked me into taking the drive back up to Dudleytown; they had been so terrified by our story that they *had* to experience it for themselves. Getting out of the car at the top of Dark Entry Road, we heard what sounded like some kind of loud growling coming from deep within the woods, followed soon by the sound of a woman wailing. We decided at that point that it was perhaps not the best night to venture into the supposedly haunted site. That winter, a friend from my original exploratory group to Dudleytown attended a lecture on ghost hunting and demonology by the Warrens (of *Amityville Horror* fame) at Central Connecticut State University. The lecture was followed by a Q & A session, during which my friend asked the ghost hunters about Dudleytown. The Warrens' response was curt: Don't ever go there, under any circumstances. Lorraine, a purported psychic, claims that the site is one of the most intense nexuses of negative psychic energy that she has ever experienced. Worse, most paranormal experts will tell you that negative energy can follow a person out of a "cursed" or "haunted" location. And so can malicious spirits.

With the technological advances of the last couple decades, one of the most recently discovered and increasingly recurring paranormal occurrences is electronic voice phenomenon (EVP). Simply stated, EVP is the sound of a noise or voice on audiotape or videotape that was not heard by investigators as they were recording live. A visit to the Ghost Investigator's Society (GIS) Web site[187] turns up dozens of professionally recorded EVP; the GIS's recordings have been featured numerous times on *Coast to Coast AM*, and many believe them to be the closest thing we have to proof of the paranormal. Sometimes the voices seem to be responding to actions or questions of those recording, sometimes they don't. For example:

> GIS member Barbara recorded this voice while we were investigating an old abandoned movie theater. One of the members had just complained about a previous occasion there, when a person most of us didn't know showed up. Jenny's words were, "I didn't even know who this guy was," and this voice replied, "I know who it was."

Sure enough, Dudleytown has had its share of EVP experiences (when the mechanical devices actually worked)—and would certainly have produced more if the site had remained open to the public. A fellow named Matt from East Hartford went into Dudley-town with a camcorder and some friends in the mid-1990s. After looking around a bit, the cameraman dropped the camera. Seeing the bemused look on the faces of his friends, the cameraman quickly tried to explain that it felt like something had physically knocked the camera right out of his hands. When they went back and reviewed the film, one can clearly hear the sound of an other-worldly growl just before the camera falls to the ground and the screen goes black. And when Jenna from Bristol went into Dudley-town for a high school project, she and her friends also brought a camcorder with them. They didn't experience any strange activity while at the site, but when they played back the tape, several min-utes of the recording had what sounded like a woman screaming or wailing in the background.

There have been well over a hundred reports of paranormal ac-tivity at the site.[188] How can this be, if, as Gary Dudley insists, there was never any curse of the town, and the bad luck of its residents had been purely consequential? As the curse legend grew, enthu-siasts of the paranormal—from curious teens to ghost hunters, Wiccans, and Spiritualists—were naturally drawn to the site. As anyone who listens to *Coast to Coast AM* regularly will tell you, many hauntings and possessions occur due to intent; the individu-als involved *want* or *expect* to experience the paranormal, so they do (or at least they trick themselves into thinking they do). Even though Ed and Lorraine Warren's depiction of the Dudleytown leg-end is by and large the least consistent with other books on the subject,[189] the famous ghost hunters come to perhaps the most reasonable conclusion: people have bought into the Dudleytown curse myth and want the place to be haunted, so they have gone to the site to perform occultist practices such as séances—exactly the kind of practices that, as the Warrens argue, invite demonic forces into the world in the first place. In a rare moment of agree-ment with the Warrens, Gary Dudley is of the opinion that if Dudleytown is haunted today (he isn't completely convinced), it is probably due more to the 20th-century visitors to the site than to any 16th-century curse:

So much has been made of the place—New Agers have chan-neled spirits there, mediums have done séances there, Satanists have done their rituals there, and add all that up, and the cliché' "if you play with fire, you are going to get burned" comes to mind. . . . I know some true paranormal investigators . . . [who] have said that IF Dudleytown is haunted now, it is be-cause of what people have brought in—not by what was orig-inally there.[190]

So, is Dudleytown a cursed plot of land, a nexus of negative en-ergy that has the potential to inflict horror and death on all who tread within? Is it a self-fulfilling prophecy, a town that became haunted *because* of its legend? Or is Dudleytown simply an aban-doned settlement like any other and no more dangerous than any other parcel of woods in New England? Perhaps Dudleytown is simply a spot that, as Susan Smitten suggests, was conjured up by overactive teenage male imaginations to scare their girlfriends when they parked at the top of Dark Entry Forest Road?[191] Although its history remains in debate, there have been far too many reports of paranormal phenomena in Dudleytown to deny its reputation as a haunted location; perhaps it *is*, as Dan Aykroyd claims, the most haunted place on Earth.

How to find it: Dudleytown is located in Cornwall, which is in Litchfield County. The closest roadway to Dudleytown is Bald Mountain Road (formerly Dark Entry Road), which is off CT 45, near Mohawk Mountain Ski Resort. Head south down CT 7 through the village of Cornwall Bridge. Take a left on CT 45; the turn for Bald Mountain Hill Road is only about a quarter mile farther. Unfortu-nately, due to some isolated incidents in the 1990s, the private land on which Dudleytown resides is now closed to the public. Any cars parked at the top of Bald Mountain Road are subject to towing, and any trespassers are subject to fines and arrest. However, the wooded path that leads to Dudleytown from the *opposite* direc-tion is still open to the public during the day and is a popular hik-ing trail. It seems that visitors are evaluated on a case-by-case basis by authorities; if the visitor seems to be in the woods looking for

Dudleytown (especially at night), they might find themselves in trouble; but if the visitor is hiking on the popular trail in broad daylight, the authorities are apparently lenient.

Despite this, it is not advised that anyone attempt to find Dudleytown while it's still closed to the public. It *is* private property, and any attempts to check the place out constitute trespassing. Moreover, if one listens to Ed and Lorraine Warren, visiting Dudleytown isn't a good idea anyway, whether it's open to the public or not.

Fairfield Hills Asylum (Newtown)

What was once known as Fairfield State Hospital, Fairfield Hills Asylum is a sprawling complex of buildings—complete with dark, underground tunnels connecting them—that housed nearly four thousand mentally insane inmates.[192] Perhaps not surprising considering the hospital's reputation (it was known to be one of the leading institutions in the study and implementation of shock therapy and was reputedly the first U.S. hospital to perform a lobotomy), since its closing, Fairfield Hills has earned a reputation for being quite haunted. Wailing screams and insane laughter have reportedly been heard echoing throughout the hospital's abandoned, crumbling underground passages. Fairfield Hills' reputation as a paranormal hotspot has grown in recent years due to an episode of MTV's hit show *Fear* being filmed within; the hospital was also the site of the 1996 film *Sleepers*.

How to find it: The Fairfield Hills complex lies dormant on Main Street (CT 25 and CT 6) in Newtown. From I-84, take exit 10, which will lead right onto CT 6. However, Fairfield Hills is private property, and trespassing is illegal. The property is patrolled by security officers and the Newtown police at all times. The town of Newtown is currently trying to figure out exactly what to do with the abandoned campus.

Guntown Cemetery (Naugatuck)

As if the setting of a graveyard in a rural area of Connecticut weren't eerie enough, Naugatuck's Guntown Cemetery has earned a reputation for strange sights and sounds that have no logical explanation. There have been numerous reports of a black dog roaming the cemetery, which many interpret to be a foreboding sign of death (sometimes only one person in a group actually sees the dog). Children's laughter has been heard in the middle of the night, and the sound of music has been heard coming from the woods, growing louder and closer until it could only be emanating from some unseen source within the cemetery.[193] Some recent visitors to the cemetery report that although they have no cell phone reception (yes, it's a dead zone), they have received a call with no number while standing in the cemetery, and all they could hear on the other end has been heavy breathing.

How to find it: From I-84, take exit 16 to CT 188. Take a right onto Whittemore Road, then another right onto South Street. Follow South Street until it comes to a four-way intersection, and bear right onto Guntown Road, which is less than a mile long and connects South Street and Griswold Road. The cemetery will be on the right side of the road.

eastern connecticut and the quiet corner

Bara-Hack Village (Pomfret)

Even though Dudleytown gets all the attention in terms of New England's haunted abandoned settlements, Connecticut is home to the remains of yet another deserted ghost village. In the "Quiet Corner" of northeastern Connecticut, in the deep isolation of the Pomfret woods lies what used to be the Bara-Hack settlement. Although the site has long been abandoned, on arriving in what was once Bara-Hack, visitors and investigators report hearing the sounds of daily life as it might have existed in the 19th century.

The first settler of Bara-Hack—a name derived from the Welsh term for "the breaking of bread"[194]—was reputedly one Obadiah Higgenbotham, a British soldier who deserted his army during the

Revolutionary War and sought isolation deep in the northeast Connecticut woods. Shortly thereafter, Higgenbotham was joined by one Jonathan Randall from Rhode Island, who settled nearby with his family and a number of slaves. According to the book *Passing Strange* by Joseph Citro, it was Randall's slaves who reported the area's first examples of what might have been paranormal phenomena—the slaves had begun to see the apparitions of recently departed loved ones in and around what would become the town cemetery.[195]

Unlike the Dudleytown settlement, the demise of Bara-Hack wasn't due to a supernatural curse or negative energy—unless one considers a weak economy to be either of those. Following the Civil War, a U.S. depression forced many rural dwellers to abandon their homes and move to the city to find work. According to Susan Smitten's book *Ghost Stories of New England,* the last interment in the Bara-Hack cemetery was dated 1890; the town had lasted barely a century.

Still, the town's death gave life to a new legend as tales about visitors to the site experiencing strange phenomena have been circulating for the last few years. What is probably the most popular story about the abandoned settlement was a favorite campfire story for children growing up in suburban Connecticut, which is retold in Smitten's book:

> One of the popular stories concerned a trapper who came to the village to find supplies in what appeared to be a completely deserted village. In some of the homes and buildings, he found warm food that had been laid out on tables. Yet no people were anywhere to be found. He was so frightened by the scene that he ran away from the town.[196]

That story of evidence of recent habitation in a deserted village is unique, but other visitors to the site have reported experiencing comparatively more subtle phenomena, which hinted that the woods they were standing in was once a bustling village.

In 1927 naturalist Odell Shephard reported hearing the voices of women talking in the lonely woods. Paranormal researcher Paul

Eno visited the Bara-Hack site in 1971, and his team reported hearing dogs barking, cows mooing, and human voices. Eno's group reportedly also saw various apparitions:

> The team claims to have spent seven minutes watching a bearded face hover over a wall of the cemetery. But what really unnerved them was the sight of a babylike figure resting in the branches of the old elm tree.[197]

It is easy to see from these reports how Bara-Hack earned its other nickname: "The Village of Voices." More recently, paranormal investigator Thomas D'Agostino visited Bara-Hack and reported similar findings to those of Eno and Shepherd:

> Group members claim they could hear a bubbling brook, although the creek had long since dried up. The sound of wagon wheels and the crunch of horses' hooves approached, and then, to the group's astonishment, the [invisible] noisy vehicle passed right by and continued down the road. Some members of D'Agostino's team claimed to hear mothers calling out to their children.[198]

Like Dudleytown, Bara-Hack represents the skeleton of a thriving settlement that was unable to survive into the current century. But unlike Connecticut's more notorious ghost village, Bara-Hack is not a nexus of negative energy and possible malicious intent. Bara-Hack is merely haunted—if it is indeed haunted—by the reminders of a long-past day-to-day life that the settlement once enjoyed.

Paul Eno believes that people are indeed seeing and hearing things in Bara-Hack, but what they are hearing and seeing has little to do with what we conventionally refer to as "ghosts." Instead, referring to quantum physics and the nature of time, Eno believes what people are witnessing in Bara-Hack are glimpses into another time or a parallel universe—history being played back like a hologram or a CD.[199] Whatever the explanation for the various experiences in the Pomfret woods, what is clear is that they are simply a peek into a village's past life and not the more nefarious forces that may be at work in Connecticut's *other* ghost village.

How to find it: At the intersection of CT 44 and CT 97 in Pomfret, take CT 97 north to a side street on the left. The entrance to Bara-Hack is a grown-over footpath on the right, just beyond a small brook, which you would follow for ¼ mile before stumbling on the remains of the settlement (which is basically only a couple of cellars, foundations, and a cemetery). However, this land is private property, and trespassing is prohibited.

Benton Homestead (Tolland)

Although perhaps not as historically relevant as, say, Pettibone's Tavern or the Hale Homestead, the Benton house in Tolland was the site of more than one interesting and touching tale since its construction in 1720, and the ghosts that have been seen in and around the building are testament to the house's storied past. Men's voices have been heard in the dwelling's basement, a woman wearing a wedding gown has been seen sobbing, and uniformed Hessian soldiers have been spotted roaming the building's grounds.

During the Revolutionary War, Daniel Benton's grandson Elisha reportedly contracted smallpox as a prisoner of war. After being released, nobody in the Benton family was willing to care for the ailing Elisha due to their fear of contracting the potentially fatal disease. The only one to step forward was Elisha's 17-year-old girlfriend, Jemima, whom the family had refused to let the boy marry. Not long after Elisha passed on, Jemima also fell victim to the disease. Out of respect, the family buried her on the family plot—but separated by a driveway, for it was customary that only married couples be buried side by side.[200] Some paranormal researchers believe that the wedding-gown-wearing apparition is none other than Jemima, pining for the marriage that never came to be.

According to Cheri Revai's *Haunted Connecticut,* the Benton homestead had also housed Hessian soldiers who were passing through Connecticut on their way to ships in Boston that would take them back to Germany; historical records indicate that many soldiers met their future wives in the Tolland area and decided to settle in Connecticut instead of sailing out of Boston. This might

The Daniel Benton Homestead in Tolland is now a museum—and the reputed home of many ghosts.

explain the uniformed soldiers that have been seen in and around the home.

How to find it: The Benton Homestead, now a museum that captures how life would have been for the Benton family during the 18th and 19th centuries, is located on Metcalf Road in Tolland. From I-84, take exit 68 toward Tolland/Mansfield. Go right off the exit onto Merrow Road (CT 195), right again onto Goose Road (after the gas station), and another right onto Anderson Road, which becomes Metcalf Road. The Benton Homestead will be about ½ mile down the road on the right. The Benton Homestead Museum is open seasonally; for more information, call 860-974-1875, or visit pages.cthome.net/tollandhistorical/Benton.htm.

Hale Homestead (Coventry)
The childhood home of Revolutionary War hero Nathan Hale—who famously exclaimed, just before being put to death by his

British captors, "I only regret that I have but one life to lose for my country"—resides on a 12-acre plot of south Coventry, alongside the 500-acre Hale State Forest. The mansion's original owners, Richard and Elizabeth Hale, had 12 children (including Nathan)— and when Elizabeth died, Richard remarried Abigail Cobb Adams, who had 7 children of her own. To accommodate the large family, the original 1746 mansion was enlarged over the decades, including the addition of a schoolroom. As a result of the home's large size, many generations of Hales occupied the grounds over the course of time until 1914, when it was sold to George Dudley Seymour, who would restore and remodel the mansion.

The earliest clues that the Hale Homestead might be haunted appeared shortly after Seymour purchased the home. A friend of his rode with him to the then-abandoned mansion; when the friend peered in the schoolroom window, he came "eyeball to eyeball with an elderly gentleman dressed in colonial-style garb. The entity stepped back inside the room and vanished."[201] Later, when the friend viewed a portrait of patriarch Richard Hale, he realized that the man he had seen looking back at him through the schoolroom window was none other than the mansion's original owner.

Throughout the years, other members of the Hale family—including Richard's son Joseph as well as his brother John and John's bride, Sara—have been seen roaming the mansion's halls. Also apparently still residing within the Hale homestead along with the ghosts of the Hale family is a former servant—a lady in white who is occasionally seen sweeping the halls and tidying up the kitchen. According to neighbors, the apparition is likely to be Lydia Carpenter, the Hale's family servant for many years, who was known to eavesdrop on the conversations of family members.[202] Perhaps not surprising, the lady in white has also been seen loitering barely within sight just outside doorways and around corners, almost as if she is still eavesdropping. Old habits die hard—especially in the state of steady habits.

Besides sightings of apparitions moving throughout the house, strange sounds are often heard, even when the house is otherwise

Apparitions in Colonial-style attire and the sound of rattling chains have given the Hale Homestead in Coventry a well-deserved reputation.

empty, such as chains rattling in the basement and the noise of heavy footfalls coming down the home's back stairwell. The house is now under the care of the Antiquarian and Landmarks Society, and although visitors occasionally claim to see and hear things they cannot explain, the home's current administrator, Desiree Mobed, has not experienced anything otherworldly at the Hale Homestead since taking the position in 1995.[203]

How to find it: The Nathan Hale Homestead, located at 2299 South Street in Coventry, is now a museum open seasonally to visitors. Take route I-384 east until it ends, becoming CT 44 and CT 6 east. Continue on CT 6 for about 3 miles, until you reach South Street on the left. The Hale Homestead is visible just a short distance down South Street. For information and tour arrangements, call 860-742-6917, or visit www.ctlandmarks.org/hale.php.

Homespun Farm (Griswold)

Built in 1740 by Simon Brewster—a descendant of *Mayflower* passenger William Brewster—the Homespun Farm is now a popular
bed & breakfast. It is currently home to Kate and Ron Bauer, who
purchased the property in 1996, and it might very well still be home
to its original inhabitants. The Bauers and guests often hear soft
footfalls that they attribute to Mrs. Brewster walking up and down
the stairs, and both Kate and Ron have reported that the apparition of Simon Brewer appeared to them in the garden to offer sub-
liminal gardening advice! The Bauers seem fine with the idea of
owning a haunted inn and consider their ghosts to be of the
friendly "watchful spirit" variety.[204]

How to find it: The Homespun Farm is located at 300 Preston
Road (CT 164) in Griswold. From I-395, take exit 85. Go right at the
end of the exit onto CT 164, Preston Road. Homespun Farm is
about ¼ mile down this road on the right. For information or reservations call 860-376-5178 or 888-889-6673, e-mail relax@homespun
farm.com, or visit their Web site at www.homespunfarm.com.

Notch Hollow (Tolland)

Notch Hollow was a granite-quarry settlement, complete with a
railway line, dating back to the early 20th century. Following the
construction of CT 6, however, the town declined to the point
where only one of the original settlement's buildings today remains. Nowadays Notch Hollow is best known for extremely localized weather anomalies that elude explanation. One of the most
frequently reported incidents involves car windows either freezing
up or misting up (depending on the season) as people drive over
the now-abandoned railway line. The apparition of a ghostly steam
engine has also been witnessed on more than one occasion, and
many visitors, while standing down in the gulch of the quarry itself,
report hearing a voice singing from the ledges above. According
to Cheri Revai's *Haunted Connecticut,* Notch Hollow was the home
of a few quarry accidents as well as a couple of unsolved murders:
a young Dutchman was murdered by fellow colonists after break-

ing the rules and falling in love with a Native American woman, and the chief of the Pequot tribe was killed with a tomahawk at the end of the Pequot War.[205]

How to find it: Notch Hollow is a former quarry located along Quarry Road in "Quarryville" or Bolton Notch, which itself is part of Tolland. Take I-384 eastward until it ends, splitting into CT 44 and CT 6. After about 1,000 feet there's a five-way intersection at which CT 44 and CT 6 split; bear left onto Quarry Road, keeping Bolton Notch State Park on the left. Notch Hollow used to exist along the first mile or so of this road.

Putnam Science Academy (Putnam)

Nestled in the serene northeast section of Connecticut known as the Quiet Corner, the Putnam Science Academy is now a private boarding high school focusing on science and mathematics. Before the academy opened in 2003, the building had been used as a Catholic high school and a hospital. When the building was being renovated during the first years of the new millennium, construction workers and electricians complained about hearing the sound of children's laughter coming from the building's basement. An electrician named Mark claimed that he and his coworkers witnessed a strange light coming from the basement even though there was no electricity in the building. As he was walking up the stairs one day, he also claimed to have felt a force behind him pushing him up, almost as if a presence were trying to force him out of the basement area.

How to find it: The Putnam Science Academy is located at 18 Maple Street in Putnam. From I-395, take exit 95 onto Kennedy Drive. Go left onto Pomfret Street, then right onto Church Street and left again onto Maple Street. For more information, call 860-928-5010, e-mail at info@putnamscience.org, or visit the school's Web site at www.putnamscience.org.

At the Avon Old Farms School, a little girl is said to search eternally for her mother.

GReateR HaRtfORD anD tHe faRminGtON vaLLey

Avon Old Farms School (Avon)

A private boarding school tucked away in the woods of the affluent Connecticut town of Avon, Old Farms School holds an excellent academic reputation. But it is also purportedly home to the apparition of a little girl who has appeared in the early hours of the morning in one of the homes attached to the dorm building. Local legend states that she is searching for her mother.[206]

How to find it: Avon Old Farms School is about halfway down the narrow, winding Old Farms Road, which connects CT 167 to CT 10. Coming from Hartford, take CT 44 over Avon Mountain to CT 10 on your left. Old Farms Road will be the first light, on the right. From

Canton, take a left on CT 167, and Old Farms Road will be on the left.

Church of Eternal Light (Bristol)

In a plot of thick woods between the hamlets of Bristol and Burlington sits a plain white church, looking lonely in its solitude and silence. The Church of Eternal Light houses a "pagan spiritualist" denomination,[207] as evidenced by the Maypole in the church's front yard. Perhaps the church's embrace of the spiritual has created a welcoming atmosphere to the departed. Passersby, on late summer nights, have reported viewing a spectral maiden in white standing alone in the church's bell tower. In the 1990s the original bell tower was replaced (reputedly due to a lightning strike) and now sits behind the church, just on the edge of the thick woods. Since then, there have been reports of the apparition being seen in both the old bell tower near the woods and the new one atop the church.

How to find it: The Church of Eternal Light is located at 1199 Hill Street, on a country road that connects Bristol to Burlington. From CT 69 in Burlington heading toward Bristol, take a right onto Scoville Road. This road will take a hard, nearly 90-degree left turn, at which point it becomes West Chippens Hill Road, a curvy country byway that eventually straightens out before reaching Bristol. The Church of Eternal Light will be on the right, just after the Bristol town line. From CT 72, take a left onto Marsh Road, which borders a reservoir on the left. This road runs past Chippanee Golf Club on the left, after which you will turn left onto Hill Street. Hill Street becomes West Chippens Hill Road at the Burlington line; The Church of Eternal Light, from this direction, will be on the left-hand side of the road.

Gay City (Bolton)

Gay City was founded in 1796 by a religious sect made up of some 30 settlers, led by Elijah Andrus. After Andrus packed up and left following a series of disputes with his disciples, John Gay became

The resting place of Elisabeth Palmiter in Burlington's Green Lady Cemetery, where the ghost of the graveyard's eponymous "Green Lady" is said to be searching for her lost love.

the community's leader—and the town took his name. A man named Henry Sumner took over the religious and spiritual leadership of the community, but unfortunately "their families behaved like the Hatfields and the McCoys."[208] The settlement struggled for many years following its inception—that is, until a wool mill was constructed just downstream of a pond that had been dug for water collection. Bizarrely, the water running to the water wheel that supplied the mill with water power was said to have run uphill—which some considered a sign of the devil. Despite the mill, Gay City nonetheless struggled to survive, and the population dwindled. When the mill burned down in 1830, it represented the final blow, the nail in the coffin that would toll the town's death knell.

Today the area is preserved as Gay City State Park and is home to a couple of strange apparitions: a skeleton standing over a charcoal pit and a man who runs through the forest headless, carrying his very own head in his hands.[209] Around the time of the Civil War, a jewel peddler's corpse was found disposed of in the charcoal pit, and a young man was apparently slashed to death and then decapitated by the village blacksmith. Neither case was ever brought to trial.[210] Perhaps that's why these spirits have found no rest.

How to find it: What was once Gay City, now part of Gay City State Park, is just south of Bolton, near New London. From I-84, take exit 59 (I-384 east), and follow I-384 for about 8 miles. Take exit 5 to merge with CT 85, and continue on CT 85, taking two rights—first onto Bolton Center Road and then onto Clark Road. Gay City itself is within the state park; the park's pond was once the millpond for the water wheel and was said to have flowed uphill.

Green Lady Cemetery (Burlington)

A small, disused cemetery off a dirt road in rural Burlington has become well known locally for visions of a strange anthropomorphic mist—known as the Green Lady—traveling along the road near the graveyard. The cemetery—also called the Seventh Day Baptist Cemetery—was built as a plot for the members of the nearby Seventh Day Baptist Church. Local legend states that the ghost belongs to Elisabeth Palmiter—probably largely due to a young couple, who, on developing a roll of film discovered a greenish-yellow apparition standing behind them over this young woman's tombstone.[211] It is widely believed that some time in the early 1800s, Elisabeth drowned in the nearby swamp when she went out searching for her husband, who had gone out to get supplies during a winter storm, and she still haunts the area to this day.[212]

How to find it: The Green Lady Cemetery is a small plot of headstones on Upson Road in Burlington. From CT 8 or CT 72, take a right onto CT 4 east toward Farmington and Avon. Upson Road will be on the left. After passing swamplands on both sides, the cemetery will be just a couple hundred feet up on the left side of Upson Road, enclosed by a low stone wall.

The Huguenot House museum in East Hartford reportedly has mischievous spirits residing within its centuries-old structure.

Huguenot House (East Hartford)

Now a museum that displays the furnishings and amenities of Connecticut life in the 18th and early 19th centuries, Huguenot House is quite possibly still the home of one of its original residents—despite the dwelling having been moved from its initial location.

Built in 1761, Huguenot House belonged to the family of Edmund Belmont and, later, his son Makens.[213] In the early 1980s the Historical Society of East Hartford began a renovation on the house that proved to be the beginning of the building's haunted reputation. Workers who had been alone on the bottom floor reported hearing the sounds of hammering upstairs; on investigation, nobody was there. Likewise, one worker arrived early one morning to hear the sounds of hammers coming from within, although the house was still locked from the day before and nobody was inside. When Herman Marshall, the consultant in charge of the restoration, attempted to activate the home's alarm system over the phone, he was told that the alarm company could not do so due to the sounds of hammers being picked up on the supposedly empty home's microphone!

Several unexplainable incidents have taken place in the home over the years. During a routine tour, a spinning wheel located in one of the rooms began rotating on its own. There have also been strange sightings in and around the house at night when the home was locked up and supposedly empty, such as sparks within the unused fireplace as well as the apparition of a girl holding a candle in one of the upstairs bedrooms.[214]

How to find it: The Huguenot House, also known as the Makens Belmont House, now stands at 307 Burnside Avenue in East Hartford, although this wasn't the home's original plot of land. During the summer months, tours are given of this museum that illustrates 18th- and 19th-century life. Take I-84 to exit 58. From Roberts Street, go left onto Hilldale Street, then another left onto Burnside Avenue (CT 44). Burnside Avenue bears left, and the Huguenot House will be on the left. For information call 860-568-7645, or visit the East Hartford Visitors' Info Web site at www.ehworks.com/visitorinfo.php, which encourages visitors to "ask about [the house's] friendly ghost."

Lake Compounce (Bristol)

The longest continually run amusement park in the nation has in recent years become known for a string of unfortunate, seemingly random deaths during the park's operating hours. Local legend states that the original owner of the land, a Native American chief named Compounce, drowned himself in the lake that was subsequently named for him just as the property was about to change hands.[215] Although apparitions have been seen all over the park and the surrounding land, especially by the numerous security patrols that roam the park at night, reports indicate that the most haunted building in the park is the Starlight Ballroom because numerous apparitions have been reported there by many people at all hours of the day.

How to find it: Lake Compounce is a popular and busy amusement park open from May to October. The park's main entrance is on 217 Enterprise Drive. From I-84, take exit 31. From there you will see signs to the park. For information call 860-583-3300, or visit the park's Web site at www.lakecompounce.com.

The Old State House (Hartford)

America's oldest standing state capitol building, the Old State House is where the first draft of what would later be revised into the U.S. Constitution—known as the Fundamental Orders—was written by founding English colonists in 1639. The Old State House was used as the capitol until the new capitol building was completed in 1878, during which time the third floor was home to one Joseph Steward's portrait gallery and museum of natural curiosities. It was there that Steward would display oddities such as a two-headed calf and a unicorn horn, and it is said that his footfalls are still heard overhead by guests standing on the second floor.

How to find it: The Old State House at 800 Main Street in downtown Hartford is now a museum open year-round. Its hours are Tuesday through Friday 11–5 and Saturday 10–5. Take I-84 to exit 50 onto Chapel Street, and turn right onto Main Street. For more information, call 860-522-6766, or visit the Old State House Web site at www.ctosh.org.

Abigail's Grille (Simsbury)

Once the meeting place for Revolutionary War heroes such as Ethan Allen, the Green Mountain Boys, Joseph Phelps, and (it is believed) George Washington, the former Pettibone's Tavern had operated continuously in one form or another from 1780—until, sadly, a fire ravaged the interior in January 2008. Thankfully a new owner has restored the establishment and renamed it Abigail's in honor of the spirit who is said to haunt the place.

Pettibone's Tavern in Simsbury is reputedly the home of a vengeful ghost named Abigail. Perhaps it was Abigail who started the recent fire that resulted in extensive water damage to the interior, causing the historic tavern to close.

Although its connection with major events in history is well documented—the siege of New York's Fort Ticonderoga was reputedly planned at Pettibone's, and the tavern was apparently a stop on the Underground Railroad—it became best known locally for the widespread rumors of its haunted nature. According to local legend, a woman named Abigail had married Captain Pettibone's son, Jonathan. Apparently this woman was not faithful, and the story goes that Jonathan came home one day to find her with her lover, at which point he flew into a rage and murdered them both. However, this is but one of the tales surrounding the house. According to Susan Smitten, the Simsbury Historical Society claims that there never was an Abigail Pettibone, but there very well

might have been a small boy killed on the property. Still other accounts claim that a local witch was able to "turn herself into a bird
and enter rooms through keyholes."[216]

Whatever the origin of the restaurant's rumored hauntings, it is
clear that strange experiences at the restaurant were hardly few
and far between; indeed, to the tavern's employees, strange occurrences were the norm and very nearly part of the daily routine. The
lights regularly turned themselves back on after the restaurant was
closed, and employees were locked in and out of rooms and reported feeling the touch of an unseen hand or a chill like a cold
breath on the back of their neck. And weird experiences weren't
limited to the restaurant's employees—diners regularly complained
about getting poked in the ribs, of being shoved forward by an unseen assailant, of candles relighting after being blown out, and of
smelling the distinct scent of a wood-fired stove even though the
restaurant only used gas heat for a number of years. There were
even reports by female guests seeing, in the women's room mirror,
the apparition of a young woman standing behind them.

A former employee named Mike recalled that when the restaurant changed ownership, a new set of framed paintings was going
to be hung on the walls. In preparation, these paintings were left
leaning against their respective walls when the night manager ex-
ited the building. Apparently Abigail, or whoever had caused the
mischief all those years, didn't like the change, for the next morning the day manager the found the paintings piled face down in
the center of the room. This wasn't the first case of furniture being
moved by unexplainable means: a Halloween séance was held
there on air by Connecticut's WTIC FM radio station, and the next
morning the manager found chairs stacked together so forcefully
that some had been broken.[217]

According to Susan Smitten, the Connecticut Paranormal
Research Society conducted an investigation of Pettibone's in 1998
and collected a pile of evidence suggesting that the restaurant was
indeed haunted. Many photographs taken by the society show
globes of light hovering around a psychic who claimed to contact

three different spirits (none of whom, incidentally, went by the name Abigail), and a photo taken in the basement showed a dark, shadowy figure in the exact site where a cold spot was felt by the investigators.[218] After that investigation (or possibly because of the investigation), reports of activity at Pettibone's actually *increased*—guests and workers alike reported hearing voices and the giggling of a small child in addition to the normal "routine" of lights switching themselves on and off and candles relighting themselves.

How to find it: Abigail's Grille is at the intersection of CT 10 and CT 185 in Simsbury. Coming from Hartford, take CT 44 through West Hartford and over Avon Mountain and take a right onto CT 10. Abigail's will be on the right about 5 miles down CT 10, about 1 mile before the Granby town line.

St. Paul High School (Bristol)

The late 1990s saw a melancholy patch for this small parochial school when the community lost two of its elderly teachers and one student—a senior—in the span of just a few months. In 2000 or 2001, after being closed for unknown reasons for a number of years, a section of the school's basement hallway was reopened due to an expansion that included a new middle school as well as a expanding drama/theater club. Shortly thereafter, students and teachers alike began to report visions of an apparition standing at the end of the school's newly reopened area. In what might be the first of these sightings, a small group of students who were waiting in the parking lot after the school's closing saw the apparition of a teenage girl materialize in one of the basement windows and then disappear. Whether these sightings have any connection to the unfortunate deaths in the 1990s or some other event in the more distant past is not clear; it is apparent, however, that the sightings coincided closely with the reopening of the basement hallways.

How to find it: St. Paul Catholic High School is on Stafford Avenue in Bristol. Take I-84 to exit 37 onto CT 6. Follow CT 6 until you come to Stafford Avenue on the right. St. Paul will be about ½ mile down on the left, behind and past St. Gregory's Church. For more information, call 860-584-0911, or visit the school's Web site at www.spchs.com.

Trinity College (Hartford)

The students at Trinity College are surprisingly tight-lipped about the strange goings-on that have occurred within the confines of its picturesque Hartford campus throughout the years. But one visit to the school confirms that it's exactly the sort of college one might expect to be home to a number of ghosts: the dorms, the on-campus chapel, and many of the classroom buildings are perfect representations of Gothic and neo-Gothic architecture.

Most of Trinity's ghostly rumors revolve around "the Hall," which is perhaps best described as the school's own version of Yale's Skull and Bones secret society. The Hall, located on Gallows Hill, is the oldest building on campus and is reputedly built on a site where witches were hung hundreds of years ago. According to rumor, the gray tiled floor contains three red tiles that mark the sites of various hangings. The imposing-looking building—on the border of Trinity campus and overlooking the starkly eerie Mount Zion Cemetery—also has etchings of a skull and crossbones within plain view of passersby on Summit Street, and above the large bay windows of the Hall's dorm building, Ogilby, are etchings of people being hung. It is within the Hall that members have been said to have seen the apparition of an old man; his connection to Trinity, the Hall, or Hartford's storied past are either unknown or shrouded behind the same veil of secrecy that surrounds the Hall itself.

How to find it: Trinity College is located on Summit Street, in the west end of urban Hartford. From I-84, take exit 44 and merge onto Caya Avenue. Go right onto Prospect Avenue, then right again onto New Park Avenue. After about 1½ miles, take a left onto New Britain Avenue. The entrance to Trinity College campus will be on the left. Summit Street is a road that runs along the westernmost end of campus. The Hall and the Ogilby building are at the end of Summit Street, on Gallows Hill: the Hall on the corner of Summit and Allen Place and Ogilby on the corner of Summit and Vernon Street. Trinity College campus is open to the public, but the Hall and Ogilby are private buildings. For more information about the school, call 860-297-2000, or visit the school's Web site at www .trincoll.edu.

greater new haven and the gold coast

Albertus Magnus College (New Haven)

Many of the dormitories of Albertus Magnus College, a small liberal arts school near Yale University, are actually 19th-century residential mansions that were converted into dorms following the college's inception in 1915. As is the case with many New England mansions, those of Albertus Magnus College have more than their fair share of ghost stories. Besides the more mundane reports of lights and stereos turning themselves on and off, of knocking and footfalls coming from presumably empty spaces, of doors slamming, and of disembodied muttering voices, there have also been accounts of the apparition of a young boy running through the halls as well as a woman in green. Students in McAuliffe Hall have reported incidents in which students not holding onto the rail while climbing the front stairwell have been shoved down the stairs by an unseen assailant.[219]

How to find it: Albertus Magnus College is located in New Haven, at 700 Prospect Street. Take I-91 to exit 3 onto Trumball Street, which will bend to the right and become Prospect Street.

Charles Island (Milford)

Charles Island, off the coast of Connecticut's Silver Sands State Park, is an island on which apparently no settlement can thrive— although some have tried: an inn and restaurant were opened there and were swiftly destroyed by fire, a monastery was opened there and was quickly abandoned due to repeated accidents and unexplained deaths. It is said that the antagonistic nature of the island to would-be inhabitants is due to a curse, but there is some disagreement as to where the curse came from. Some claim that it was put on the island by the chief of the Paugussett tribe when English colonists forced him off, some claim that Captain Kidd buried his treasure there and put a curse on the area to make sure that his booty lay undisturbed, and still others maintain that a group of sailors stole the treasure of a Mexican emperor—who then proclaimed a curse on it—and brought it to the island.[220]

Whatever the origin of Charles Island's curse—if, indeed, there is a curse at all—the fact remains that any and all attempts to settle the island have ended in misfortune, and reports of ghostly apparitions have been widespread. Glowing, spectral skeletons have been seen flying through the air by would-be treasure hunters, and the noises of a festival or party have been heard emanating from an unseen source within the woods. Today Charles Island is fenced off, and NO TRESPASSING signs line the perimeter of the island.

How to find it: Charles Island is about ½ mile off the coast of Silver Sands State Park in Milford, Connecticut. To access Silver Sands State Park, take I-95 south to exit 35 onto Schoolhouse Road. Follow Schoolhouse Road south to US 1 (Bridgeport Avenue), turn left onto US 1, and then right onto Silver Sands Park Way. This crosses Meadowside Road and continues downhill to the state park's main parking lot. During low tide, a sandbar connects Charles Island to the mainland, but the island is currently off limits and patrolled by round-the-clock security. For information on Silver Sands State Park, call 203-735-4311.

Fort Nathan Hale (New Haven)

Rebuilt after the British burned down the original Black Rock Fort during the Revolutionary War, Fort Nathan Hale was used to defend New Haven's ports all through the War of 1812. In the contemporary era, apparitions of Revolutionary-era soldiers have been seen wandering the barracks, and more than a few visitors to the fort have come home with photographs featuring floating, glowing orbs.

How to find it: Fort Nathan Hale, owned by the city of New Haven, is open daily as a museum. From I-95 east, take exit 50 and turn right onto Woodward Avenue. From I-95 west, take exit 51 and turn left onto Woodward Avenue. From Woodward Avenue, follow the signs to Fort Nathan Hale.

The Hanging Hills (Meriden)

Practically every region in the Western world has a "Black Dog" legend: a dark canine—usually a Labrador—that would appear from nowhere, bark soundlessly, and flash glowing red eyes. These harbingers are generally considered to be warnings of impending death, and although the Black Dog of the Hanging Hills has been reported to be a friendly, smaller variety—a spaniel, perhaps—the potential status of Connecticut's own Black Dog as a harbinger is secure. Local legend states that if you see the Black Dog once, you will experience good fortune; if you see the Black Dog twice, you will either fall ill or experience some misfortune; if you see the Black Dog a third time, your fate is sealed, and death is both imminent and inevitable.

W. H. C. Pynchon—the grandfather of celebrated novelist Thomas Pynchon—was a geologist from New York who taught at Trinity College and liked to hike Meriden's Hanging Hills. Pynchon was trekking through the woods one day when a small, happy black dog appeared and soundlessly tailed him for some length of his journey. A geologist friend who had twice seen the spectral canine had told him about the Black Dog legend, but Pynchon never suspected that this cute little fellow could be *that* Black Dog. A few years later, Pynchon and the very same friend were hiking the same trail when the little black dog appeared again. Not long after this sighting, Pynchon's friend lost his footing on one of the more treacherous sections of the trail and fell to his death. A few years after this, Pynchon, alone, attempted one more hike of the Hanging Hills. His frozen body was discovered weeks later, not far from where his friend had fallen.[221]

Over the years an inordinate number of hikers, hang gliders, and rock climbers have met their fate in Meriden's Hanging Hills. Whenever such a tragedy occurs, there is widespread speculation among those in the know as to whether the Black Dog was again to blame.

How to find it: The Hanging Hills feature access to the popular Metacomet hiking trail as well as an attraction known as Castle Crag—a medieval-looking tower overlooking the green valley below. To access the area, take exit 4 off I-691, and follow West Main Street for about ¼ mile until it reaches Hubbard Park. Keeping the pond to the right, bear right at the first intersection, and turn right at the stop sign. Beyond the concrete roadblocks is an abandoned road that leads into the Merrimere Reservoir area and the Hanging Hills.[222]

The Phelps House (Stratford)

Like a scene out of the 1982 film *Poltergeist,* the haunting of the Reverend Eliakim Phelps house began with an event that seemed comparatively innocuous, considering the mayhem that would follow. In the movie, the first clue that something is amiss arrives in the form of chairs that moved themselves around the kitchen. The family in question are initially excited and curious about their haunting—until things take a turn for the worse, and they are forced to flee in terror. Also like the popular horror film, the events that transpired in the Phelps mansion were more symptomatic of poltergeist activity than a traditional haunting.

After relocating from Philadelphia to Connecticut, the Reverend Phelps returned home from church on March 10, 1850, to find the doors of his large house wide open, though he was positive that he had locked them before leaving. Suspecting thieves—who would naturally target such a grand house that suggested great wealth—the clergyman searched his home. But the only sign of intrusion was his wife's night clothes laid out on the bed in the master bedroom, arms folded as if the clothes were on a corpse ready for burial. Acknowledging that the mischief makers might return after the family had gone back to church for the afternoon services, the Reverend Phelps sent his family into town while he armed himself and stayed behind. When nobody turned up after several hours, Phelps made another tour of the house, this time discovering that several life-sized effigies made out of his family's clothes were now set up around the kitchen table, poised as if they were in prayer. And that was just the beginning.

The weeks to follow would be a trying ordeal for the Phelps family as forceful knocking—so forceful that it would often rattle the panels of the doors being knocked on—would be heard throughout the house, originating from empty rooms and even small closets. After some time, the knocking progressed into objects such as fire pokers and bricks hurtling themselves across rooms—often with multiple witnesses present. Small objects rattling harmlessly against the walls evolved to large pieces of furniture being thrown against walls and smashing into bits. Eventually the level of danger in the house rose to the point where the sound of a slap would be heard, and a hand-shaped welt would appear on the face of one of the Phelps children. The good reverend knew at this point that it was time for his family to relocate back to Philadelphia.

The incidents at the Phelps house—which would come to be known as the Stratford Knockings—got widespread media coverage, both positive and negative. It was, in many ways, the 19th-century equivalent to the purported events of the now infamous Amityville, New York, house in the 1970s. The parallels are fairly uncanny in that the details of the haunting escalated to the point that the family had no choice but to abandon their home, and the frenzy of media coverage in the ensuing weeks led to widespread speculation over the events' authenticity. In fact, if the events of Amityville were embellished—or, as some skeptics claim, outright faked—it is within the realm of possibility that the Phelps mansion incidents provided some inspiration. If both cases were authentic, however, it is clear that they were caused by something more severe than a "regular" haunting.

Poltergeist activity or demonic invasion—if these are indeed within the realm of possibility—represent two very scary scenarios. Many paranormal researchers believe that poltergeist activity is actually the unconscious telekinetic manifestations of a young person going through a turbulent time, such as puberty. Considering that both Eliakim Phelps and his second wife brought multiple children into their marriage, this hypothesis would fit within the context of the Phelps mansion haunting. Considering also that the reverend was rumored to be interested in mysticism and that he was said to have held a séance less than a week before the occurrences of March 10, 1850, the idea of a demonic entity would be just as plausible.

How to find it: The Phelps mansion once stood at 1738 Elm Street in Stratford. The mansion changed hands a number of times and eventually was converted into a nursing home. None of the owners of the nursing home noted any strange events, but in the early 1970s, the home's residents complained of strange knocking and gurgling sounds, and fire alarms would go off without explanation. The nursing home closed in the 1970s when the owners ran into financial difficulty. Unfortunately, nobody will ever know whether the haunting at the Phelps mansion was authentic or not, for it was either "demolished" or "burned to the ground," depending on whom you ask.

The Shakespeare Festival Theater (Stratford)

For many years the Shakespeare Festival Theater in Stratford was a thriving dramatic theater that hosted such notable actors as Katherine Hepburn, Ed Asner, and Roddy McDowell; it has also been host to some unexplained phenomena. Ropes have been said to swing on their own, unexplainable laughter has been heard echoing throughout otherwise empty space, and the apparition of a young woman has been seen in one of the very old administration building's upstairs windows.[223]

How to find it: The Shakespeare Festival Theater is located at 1850 Elm Street in Stratford. Although the theater is currently closed, the theater's ownership was transferred to the town of Stratford in 2005, and tentative plans are in place to reopen it. To get to Elm Street in Stratford, take I-95 to exit 31 on South Avenue eastbound. Go left onto Main Street, then a quick right onto Shore Road, and another left onto Elm Street.

Union Cemetery (Easton)

One of the country's most famous haunted cemeteries has had a long, storied history that has been corroborated by audio and video evidence. Easton's Union Cemetery is also significant for being home to not just one notable and frequently encountered apparition but two: the White Lady and the Red-Eyed Creature from the Woods. Most would-be paranormal researchers visit Union Cemetery in hopes of encountering the former.

The main topic of Ed and Lorraine Warren's book *Graveyard,* the White Lady of Union Cemetery is thought to have been a young woman murdered by either an adulterous lover or a love-struck stalker,[224] depending on the teller of the tale. The White Lady has appeared to the graveyard's visitors in various forms, ranging from the visitor simply hearing the sound of a woman sobbing to appearing as an apparition in plain sight. The White Lady has appeared on film when no one present had seen her with their naked eyes, and her sobbing has been heard in EVP recordings captured in and around the cemetery.

Perhaps the most interesting recurring White Lady sighting involves a witness driving along Route 59 near Union Cemetery when suddenly a luminous lady in white materializes in the middle of the road. Although it initially appears that the witness has run the apparition over, she nearly always seems to pass harmlessly through the car and disappears without a trace. I write "nearly always" because one case was apparently the exception to the rule: A fireman claims that he was driving his pickup truck one night near the cemetery when the road took on a reddish glow. The next thing he knew, a man who appeared to be a farmer was sitting next to him in the passenger seat, and the White Lady had materialized in the road in front of his truck. Instead of her passing harmlessly through the vehicle, however, the fireman heard a thud and slammed on the brakes. Sure enough, on coming to a stop, the farmer and the

White Lady had disappeared without a trace—except for the dent in his truck's front bumper.[225]

Union Cemetery's other unexplained resident is known as the Red-Eyed Creature from the Woods—which, from all accounts, is precisely what it sounds like: The witness inside or near the graveyard looks into the nearby woods and sees a pair of glowing red eyes staring back. There have even been reports that people who see the eyes and run away in terror can hear the sound of running footfalls behind them, although there is nothing to see when they look over their shoulder. The red eyes might belong to a man who one night provided his name (although the name was either never repeated or was lost to the annals of history) "and a number of choice expletives" to a group of young ghost hunters that caught, via EVP, a male voice on audiotape.[226]

How to find it: Union Cemetery is located at the intersection of CT 59 and CT 136 in Easton. The still-used public graveyard is open during daylight hours but closes at sundown. Although many would-be ghost hunters have attempted to access the cemetery at night, a "no trespassing after dusk" policy is strictly enforced. Those who break this rule will be, and have been, fined or arrested.

Union Trust Building (New Haven)

"You moved the cemetery, but you left the bodies, didn't you? You son of a bitch, you left the bodies, and you only moved the headstones. You only moved the headstones. Why? Why?!?"

—Craig T. Nelson, in Poltergeist (1982)

In the 1982 film *Poltergeist*, the disturbances experienced by the Freeling family in and around their home are eventually explained to be the result of a greedy real estate developer's cost-cutting measure of relocating a cemetery's headstones but not the bodies when the land in question was to be developed into the suburban neighborhood in which the Freelings would eventually reside. This practice might seem to be merely a clever horror movie plot device, but, in fact, when the piece of land known as the New Haven

Green burial ground was built on, the headstones were moved to Grove Street Cemetery but the bodies were left behind. The results may very well be similar in reality, as well, for the old Union Trust building, the adjacent Emerson apartment building, and the surrounding area have been host to dozens of reports of unexplained phenomena over the years—well over 60 reports since the late 1990s alone.[227]

The old Union Trust building, a massive 13-story structure that occupies the entire corner of Church and Elm streets, seems to be home to a particularly noisy set of ghosts—people hear their names called when they are alone in the building, loud banging noises emanate from nowhere in particular, pitiful moans have been heard in all parts of the building, footfalls are heard coming down empty corridors, toilets flush on their own, and lights turn themselves on and off with frightening regularity. The most often recurring phenomenon in the old Union Trust building is the sound of walls being slapped by unseen hands within the series of unused tunnels and rooms in the building's basement known as the Maze: several people have reported hearing the sound of "an open hand striking the wall of the basement hard and always three times in rapid succession."[228]

The old Union Trust building and the surrounding area is also home to a variety of repeatedly seen apparitions, many of which are a bit more unique than the average ghost. Dark shapes known as Shadow People have been seen materializing as if from the ether and just as quickly dissolving; dwarves have appeared from nowhere and then suddenly vanished; an elderly man who is said to have died in the Emerson apartments has been seen in the building as well as on the street (including peering into the window of his favorite local diner![229]); and a tall, dark man has been seen roaming the grounds around the Union Trust building and the Emerson apartments just before dawn.

How to find it: The Union Trust building is in New Haven, just off of Yale University's campus, on the corner of Church and Elm streets, and the Emerson apartments are directly behind the Union

Trust building, on Crown Street. From I-91, take exit 2 onto Grand Avenue, and then stay straight onto Elm Street.

Yale University (New Haven)

With Yale being home to the elite Skull and Bones society, students of the prestigious Ivy League school are not strangers to being secretive. Perhaps it shouldn't be surprising then that—as with Trinity College—it's difficult to obtain clear information on Yale's many purported ghosts. Even as eminent a source as noted paranormal expert Hans Holzer has been unable to unearth many details about Yale's ghosts, and for the insights he *has* been able to glean, his informants have chosen to remain anonymous.[230]

What is well known, however, is that the organ in Yale's Woolsley Hall—the fifth-largest pipe organ in the world—is said to be watched over by a protective spirit whose presence has been felt by many, and that strange events such as the viewing of orbs and ghostly mists have occurred within the stacks of Yale's very Gothic Sterling Memorial Library. The source of the library's purported spirits is unknown, but the Woolsley Hall ghost is said to be that of one Henry Jepson, a Yale music professor who was forced to retire against his wishes sometime in the 1940s.[231]

How to find it: Yale is a preeminent Ivy League university located in New Haven. Yale's campus occupies several blocks of the city, with Prospect Avenue bisecting the campus. From I-91, take exit 2 onto Grand Avenue; then stay straight onto Elm Street. Yale will be directly ahead.

CONNECTICUT RIVER VALLEY AND THE SOUTHEAST COAST

Captain Grant's, 1754 (Poquetanuck)

The quaint inn now known as Captain Grant's, 1754 was built by William Gonzales Grant in, yes, 1754 as a home for himself and his family; unfortunately, Captain Grant died at sea at the too-young age of 32 while his wife, Mercy Adelaine Avery, was pregnant with their third son. The boy was named Captain William Gonzales Grant II, and Mercy raised him and his siblings in the house until she passed away well into her 80s. Father and son are buried side by side on the property.

A frequent occurrence at the inn is a loud knocking on the building's front door that on investigation opens to an empty front porch. Most of the inn's disturbances, however, seem to occur within the Adelaine Room—"The shower curtain falls inexplicably, and the TV turns on and off on its own. . . . Many guests have captured orbs on film, and [inn owner Carol Matsumo] has photographed 'an actual electrical outline' of a ghost."[232]

How to find it: Captain Grant's, 1754 is located at 109–111 CT 2A in Poquetanuck. From I-95, take exit 92 onto CT 2 heading west. After traveling about 12 miles—and passing the massive Foxwoods casino resort—take a left onto CT 2A. Captain Grant's will be just over 1 mile down on the right. For information or reservations, call 860-887-7589 or 800-982-1772, or visit the inn's Web site at www.captaingrants.com.

Gillette Castle (East Haddam)

Now part of Gillette Castle State Park, Gillette Castle—constructed of stone and resembling a medieval European fortress—was built by stage actor William Gillette, best known for his portrayals of Sir Arthur Conan Doyle's detective Sherlock Holmes. The castle is a museum of sorts, full of creative design touches such as couches built right into the walls, a table that runs along on tracks, and a secret room right in the center of the house. According to Elaine Kuzmeskus's *Connecticut Ghosts*, the spirits of Gillette and his Japanese gardener may very well still wander throughout the castle,[233] as apparitions matching the description of both men have been reportedly seen casually strolling throughout the castle grounds.

How to find it: Gillette Castle rises imposingly from 67 River Road in East Haddam. Take I-91 south from Hartford to CT 9 south. From CT 9, take exit 7 onto CT 82 eastbound; River Road will be a right-hand turn. The castle is difficult to miss. For tour information, call 860-526-2331.

Gungywamp (Groton)

An area that has reputedly caused inexplicable mental anguish to some visitors—who have been said to become so suddenly overcome with grief that some have actually burst into tears—as well as such physical discomforts as nosebleeds, bleeding gums, and splitting headaches, Gungywamp is the site of mysterious stone structures and shifting magnetic fields that represent the closest thing that the Northeast has to a marvel like Stonehenge.

Massive boulders, rock cairns, stone circles, and stone foundation cellars with astrological significance occupy the site. Perhaps the most noteworthy structure in Gungywamp is the "Calendar Chamber," which indicates that the site might very well have been used for a functional purpose, possibly even as a location for ceremonies or as a predictor for harvest and planting times:

> [The Calendar Chamber] has an opening facing east, which, only during the spring and fall equinoxes, allows the sunlight to penetrate through the larger chamber and directly into the entrance of a small, beehive-shaped internal chamber. The lone ray of light then reflects off a pale wall of stone with heavy garnet concentrations, which illuminates the interior of the smaller chamber twice a year. In this way, the configuration of stones acts as a reliable calendar, just like the similar structures in sixth- and seventh-century Ireland.[234]

There are no known reports of apparitions or strange noises in Gungywamp, just alleged changes in visitors' moods and the occasional physical discomfort. These factors, as well as the mysterious nature of the site itself and the Calendar Chamber in particular, suggest that it would be a location of interest for readers of this book. However the Gunywamp Society states on their Web site that they "do not represent or encourage any kind of religious/ spiritual or paranormal interpretation of the Gungywamp area."

How to find it: Gungywamp is on private property in the woods of Groton, however, the Gungywamp Society gives periodic tours of the area. For more information, contact the Gungywamp Society at P.O. Box 592, Colchester, CT 06415 or by visiting www.gungy wamp.com.

John York House (North Stonington)

Named for its original owner, who built it in 1741, the eponymous John York House is now an inn that reportedly houses some very restless spirits left over from its days as a Revolutionary War–era tavern. That George Washington was rumored to have slept there[235] has attracted many an American-history buff, but the rumor that two Revolutionary War–era soldiers might have made the John York House their permanent residence attracts an even greater number of amateur ghost hunters. Apparently, two colonial soldiers got into an argument over a woman at the John York House, and the argument escalated into a murder followed by a grief-driven suicide. Subsequently, cold spots have been felt, shadows have been seen out of the corners of visitors' eyes, and unexplainable sounds have been heard echoing throughout the building.

During the 1960s, the building's owner decided to hold a séance to discover the cause of the strange disturbances that she had been experiencing within the house. As often happens, the séance opened doors that should have been left shut, and the disturbances worsened, culminating in a series of terrifying incidents that led the family to call in a team of psychic exorcists:

Furniture was flipped over by unseen hands, a barometer repeatedly became a projectile . . . locked doors were found
opened, electrical objects turned themselves on and off, tobacco smoke was smelled, and loud bangs like cannon fire
were heard. . . . The climax for that particular family was when
their son awoke screaming one night, and his parents found
him gagging, with red welts forming around his neck, as if
someone were trying to strangle him right in front of them.[236]

The disturbances have lessened in frequency and severity since
the psychic exorcism, but strange noises are still heard—such as
people hearing their names called when there is nobody else
around—and unsettling poltergeist-type activity has occurred, including a van window suddenly exploding outward for no apparent
reason.

How to find it: The John York House is now a bed & breakfast located at 1 Clarks Falls Road in North Stonington. From I-95, take
exit 92 onto CT 2; go left at Liberty Street, following CT 2 until the
intersection of CT 184. Take CT 184 east toward Providence and
the New London Turnpike. Turn left at Pendleton Road (CT 49) and
then right onto Clarks Falls Road (CT 216). For information or reservations, call 860-599-3075.

Ledge Light (Offshore from Groton and New London)

Seemingly floating on the ocean where Fisher's Island Sound, the
Thames River, and Long Island Sound all meet, Ledge Light marks
the intersection and warns incoming vessels as they approach the
rocky shores. Besides hearing the ghostly foghorn of the steamship
Atlantic, which crashed into Fisher's Island in 1846, killing its 42 passengers in the process, the lighthouse keepers and visitors also report seeing and hearing a ghost that they reckon to be John
"Ernie" Randolph.

Local legend states that Ernie married a young and attractive
woman in 1936, and she moved into the lighthouse with him. After
just a few months, the woman grew lonely and stir-crazy in the secluded environment and sought escape. The two argued until fi-

nally the woman did escape, and the grief-stricken Ernie was said to have slit his own throat and fallen from the roof of the house onto the rocks below. Since then, the house's television and the foghorn turn themselves on and off, doors open and close themselves, boats securely tied to the docks drift off during the night, and the decks even wash themselves. An apparition has also been reported—strangely enough only by women and children—of a bearded man dressed in rain gear.

The Ledge Light became fully automated in 1987, and the final log entry of its manned era read: "A rock of slow torture, hell on earth . . . it's Ernie's domain now."[237]

How to find it: The Ledge Light is a fully automated, remote lighthouse in New London Harbor, with its closest shore being that of Groton, Connecticut; it is currently controlled by the U.S. Coast Guard and maintained by the New London Ledge Lighthouse Foundation. The only way to tour the Ledge Light is through the Project Oceanology of Groton summer tour. Project Oceanology tours can be arranged by calling 860-445-9007 or 800-364-8472. For more information on the tours, visit www.oceanology.org. The New London Ledge Lighthouse Foundation can be contacted at P.O. Box 855, New London, CT 06320.

Lighthouse Inn (New London)

Originally a mansion, named "Meadow Court," built by steel magnate Charles S. Guthrie, the Lighthouse Inn is now a resort and conference center with a half-circle design that allows nearly every room in the house a spectacular view of either the ocean or the wildflower-strewn gardens. When Meadow Court opened as an inn in 1927, it attracted representatives of high society and movie stars such as Joan Crawford and Bette Davis, and it became *the* location to hold a wedding or reception for New England's upper crust.

Local legend states that a bride—whose name is no longer remembered—fell down the long, winding grand staircase on her wedding day, broke her neck, and died while her groom was waiting for her at the bottom of the stairs. Whether this tragic event actually happened or not remains one of history's mysteries, but it would certainly explain the apparition of a bride, in full wedding attire, that has been seen roaming through the Lighthouse Inn's hallways, entering and exiting rooms, reading in a guestroom, and reportedly even once again descending the grand staircase. The Lighthouse Inn experienced a sort of renaissance in popularity among the paranormal community when an episode of the Sci-Fi Channel's *Ghost Hunters* was filmed there, and The Atlantic Paranormal Society (TAPS) experienced anomalies such as unexplained temperature drops. One of the TAPS members even felt an unseen hand touch him on the back, though nobody was behind him.[238]

How to find it: The Lighthouse Inn is located at 6 Guthrie Place in New London. If you are traveling north on I-95, take exit 82 and turn right onto Broad Street. At the second traffic light, turn right onto Colman Street. If you are traveling south on I-95, take exit 83 (Frontage Road), and then take the exit for Colman Street. At the stoplight at the end of the ramp, turn left onto Colman Street. Follow Colman Street for about 2 miles, and then turn left onto Bank Street. At the third light, go right onto Montauk Avenue. Follow Montauk Avenue for about 2 miles, turn right onto Pequot Avenue, then take the second right onto Guthrie Place. For reservations or more information about the beautiful Lighthouse Inn call 860-443-8411, e-mail reservations@lighthouseinn-ct.com, or visit the inn's Web site at www.lighthouseinn-ct.com.

Mount Tom (Moodus)

The town's name, Moodus, allegedly comes from a Native American word[239] meaning "Place of Bad Noises,"[240] which is not surprising, considering the phenomenon—known as the Moodus Noises —that has been occurring within the area surrounding Mount Tom since at least the first half of the 18th century.

The Moodus Noises, loud yet muffled explosions or groaning, were first attributed to Native American gods being angry that the Englishman had brought his God into their home; later, during the age of witch trials, it was believed that the good witches of

Haddam were battling the evil witches of Moodus atop Mount Tom. Today, the prevailing theory is that small "micro-earthquakes" were the cause of the Moodus Noises. Whatever the basis, the reports of strange noises coming from Mount Tom have diminished over the years—some even believe that an Englishman named Dr. Steel came to Mount Tom to solve the problem of the strange noises and managed to do exactly that.

How to find it: The Moodus Noises weren't limited to a specific point; Mount Tom in Moodus generally referred to the wooded, hilly areas around the town. To access Moodus, from CT 9, take exit 7 onto CT 82. Follow CT 82 over the Connecticut River and into East Haddam, and then take the first left onto Main Street (CT 149). CT 149 will lead directly into Moodus.

Randall's Ordinary Landmark Inn (North Stonington)

Room 12 of Randall's Ordinary Landmark Inn is said to have an unregistered guest, the description of whom has remained remarkably consistent over the years. The Landmark Inn was originally a North Stonington farmhouse built by wealthy silk merchant John Randall way back in 1685. It was turned into an inn, owned and operated by the Mashantucket Pequot Tribal Nation, in 1987. Since then, guests have reported witnessing the apparition of a tall, slim gentleman with long hair and a forlorn expression wearing a soldier's uniform and carrying a blunderbuss—a long-barreled musket whose business end curves out like a tulip.[241] The man always looks the same, but for one variation: he has sometimes been seen with the specter of a small child clinging to his leg.

Room 12 is the most common site for unexplained phenomenon at the Landmark Inn, but guests staying in rooms 6 and 11 have also had eerie experiences, such as strange noises from nowhere as well as witnessing someone sitting at the end of the bed, getting up, and walking right through the room's closed door as if it were open.

How to find it: Randall's Ordinary Landmark Inn is located at 41 Norwich/Westerly Turnpike (CT 2), also listed as Norwich Westerly

Road, in North Stonington. From I-95, take exit 92, going right onto CT 2 at the end of the off ramp. The inn will be just a few hundred feet up, on the left side of CT 2. For more information or to make reservations, call 860-599-4540.

Red Brook Inn (Mystic)

The coastal Connecticut village of Mystic is a popular tourist destination due to its seaport museum, its large aquarium, the quaint curio shops that line the downtown area, and, undoubtedly, a small pizzeria that shares its name with a cult-classic movie. Like the seaport and many of the old buildings that make up Mystic's downtown riverside area, the Red Brook Inn is an unspoiled visual reminder of the designs of colonial New England.

When Bob Keyes first took possession of the inn, he wrote off the odd knocking sounds and cold spots as simply being idiomatic to old houses—but when more than a few of the inn's customers came to him with stories of an elderly woman wrapped in a black shawl waking them up in the middle of the night[242] or of being awakened by a room inexplicably full of smoke or both[243]—Bob and his wife, Ruth, had no choice but to consider the possibility that their inn might be haunted. Unlike the random and infrequent paranormal encounters experienced at many other presumably haunted New England inns and restaurants, a great many guests of the Red Brook Inn have reported unexplainable occurrences.

How to find it: The Red Brook Inn is located at 2800 Gold Star Highway in Mystic. From I-95, take exit 89 onto Mystic Street northbound. Bear left onto Cow Hill Road, and then go right onto Gold Star Highway (CT 184). The inn will be just a few hundred feet up on the left. For more information or to make reservations, call 860-572-0349

part six
spirits by the sea:
haunted
rhode island

The bucolic Chestnut Hill Cemetery in Exeter is reportedly haunted
by the ghost of a girl who was accused of being a vampire.

In many ways, Rhode Island (and Newport especially) was home to New England's "royalty" for a good portion of the 19th and 20th centuries. Names as prominent as Astor, Belmont, Sprague, and Vanderbilt built vast, sprawling mansions in the fashion of their European ancestors to help create and secure a legacy within our still-young nation. As the entries within this chapter prove, the Rhode Island wealthy were immensely successful in establishing that legacy—although probably not in the form in which they had intended. The mansions of some of New England's most powerful families—indeed, some of the wealthiest individuals in our nation's history—are now well known for being as haunted as the European castles and manors that they were intended to emulate.

The haunted mansions of Rhode Island are not the state's only paranormal attractions, however. Indeed, it's very likely that, being the smallest state in the U.S., Rhode Island might be able to claim to the densest spirit population in the country. And Rhode Island's ghosts aren't always the anonymous ghosts of the past that one might expect—with names like Vanderbilt, Dorr, Lovecraft, and Poe, the state's ghosts may be very possibly the most *famous* in the country, as well.

eastern rhode island

Buck Hill Road (Pascoag)

Unlike the Black Dog of Meriden, Connecticut, Rhode Island's "Gray Dog of Buck Hill Road" doesn't seem to be a harbinger of bad fortune; as local legend states, the dog is simply the apparition of a canine who was cut down by a careless driver in the middle of the night long ago. The most popular form of the tale involves motorists coming across an apparently dead gray dog lying in the middle of the road. As the concerned drivers get out of their cars to check the dog, the animal simply vanishes before their eyes. Thomas D'Agostino, in his *Haunted Rhode Island*, presents another version of the story. It seems that more than a few drivers traveling down Buck Hill Road have had the gray dog suddenly appear in front of their car, its eyes glowing green and its teeth bared as if ready to attack. As the motorist hits their brakes to avoid hitting the animal, it suddenly disappears.[244]

How to find it: Buck Hill Road is in Pascoag, about 2 miles west of the town of Burrillville, just a couple of miles south of the Massachusetts state line and a couple of miles east of the Connecticut state line. From I-395 in Connecticut, take exit 100 to CT 193 south; follow CT 193 southbound a short distance, and then take a left onto Porter Plain Road. Go right onto Sand Dam Road, another quick right onto East Thompson Road, then a quick left onto Quaddick Town Farm Road. Buck Hill Farm Road will be a left-hand turn that crosses the Connecticut/Rhode Island line; the phantom dog of Buck Hill has been seen all along this road.

Burdick Cemetery (Charlestown)

More often than not, it isn't thrill-seeking teenagers but rather hunters who report the phantom voices and ghostly apparitions that are said to inhabit Charlestown's Burdick Cemetery after dark. The cemetery, it seems, is right on the border of the Burlingame Wildlife Management Area—a hotspot for hunters. According to reports, the nearly ancient plot is also a hotspot for illuminated, floating orbs, human-shaped apparitions, and voices from seemingly nowhere.

How to find it: Burdick Cemetery is located on Buckeye Brook Road, at the edge of the Burlingame Wildlife Management Area. From I-95, take exit 91 onto RI 234, the Pequot Trail. Bear right onto US 1 (Granite Street, later Old Post Road and Post Road), and continue on this route eastbound. Go left onto RI 216 (Ross Hill Road) and then right onto Buckeye Brook Road. The Burdick Cemetery is about 1/2 mile down Buckeye Brook Road, just before reaching the Burlingame State Park.

Chestnut Hill Cemetery (Exeter)

Officially known as Historical Cemetery #22, this cemetery located on Chestnut Hill in Exeter has long been host to visitors who have

The grave of Mercy L. Brown in Exeter's Chestnut Hill Cemetery; the young woman incited a vampirism scare during the late 19th century and may have inspired Bram Stoker to write *Dracula*.

reported witnessing a brightly glowing globe of blue light or the apparition of a young woman near the Brown family burial plot. These sightings are generally attributed to be the ghost of one Mercy Brown, who, like her entire family except her father, passed away from tuberculosis in the late 1800s. During the 19th century, the symptoms of tuberculosis—usually called "consumption"—— were sometimes thought to be the effects of vampirism due to the slow wasting away of the body.

Mercy Brown passed away not long before her older brother, Edwin, contracted the disease. Desperate to cure his son and willing to try anything, George elected to have the bodies of his deceased loved ones exhumed to see if any of the three displayed signs that, in those days, were considered to be telling of vampires. On exhumation, his wife and other daughter were found to be in advance states of decay; Mercy Brown, however, looked very well preserved, and, shockingly, had, according to legend, moved herself from a slab within the family's crypt into a coffin. A doctor who accompanied George performed an autopsy on the corpse and found that Mercy's heart still held a large amount of blood. Nowadays this would not be considered abnormal by those with medical knowledge, but back then it was believed that the fresh blood—and the significantly more troubling claim that Mercy's body had somehow moved itself into a coffin—was evidence enough that George had found his family's vampire.

The story received a great deal of media attention and was even said to inspire both H. P. Lovecraft's *The Shunned House* and Bram Stoker's *Dracula*—after Stoker's death, newspaper articles about Mercy Brown were found in his personal files.[245] Claims of vampirism might be easily dismissed today, but the apparitions that have appeared to many visitors of Historic Cemetery #22 are not so easily explained. The brightly shining orbs and the apparition of a young woman continue to be seen into the present decade, and many recent reports indicate that—much like my own experiences at Dudleytown in Connecticut—people driving by the cemetery have experienced inexplicable car trouble.

How to find it: The Chestnut Hill Cemetery is adjacent to the Chestnut Hill Baptist Church in Exeter. From I-95, take exit 9 onto RI 4 southbound, and then take exit 5 onto RI 102 westbound. The Chestnut Hill Baptist Church and the cemetery will be on the right side of the road, about 3 miles down RI 102.

Dolly Cole Bridge (Foster)

A small, unassuming bridge spanning a small, unassuming brook has been the site of numerous reports of a pretty young brunette apparition wearing a 19th-century dress. Local speculation states that the ghost belongs to one Dorothy "Dolly" Ellen Cole, whose body was found in the woods near the bridge in 1893. Both the bridge and the brook are named in her honor.

How to find it: The Dolly Cole Bridge is located on the Danielson Pike (RI 6) on the border of Foster and North Scituate. From I-395, take exit 90 onto the Governor John Davis Lodge Turnpike, which eventually becomes RI 6 (Danielson Pike). The bridge will be near the intersection of Tucker Hollow Road.

Exeter School (Exeter)

Now an abandoned complex on Allentown Road in Exeter, the Exeter School started off as a small farm colony but eventually became a school for the mentally handicapped, known alternately as the Exeter School, the Joseph P. Ladd School, and the Rhode Island School for the Feeble Minded. Legends abound about the old school, with stories about living conditions nearing torture—apparently Mr. Ladd, for whom the school was at one time named, felt that the mentally handicapped were a burden upon the community and were to be considered lower-class citizens. (Thomas D'Agostino writes about "patients having teeth pulled without any local anesthetics to save money."[246]) Whether or not these stories are true, it is fact that the school eventually had to close in 1982 due to a multitude of wrongful-death suits and human-rights inquiries.

Multiple unexplained phenomena have been reported at the school's former campus over the decades. Investigators and other curious parties have claimed to see apparitions and dark shadows roaming the grounds, eyes glowing from the windows of many of the former campus's 10 buildings, and orbs of light bobbing in and around the buildings. Witnesses have also claimed to hear the sounds of footfalls echoing down empty corridors as well as strange scraping and dragging sounds, and electronic voice phenomenon (EVP) recordings have picked up the sounds of voices ranging from whispers to screams.

How to find it: The former Exeter School, located on what was once Allentown Road, in the Sheffield Hills area of Exeter, is now closed to the public, but several investigative teams have gotten special permission to enter the campus. From I-95, take exit 9 onto RI 4 southbound, and then take exit 5 onto RI 102 eastbound. Go right onto Haville Road, then right again onto Sheffield Hills Road. The former school will be located just a few hundred feet down Sheffield Hills Road.

Gorton's Funeral Home (Coventry)

It only makes sense that a funeral home would have more than its fair share of ghosts, but what paranormal investigator Thomas D'Agostino witnessed there over several years—his band used the abandoned establishment as a makeshift recording studio—was certainly beyond expectation. The startling, otherworldly banging and knocking that emanated from the otherwise empty mortuary was almost certainly frightening enough on its own; what must have been downright scary were the multiple apparitions that he and his bandmates witnessed: a tall man wearing old-fashioned baggy clothes who kept walking through walls as well as a small, bespectacled old man (who matched to a T the portrait of one of the funeral parlor's original undertakers) who shut a door behind the musicians just before disappearing into thin air.[247] But reading D'Agostino's account, what really sends a shiver down one's spine are the reports of the screaming and shrieking, both heard in person and recorded as inadvertent EVP:

> One of our taping sessions was interrupted by the boom of the double doors leading to our rehearsal space/former embalming room/recording studio. When we replayed the tape to see if the recorder had picked up the possible nuisance, we heard, to our astonishment, not only the doors rushing open but the wailing and pleading of a female's voice as well. Yes, as usual, the doors were locked.
>
> Frightful shrieks and unearthly moans would saturate the confines of the sepulture at all hours as if history was replaying the mourning of passed loved ones. One night three of us crept up to the third floor to see who was screaming tumultuously. It was such a clamor that we heard it from the basement. When we reached the large open room, we flicked on

the light. . . . The screaming stopped the very moment the light illuminated the chamber.[248]

Gorton's Funeral Home itself moved to a larger, more modern structure down the street; the old building has been mostly abandoned for several decades now and has fallen into a state of disrepair. Still, those who do still use the place from time to time continue to report strange occurrences, such as lights flicking themselves on and off as well as the occasional ghostly apparition.

How to find it: Located at 700 Washington Street in Coventry, the old Gorton's Funeral Home is now a more-or-less abandoned space that is rented out for miscellaneous uses (such as a makeshift recording studio). From I-95, take exit 10A onto RI 117 westbound. RI 117 (Centerville Road) will eventually turn into Washington Street.

Quidnessett Memorial Cemetery (North Kingstown)

Many sources name the Quidnessett Cemetery as the most haunted burial ground in Rhode Island, as there are frequent reports of glowing orbs of light and dark, misty, vaguely anthropomorphic shapes moving in and around the graveyard. Speculation is that many of these apparitions belong to the 54 former soldiers who are buried there in a mass grave. A plaque hanging on a boulder in the graveyard tells the tale: ERECTED A.D. 1941 TO MARK THE BURIAL IN THIS PLOT OF THE REMAINS OF FIFTY-FOUR UNIDENTIFIED BODIES MOVED HERE FROM OLD BURIAL PLOTS LOCATED ON LAND ACQUIRED BY THE GOVERNMENT FOR THE SITE OF THE UNITED STATES NAVAL AIR STATION AT QUONSET POINT, R.I. Quonset Point, a strategic spot with a breathtaking view of the entire Narragansett Bay, was erected during World War II as a U.S. Naval command point. According to Thomas D'Agostino, when the government took over the land, they might not have acted with as much respect toward the dead as one might expect:

> It would appear that the government took over the land with little regard to the interred. Replacing each headstone was a task that they were not about to embark on, so they made a common grave for the people they had dug up. That is where

The front gates of the expansive Quidnessett Memorial Cemetery in North Kingstown—called the most haunted graveyard in Rhode Island.

they now lay nameless and all but forgotten. It is no wonder they are now seen wandering among the stones of the grave-yard, looking for their last piece of immortality: their head-stones.[249]

Are the actions of the government, making a mass grave for those who had been previously buried correctly and respectfully, to blame for the copious number of ghost sightings reported at the Quidnessett Cemetery? It's impossible for us to say for certain, but if one is looking for a logical cause-and-effect relationship, this explanation certainly fits the bill.

How to find it: Quidnessett Memorial Cemetery is located on Post Road (US 1) on the border of the towns of North Kingstown and Quidnessett. From I-95, take exit 9 onto RI 4 southbound. Take exit 7 onto RI 402 eastbound, and then go right onto Post Road (US 1). The cemetery will be about ½ mile down US 1 on the right side of the road.

Ramtail Mill (Foster)

Every state has its share of haunted locales, but the Ramtail Mill (alternately known as the Ramtail Factory and the Foster Woolen Factory), which dates way back to 1799, might represent the only site in the country that has been officially recognized as such by a state government: Rhode Island's 1885 census officially records the now-abandoned factory as "haunted."[250]

The well-traveled story begins with factory founder William Potter taking on his son-in-law, Peleg Walker, as one of four business partners in 1813 to expand his cotton mill on the banks of the Ponagansett River. Potter would run the factory, and Walker would be the factory's keeper, watching over the building when it was unoccupied at night. Walker's last duty every night was to ring the factory's bell at daybreak, calling all the employees into work for the day. This partnership worked out fine for about nine years, until Walker got into a dispute about money with one or more of the other partners and, in his anger, shouted that the men would soon have to take the keys to the mill "from a dead man's pocket."[251] The very next day, May 19, 1822, Peleg Walker was found hanging from the bell rope that he was charged with ringing every morning; the keys to the mill were indeed in his pocket.

It wasn't long before the unique, unmistakable sound of the mill's bell awoke the entire town at midnight; when a few brave souls arrived at the mill to investigate, they found it locked and empty. Over time, the townspeople began to accept the midnight tolling of the bell as commonplace and chocked it up to Peleg Walker's ghost making his presence known. (Nobody is quite sure why the ghost opted to ring the bell in the middle of the night instead of at daybreak, when workers would typically be summoned to the mill—perhaps Peleg decided to take out revenge on his old business partners in a more mischievous than malicious fashion.) After a while, the late-night awakenings became tiresome, and some factory workers decided to remove the bell. But just a few nights later, the town was once again woken in the middle of the night—this time, all the factory's machinery had turned on, operating as if it were the middle of the day (some accounts even state that "the water wheel that was used to run the mill was turning *opposite the flow of the stream!*"[252]). Not long after that, the distinctive shape of Peleg Walker's apparition, complete with a night watchman's lantern, was seen by several townspeople who were out for a night stroll near the factory's site on the Ponagansett River.

Today, all that's left of the old factory in the woods of Foster, Rhode Island, is a set of stone foundations and a couple of stone walls. The legend of Peleg Walker lives on, however, because visitors to the property that once housed the Ramtail Mill still report hearing a metallic creaking sound, as if a night watchman's lantern were swinging back and forth, and occasionally there are reports of glowing orbs floating through the woods—perhaps it's a night watchman's lantern, bobbing as it is carried by unseen hands. Some people have even claimed to have heard the sound of Peleg Walker's bell tolling late in the night, even though the bell is long gone, and there are no longer any factory hands to call to work.

How to find it: The remnants of the Ramtail Mill are located in the woods of Foster, by the banks of the Ponagansett River. From I-295, take exit 6 onto RI 6 westbound. Turn left onto Ramtail Road. After a couple hundred feet, watch for a small brook running under an old bridge; follow the brook another couple hundred feet to the beginnings of an overgrown dirt road, which will meet the Ponagansett River. Cross the river via an old beaver dam, and the remnants of the factory will be straight ahead.

Scallabrini Villa (North Kingstown)

The Scallabrini Villa is now a health-care community for former priests and nuns in Newport, but it used to be a children's hospital known as the Rhode Island Hospital Children's Facility. Nowadays the sound of phantom kids playing throughout the halls is a commonly reported phenomenon. Although these disturbances have been experienced all over the facility, most of the unexplained phenomena tends to occur within room 103, which, perhaps unsurprisingly, was rumored to be the former hospital's intensive care unit.

How to find it: The Scallabrini Villa health-care facility is located at 860 North Quidnessett Road in North Kingstown. From I-95, take exit 9 onto RI 4 southbound. After about 2 miles, take exit 7 onto RI 402 eastbound, and then go left onto Post Road (US 1). After less than 1 mile, take a right onto Old Forge Road, which will become Forge Road. After about 1 mile on Forge Road, turn left onto North Quidnessett Road. Scallabrini Villa will be just before the Quidnessett Country Club. For more information call 401-884-1802, e-mail admin@ScalabriniVilla.com, or visit their Web site at www.scalabrini villa.com.

Sherman Family Cemetery (Pascoag)

Just off Buck Hill Road—where the ghostly Gray Dog (see the Buck Hill Road entry, page 180) is said to roam—the Sherman Family burial plot on Wakefield Road is said to be home to the ghost of a young woman who stares at cars as they pass. Local legend states that the young woman is Laura Sherman, daughter of Clark Sherman, who once owned this parcel of land. In a strange conflation of the Bloody Mary legend and details from the movie *Beetlejuice,* locals say that if someone circles Laura Sherman's grave three times during a full moon and says the name "Laura," she will appear and hover over the plot before vanishing into thin air.[253]

How to find it: What's left of the Sherman Family burial plot—not much more than one tombstone and a few divots in the earth—is on Wakefield Road in Pascoag in Rhode Island's northwestern corner. From I-395 in Connecticut, take exit 100 to RI 193 south. Follow RI 193 south a short distance, and then take a left onto Porter Plain Road. Go right onto Sand Dam Road, take another quick right onto East Thompson Road, and then make a quick left onto Quaddick Town Farm Road. Buck Hill Road will be a left-hand turn that crosses the Connecticut/Rhode Island line. Wakefield Road will be a right-hand turn off Buck Hill Road.

Smith's Castle (North Kingstown)

The plot of land that holds "Smith's Castle" has had numerous structures erected on it. First Richard Smith and Roger Williams

Smith's Castle in North Kingstown effectively captures life as it once was in New England—especially with the ghosts of colonial soldiers reputedly roaming the grounds.

constructed a trading post as long ago as 1637. Smith then built a home there, which was burned down by Native Americans in 1675. Forty-nine colonists heading to Smith's house were ambushed in the swamp by Native Americans. The natives tracked the men back to the house and burned it to the ground. Smith escaped harm because he had thought ahead and constructed tunnels underneath the property to escape just such an attack. The house was rebuilt in 1678. Just off the main property is a mass grave for those 49 men.

Today, the house is a museum, complete with actors in period clothing who reenact the daily chores of the era. The ghosts of the past live on in another way, as well, according to reports. Voices are often heard where there are no living humans to utter them, the apparition of a colonial-era soldier has appeared to witnesses on more than one occasion, and phantom slaves have even been

The mass grave of 49 men slain in a Native American attack in 1675 might well be the source of Smith's Castle's ghosts.

reported by some witnesses (Smith was a slave owner in the world of 17th-century New England).

How to find it: Smith's Castle is located at 55 Richard Smith Drive in North Kingstown. From I-95, take exit 9 onto RI 4 southbound. From there, take exit 7 onto RI 402 eastbound, and go right onto Post Road (US 1). Richard Smith Drive will be the driveway for the Castle directly off US 1.

Stagecoach Tavern (Chepachet)

The long-standing Stagecoach Tavern in Chepachet, Rhode Island, is as historically significant as it is hospitable—and if the stories are to be believed, it may be as haunted as it is historically significant and hospitable. In 1842 the Stagecoach Tavern was the site of the infamous Dorr Rebellion, in which Thomas Dorr of the People's

Party sought to overthrow the incumbent governor, Samuel King. Dorr had been newly elected governor, but King refused to step down. A battle ensued near the tavern, and Dorr was forced to flee to Connecticut while King's men took over the tavern, nearly eating and drinking owner Jedediah Sprague out of business.[254]

Today the Stagecoach Tavern is said to be home to many ghosts, the most frequently occurring of them being a woman in a 19th-century dress and a little boy who strangely appears in and around the ladies room of the tavern's dining room. For many years staff and guests alike have reported physical disturbances such as silverware and coasters flying off tables. Although many of the more "mundane" characteristics of a traditional haunting—lights flicking on and/or off, voices and sobbing from nowhere—have been reported in the Stagecoach Tavern, more alarming ones, such as glasses shattering while patrons are seated at tables, have also been reported. Perhaps not surprisingly, paranormal investigations conducted at the Stagecoach Tavern have produced pictures of glowing orbs and wispy figures, EVPs of disembodied voices, and even video recordings of apparitions walking along the tavern's grounds (one such video can currently be seen on YouTube; search for "Stagecoach Tavern Ghost" in the site's search engine).

How to find it: The historic Stagecoach Tavern is located at 1157 Main Street, also known as the Putnam Pike (RI 44), in Chepachet Center. From I-295, take exit 7B onto RI 44 westbound. The Stagecoach Tavern will be about 9 miles from the highway on RI 44, near the intersection of RI 102. For more information, call 401-568-2275.

Zambarano Hospital (Burrillville)

For many years locals have told the story of a mysterious woman dressed in a 19th-century nursing uniform who still walks her rounds in the Burrillville hospital's south corridor. The ghostly nurse has been seen on numerous occasions by both hospital employees and patients, and she is said to always walk the same hallway and always between the hours of 11 PM and 1 AM. Thomas D'Agostino had a friend who worked at Zambarano Hospital; according to this source, the phantom nurse's appearances were once so common that some staff members were unwilling to walk down the south corridor alone at night.[255]

How to find it: The Zambarano Hospital, a facility catering to people with special needs, is located on RI 100 on Wallum Lake in Burrillville. From RI 44, turn onto RI 100 northbound; the Zambarano Hospital will be visible from the road overlooking the lake, about 2 miles east of the Connecticut border and about 1 mile south of the Massachusetts border. To contact the hospital, call 401-568-2551.

Greater Providence

Brown University (Providence)

Like so many of New England's old colleges, the Ivy League Brown University has its fair share of ghosts that have been reportedly seen in dormitories and classroom buildings all over campus. The building that has garnered an undeniable reputation for being haunted, however, is University Hall—the oldest building on campus.

Throughout the years, the incidents of paranormal activity in University Hall have varied from footfalls sounding on empty floors to heavy bookcases moving themselves to the middle of a room, and from apparitions appearing in mirrors to files disappearing out of locked safes. Reputable staff members—some of them tenured professors with doctorates—have claimed to hear the sound of a man loudly crying out coming from an empty room. Several students have also reportedly seen the apparition of a man leading a horse in or around the University Hall building, only to see the strange sight vanish into a wall or thin air. Staff members have also reported hearing the sound of horses' hooves walking through the basement floor but have, upon investigation, found the space unoccupied. University Hall, according to local lore, now stands where a horse stable used to be before the university was founded.[256]

On Benefit Street, which runs through campus, many witnesses have heard the sound of a phantom horse trotting along the road. Benefit Street also lays claim to one of literature's more prominent ghosts: Edgar Allen Poe. Many witnesses have claimed to have seen the eminent yet troubled American poet and short-story writer walking along the road and stopping in front of the former residence of Sarah Helen Whitman, to whom Poe was engaged while he was living in Providence.

How to find it: Brown University is located at Waterman Street in Providence. From I-195, take exit 2 onto Main Street (US 44), and then go right onto Waterman Street. For more information, call 401-863-1000, or visit Brown University's Web site at www.brown.edu.

Crescent Park Carousel (East Providence)

Crescent Park was once such a thriving local landmark that the amusement park was known as the Coney Island of New England; people young and old would come from all over southern New England to ride the rides, play the games, or simply revel in the carnival atmosphere. But most would agree that there is something inherently and ambiguously sinister about the atmosphere of an amusement park; it's a place of youthful abandon that nonetheless lacks the childlike innocence of a playground or a Little League diamond. The feeling is difficult to put into words, but Ray Bradbury managed to capture it perfectly in his novel *Something Wicked This Way Comes,* in which two boys are pursued by an evil presence through an amusement park after its closing.

When one considers the amusement park as being a youthful yet creepy place, the calliope music of the carousel springs immediately to mind. Perhaps it shouldn't come as a surprise, then, that the crown jewel of Crescent Park's golden era was the Looff Carousel, built by Charles Looff in 1895. The merry-go-round boasts four chariots and 62 wooden horses as well as a large mechanized organ. When the park's ballroom burned down in 1969 and Crescent Park began to falter, the carousel alone was saved from destruction by concerned citizens and is now considered a National

Historic Landmark. A fee of less than a dollar lets you visit the historic carousel and take a ride into the past. Although it is only operated at night, a great many witnesses have reported seeing the lights turn on at other times within the empty, locked building and the carousel machinery start up of its own volition, complete with eerie calliope music from the mechanized organ.

Although the carousel's apparent self-regulation is the former park's most frequent reported disturbance, witnesses have claimed to see the apparition of a young woman staring somewhat forlornly into the waters of the lake on which the park was built. The possible origin of the melancholy young lady is unknown but only adds to the old park's already creepy atmosphere.

How to find it: The Crescent Park Carousel, located on the site of what used to be Crescent Park in East Providence, is now a museum and a National Historic Landmark open to the public from Easter to Columbus Day. From I-195, take exit 8 onto RI 114 southbound. RI 114 becomes Pawtucket Avenue and then Bullocks Point Avenue. After about 5 miles the carousel will be on the right-hand side of the road. For more information visit www.quahog.org/attractions/index.php?id=46.

Cumberland Public Library (Cumberland)

The building that now houses the town of Cumberland's public library was once the Monastery of Our Lady of Strict Observance, housing Trappist monks there from its construction in 1902 until a 1950 fire destroyed the complex's church and guesthouse. It appears that one of the monastery's former residents might have stayed on past his tenure, for library staff and visitors periodically witness what looks like the apparition of a monk roaming the building and its grounds, and unseen hands sometimes close books left open—often in plain view of multiple witnesses.

How to find it: The Cumberland Public Library is at 1464 Diamond Hill Road (RI 114) in Cumberland. From I-295, take exit 11 onto RI 114 (Diamond Hill Road) southbound. Travel on RI 114 for about 2½ miles, and the library will be on the right-hand side of the road.

For more information, call 401-333-2552, or visit www.cumberland library.org.

Elder Ballou Meetinghouse Road Cemetery (Woonsocket)

The most common disturbance experienced by travelers passing by the cemetery on Elder Ballou Meetinghouse Road are mournful cries originating from an unseen source. Apparitions of spectral men wearing gray or black suits in and around the old, somewhat dilapidated, and more than a little eerie graveyard have also been reported.

How to find it: Elder Ballou Meetinghouse Road Cemetery is located in Woonsocket. From I-295, take exit 10 onto Mendon Road (RI 122), and then go right onto West Wrentham Road. After traveling just over 2 miles, Elder Ballou Meetinghouse Road will be a left-hand turn. The cemetery, which has fallen into a slight state of disrepair, will be evident and visible at that turn.

Greenville Public Library (Greenville)

Greenville's Public Library is apparently home to a mischievous ghost that likes to pull individual books off shelves, startling unsuspecting patrons. One witness even claimed that she saw an entire shelf of books slide off a shelf, as if an unseen arm had swept off the whole row from behind.[257] Lights have been reported to turn on and off by themselves, and the piano in the basement has purportedly sounded a few notes, even though the basement is unoccupied at the time. Speculation is that the library's ghost is either that of Mrs. Jenckes, whose family donated the land on which the library was built in 1955, or Orra Angell, who was the town librarian in 1882, when the library was then located down the road from its current location.[258] This is just speculation, however; nobody seems to have an explanation as to why either of these women who had worked toward the library's success in life would want to risk damage to the books—which could certainly occur if they were shoved off the stacks—now that they are in the afterlife.

How to find it: The Greenville Public Library is located at 573 Putnam Pike (US 44) in Greenville. From I-295, take exit 7B onto the Putnam Pike (US 44) eastbound. For more information, call 401-949-3630 or 800-745-5555, e-mail info@greenvillelibrarymail.com, or visit the library's Web site at www.yourlibrary.ws.

Greenville Tavern (Greenville)

The Greenville Tavern was built in 1733 by a man with the odd name of Resolved Waterman. The building changed hands a number of times; nonetheless, for many decades numerous witnesses reported seeing a white and wispy male form strolling through what used to be the old inn and tavern. Local legend has an explanation for this unexplained resident: During the middle of the 18th century, the tavern/inn was so popular among travelers of the Putnam Pike route that the overnight rooms were always almost completely full. One night a weary traveler entered the tavern looking for a place to stay, and Waterman regretfully informed him that all the rooms were taken—but he could sleep in the cellar if he so wished. The traveler gratefully took what was offered to him and set out to bed down in the cellar after a customary meal and several pitchers of ale. In the morning the traveler was nowhere to be found, although his belongings were still in the basement. It was believed that he had fallen into the basement's deep well in his drunken stupor—and his spirit continued to haunt the building through all its incarnations.

How to find it: What used to be the Greenville Tavern is located on RI 44 in Greenville. Currently closed, it was once slated for renovation, but it was purchased in 2003 by the Smithfield Historical Society and will soon be reopened as a museum. From I-295, take exit 7B onto the Putnam Pike (US 44) eastbound. It's just over 1 mile to the former Greenville Tavern.

Hanton City (Smithfield)

The abandoned remains of Hanton City are proof that Connecticut doesn't hold a monopoly on haunted ghost towns nestled deep within now-unpopulated woods. Although it isn't as infamous as, say, Dudleytown or even the Bara-Hack Village (both covered in the Connecticut chapter of this volume), Hanton City—a settlement built along the Aldrich Trail that connects Providence and Woonsocket—has had many reports of phantom voices whispering through the trees to visitors who have hiked in along the old roads to see what remains of the settlement. When Route 7 was built to accommodate increased traffic between Woonsocket and Providence following the Civil War, traffic along the old trail dwindled— and with it the population of Hanton City. There is some speculation that disease played a part in the town's untimely demise, but the lack of travelers—and, hence, trade—seems a more likely proposition. Still, no matter what the cause for the town's abandonment, visitors have been reporting phantom voices in the area since at least the 19th century. Perhaps the most chilling voices belong to what sound like children running and playing through the foundations, wells, stone walls, and graves that mark an empty spot in the forest that was once alive with human activity.

How to find it: Hanton City is located in the Smithfield woods. From I-295 take exit 8B onto RI 7 westbound. Go left onto RI 116, left again onto Stillwater Road, then another left onto Lydia Road, which will become Hanton City Trail Road. After just under ½ mile, turn left onto the Aldrich Trail, which is the entrance to what used to be Hanton City.

Nine Men's Misery (Cumberland)

In the woods behind the Cumberland Public Library—another site that's said to be haunted by the ghosts of Rhode Island's storied past (see page 196)—passersby and hikers sometimes report hearing wailing and moaning emanating from among the trees, despite the apparent lack of any human presence. Paranormal investigators have visited the location and have recorded several instances of EVP, and electromagnetic and thermal readings have registered as not only abnormal but nearly off the charts.

According to local legend, the alleged source for these disturbances is a site known as Nine Men's Misery—a stone cairn that marks the burial plot of nine militiamen who entered the woods searching for a party of Native Americans who had attacked a nearby town. The posse not only found the party that they had been looking for but discovered that they were badly outnumbered and initiated a hasty retreat. According to Thomas D'Agostino's *Haunted Rhode Island,* nine of the men failed to escape, and they were tortured and executed by tomahawk (autopsies conducted on exhumed remains have confirmed this aspect of the story).[259] The anguish that was undoubtedly felt by those unfortunate men certainly would go along way toward explaining the otherworldly moans heard in and around the site of Nine Men's Misery within the Cumberland woods.

How to find it: The Nine Men's Misery cairn is marked by a plaque and can be found in the woods not far from the back of the Cumberland Public Library. To find the library take I-295 to exit 11 onto RI 114 southbound. Travel on RI 114 (Diamond Hill Road) for about 2½ miles, and the library will be on the right-hand side of the road.

Precious Blood Cemetery (Woonsocket)

Housing over 16,000 interred dead, St. John's Cemetery—better known to locals as Precious Blood Cemetery—is one of the largest in Rhode Island. As if the name of the graveyard wasn't creepy enough, it is also reputed to be one of the most haunted cemetery plots in the state and is, unsurprisingly, one of the most popular cemeteries in Rhode Island for amateur ghost hunters as well as professional paranormal investigators. Reports of floating, glowing orbs as well as anthropomorphic forms walking the cemetery aisles are common, and many investigators have recorded EVP voices within the graveyard as well as photographs depicting orbs and apparitions.

How to find it: St. John's Cemetery is located off Carrington Avenue in Woonsocket. From I-295 take exit 9B onto RI 99. When RI 99 terminates, go left onto RI 122. Staying on RI 122, bear left onto Hamlet Avenue, and then take a left onto Carrington Avenue. The cemetery will be a couple hundred feet up on the left.

Sprague Mansion (Cranston)

"It's almost like a paranormal clinic," claims Andrew Laird, a member of the Rhode Island Paranormal Research Group (RIPRG). "If you want to learn about the paranormal, this is the place to come."[260] Even though previous residents and caretakers of the Sprague Mansion have scoffed at the idea of it being haunted, a notable increase in the number of paranormal incidents at the house since the 1960s resulted in an investigation by RIPRG. The evidence that they collected during their investigation has been considered by many to be nothing short of ground breaking.

The Sprague Mansion was built by the well-known and wealthy Rhode Island socialite William Sprague in 1790. After choking on a fish bone at dinner, William passed away during surgery to remove it, and the mansion was inherited by his sons, William Jr. and Amasa Sprague. The family business thrived under Amasa's watch, and William Jr. became a U.S. senator. It seemed as though the Sprague family would be prosperous for many generations—that is, until Amasa Sprague was brutally murdered on the footbridge not far from his house. John Gordon, a member of a family that had held a long-standing grudge against the Spragues, was hanged for the murder—a crime for which one of his brothers later confessed. The state of Rhode Island had murdered an innocent man, which resulted in the abolition of the state's death penalty.

A number of disturbances and encounters have been experienced by visitors to the mansion since it was sold in the early 1920s. The apparition of a woman has appeared descending the grand main staircase, bed sheets have been pulled off sleeping guests in the middle of the night, and unexplainable blasts of cold air have sent shivers up the spines of many visitors.

During the 1960s, a séance was conducted by the home's caretaker at the time, Robert P. Lynch. Those present reportedly were able to contact the spirit of a former Sprague family butler named Charles, who urged those assembled, "Tell my story."[261] Since the Cranston Historical Society acquired the mansion in 1966 and began a restoration that would turn the house into a museum, at least one other séance has been conducted. Current curator Lydia

Rapoza brought a Ouija board into a section of the house that was off-limits to visitors and got the message: "Run! Flee! Get out of here!"[262] This certainly must have surprised the curator, whose predecessor, Alice Baxter, apparently didn't believe the house to be haunted.

It would almost certainly have been Lydia's belief in the paranormal that led to RIPRG's investigation of the house in 2003. During the investigation, which took place during two separate visits, the team's instruments repeatedly "decked" (went off the scale of normal readings), cold spots were felt all over the house, they recorded EVPs in several different rooms, and all of their radios went off at the same time. The team personally saw in a mirror the image of a man walking behind them. Photographs taken in various rooms revealed ghostly images not only of orbs but also "the shadow of a lady in a long Victorian dress,"[263] a little girl with a dog, and another woman walking up the grand staircase. Video footage picked up EVPs that were not recorded on the audiotape, although both tapes were running simultaneously. The voices on each separate tape seemed to come from a forlorn-sounding woman sighing and saying things like, "I'm alone."[264] Andrew Laird even felt someone tap him on the shoulder in the mansion's basement; when he turned to respond, the nearest team member was over 20 feet away.

"On a scale of one to ten, I would rate it as a nine," concludes Andrew Laird on the topic of paranormal activity in the Sprague mansion. If RIPRG's findings are accurate, the historical Sprague mansion might very well be one of the most haunted houses on the East Coast, if not the entire United States.

How to find it: The Sprague mansion is on the corner of Dyer Street and Cranston Street in Cranston. The museum is open to the public for tours year-round and is also available for special events such as weddings. From I-95, take exit 16 to RI 10. Bear left off the exit if you were traveling north on I-95 and right off the exit if you were traveling south. Go ¼ mile north on RI 10 to the Industrial Park/Cranston Street exit. Take a left onto Cranston Street, then right at the sixth traffic light, which remains Cranston. The entrance to the museum is the door at 1351 Cranston Street. For more information on the mansion and tours, call 401-944-9226 or visit the museum's Web site at www.cranstonhistoricalsociety.org/mansion .html.

Swan Point Cemetery (Providence)

Many of the haunted places listed in this volume have had reports of historically significant apparitions, but it is probable that none hosts quite as many recognizable ghosts as the Swan Point Cemetery in Providence. Although the graveyard's alleged ghosts are numerous, and most would be unknown to the average visitor, sightings have been reported of the apparitions of various interred notables such as General Ambrose Everett Burnside (whose idiosyncratic facial hair gave rise to the term "sideburns"); William Sprague (of the Sprague Mansion, the previous entry in this volume); Thomas Dorr, the elected governor and leader of the Dorr rebellion (see the Stagecoach Tavern, page 192); and even famed horror writer H. P. Lovecraft, who died in 1937 at the age of 47.

How to find it: Swan Point Cemetery is located off Blackstone Boulevard in Providence. From I-95, take exit 25B, going left from the off ramp onto North Main Street. Take a right onto Pidge Avenue, then bear right onto Blackstone Boulevard; the cemetery will be just a few hundred feet up on the left.

NEWPORT AND THE ISLANDS

Arnold's Point Fort (Bristol)

Although none of the soldiers stationed at Arnold's Point saw military action during World War II, it is said that apparitions wearing World War II–era uniforms can be seen walking along the old garrison. The fort was erected to protect the Quonset Point naval base and Northeast seaboard in general in case of an Axis attack on the United States. It was closed shortly after the war ended.[265]

How to find it: To find the now-in-disrepair Arnold's Point Fort in Bristol, take I-195 to exit 7, RI 114 south. Stay on RI 114 through Bristol, just a couple hundred feet past Willow Lake and the Bristol Ferry.

Astors' Beechwood Mansion (Newport)

History is literally alive in Newport's Astors' Beechwood Mansion because the historic building is now home to a theater troupe that dresses in period garb and offers tours that focus on themes such as the "gilded age" of F. Scott Fitzgerald's writing or popular "murder mystery" events. But reportedly history can also be seen at the Astors' mansion in a state that most of us would agree has nothing to do with being alive. It is chilling enough that candles blow themselves out and locked doors are found wide open throughout the stately mansion, but ghostly sighs have also become a common occurrence, and the apparition of a young woman wearing a Victorian-style yellow dress has been seen by guests as well as the mansion staff on several occasions.

Astors' Beechwood Mansion was built in 1851 for a wealthy merchant named Daniel Parrish, but it got its name when William Blackhouse Astor Jr. bought the property in 1881; William was the grandson of John Jacob Astor, considered one of the wealthiest men in American history, who made his fortune first with fur trading and then, much more substantially, in real estate. The Astor mansion became known as a society hot spot, and the end-of-summer ball was considered *the* party of the year, even more popular and

Stately Astors' Beechwood Mansion in Newport is so beautiful that some of its Victorian-era residents have apparently refused to leave.

looked forward to than any of the balls thrown by the Vanderbilt family in their mansion, Breakers, down the road.

By all accounts, life was good for the Astors when William was the patriarch of the household; it was when his son John Jacob Astor IV became the head of the household following his parents' deaths (his father in 1892 and his mother in 1908) that tragedy repeatedly transpired on the property. The first such incident, following a difficult divorce for Astor, involved a telephone repairman who was accidentally electrocuted within the mansion's basement in 1911; this led to a costly lawsuit on the part of the young repairman's mother.[266] Local legend also states that not long after this incident, a beautiful young servant committed suicide in the mansion over an unfaithful lover. Perhaps to escape the series of unfortunate events that befell those around the mansion, John Jacob Astor IV and his new bride, Madeline Talmadge, decided to honeymoon in Europe in the spring of 1912. The honeymoon apparently went splendidly, but their choice of a return vessel was not, in retrospect, the best choice they could have made: on Wednesday, April 10, 1912, John Jacob and Madeline Astor boarded the RMS *Titanic* bound for New York. The pregnant Madeline would survive the tragedy at sea. Her husband would not.

It is not clear who the apparition of the woman in the yellow dress is; perhaps it is the Madeline Astor, who lived on in the home after her husband's untimely demise in one of the most infamous disasters in modern history; perhaps it is her mother-in-law, who was known for hosting the most lavish balls on the East Coast and would therefore be dressed appropriately; perhaps it is the jilted young servant who was said to have taken her own life within the mansion's walls; or perhaps it is simply one of the mansion's many partygoers, dressed for a spectacular ball and encouraged by the property's present-day theater troupe—who look as though they are ready to party right along with her.

How to find it: Astors' Beechwood Mansion, now a museum open to the public for themed tours by reservation and an event hall that hosts weddings and other functions, is located at 580 Bellevue Avenue in Newport. From I-95, take exit 9 onto RI 4 southbound. RI 4 will end and become Tower Hill Road where it merges with US 1. Continue a short distance on Tower Hill Road to the cloverleaf intersection. There, turn onto RI 138, which crosses the Jamestown Bridge into Jamestown, and then the Claiborne Pell Bridge into Newport and Middletown. After crossing the latter bridge, take a right onto Farewell Street (RI 138A), which will become Thames Street. At the intersection of Thames Street and Memorial Boulevard, go left onto Memorial Boulevard (and staying on RI 138A) and then right onto Bellevue Avenue. For more information or to make reservations, call 401-846-3772, or visit the Astors' Beechwood Mansion Web site at www.astorsbeechwood.com.

Belcourt Castle (Newport)

Belcourt Castle is a famously haunted museum and function hall that boasts a popular ghost tour alongside its more conventional mansion tour. Belcourt was designed in 1894 by famed architect

Belcourt Castle houses what might very well be the most haunted home furnishings in New England.

Richard Morris Hunt—who also designed the Statue of Liberty as well as the Vanderbilts' Breakers mansion—for Oliver Hazard Perry Belmont, the son of entrepreneur August Belmont (after whom the Belmont Stakes horserace is named). The building, which was fashioned after Louis XIII's hunting lodge in Versailles, boasts lighting designed by Thomas Edison as well as a stained-glass window collection that is the largest in the United States.[267]

Oliver Belmont passed on in 1908, able to enjoy his beloved mansion for only 14 years, and left Belcourt Castle to his wife, who in turn left it to family when she died in 1938. The mansion stayed in the family for just two more years, then it changed hands several times until finally a newlywed couple named Harley and Donald Tinney bought the property in 1960. They have owned it since. If the stories told by the Tinneys and various guests are any indication, however, the Tinneys are far from the mansion's only occupants. The couple has on numerous occasions seen the apparition of an old man. They and multiple other witnesses have also seen the apparition of what appears to be a monk near the mansion's grand staircase, and according to Thomas D'Agostino, an entire tour group being led through the house witnessed one of the monk's appearances. After a while, the phantom monk seemed to have moved its comfort zone from the grand staircase to the home's chapel:

> [The Tinneys had] a wooden statue of a monk that Harley had placed near the grand staircase. Witnesses spotted the phantom monk on the stairs for some time. . . . A psychic told Mrs. Tinney that the statue wanted to be put in the chapel or it would never be at peace. She did just that, and the sightings of the phantom monk now remain isolated to that room.[268]

Although Belcourt Castle's apparitions are startling enough, it may well be the mansion's furnishings that truly have the ability to frighten visitors. In the mansion's ballroom is a pair of thronelike chairs that reportedly emanate powerful waves of negative energy—local legend states that visitors who touch the chairs often feel an intense chill or might even experience the sensation that the blood is fleeing from their hands. One woman was reportedly even launched across the ballroom on touching the chairs. (Today the chairs are roped off, and visitors are not allowed to touch them.)

Also, a suit of armor in the ballroom reportedly screams and moans. On numerous occasions, often when noticing that the ballroom lights had apparently turned on of their own accord, the Tinneys or their guests have heard loud shrieking or deep, sorrowful moaning coming from within the suit of armor. Although this might seem like the plot to a bad 1930s horror movie (or an episode of *Scooby-Doo*), the noises have been heard by the Tinneys, their guests, and even tour guides. Reportedly, the armor sometimes even raises one arm as it is screaming, as if it were trying to level an accusation. The back of the helmet apparently has a deep gash, possibly from a broadsword or a battle-ax; speculation is that the armor's original owner was killed in the suit and still haunts it, screaming in agony.

How to find it: Belcourt Castle is located at 657 Bellevue Avenue in Newport. Although a private residence, the historic mansion is open to the public for tours as well as special events such as weddings. From I-95, take exit 9 onto RI 4 southbound. RI 4 merges with US 1 and becomes Tower Hill Road. Continue a short distance on Tower Hill Road until the cloverleaf intersection; there, turn onto RI 138, which crosses the Jamestown Bridge into Jamestown and then the Claiborne Pell Bridge into Newport and Middletown. After crossing the latter bridge into Newport, go right onto Farewell Street (RI 138A), which becomes Thames Street. At the intersection of Thames Street and Memorial Boulevard, take a left onto Memorial Boulevard (which remains RI 138A). Go right onto Bellevue Avenue to the mansion.

Black Duck Inn (Newport)

Just a short walk from the shops, restaurants, and seaport that make up Newport's popular tourist region, the Black Duck Inn is named after a notorious rum-running ship that had gained the favor of the public but the loathing of the U.S. Coast Guard. Many of the inn's guests over the years have claimed to find doors that were left unlocked have had their deadbolts securely bolted, that lights have turned themselves on and off, and even that guestroom alarm clocks mysteriously changed their settings.

How to find it: The Black Duck Inn is located at 31 Pelham Street in Newport. From I-95, take exit 9 onto RI 4 southbound. RI 4 becomes Tower Hill Road where it merges with US 1. Continue a short distance on Tower Hill Road until the cloverleaf intersection; there, turn onto RI 138, which crosses the Jamestown Bridge into Jamestown and then the Claiborne Pell Bridge into Newport and Middletown. After crossing the latter bridge into Newport, go right onto Farewell Street (RI 138A) and then another right onto Pelham Street. For more information or to make reservations, call 401-841-5548 or 800-209-5212, or visit the inn's Web site at www.blackduck inn.com.

The Breakers (Newport)

Now one of Rhode Island's most famous and most visited tourist destinations, the Breakers—an enormous (65,000 square feet) sprawling, mansion overlooking the Atlantic—was once the summer home of the Vanderbilt family, who made their fortune building railroads. The home was built for Cornelius Vanderbilt II, the grandson of tycoon and railroad magnate Cornelius Vanderbilt, by renowned architect Richard Morris Hunt—who also designed the Statue of Liberty—from 1893 to 1895. A previous mansion stood on the same property until it burned down in 1892; as a result, Vanderbilt insisted that no flammable materials be used in the construction of the almost all stone-and-brick mansion. At the time, the Breakers in Newport—considered to be the capital of American social prestige—was the largest and most opulently decorated summer home in the United States; in today's dollars its construction cost would be $150 million.

There have been reports of an apparition of an ornately dressed woman roaming the Breakers' vast halls. It's widely speculated that the apparition is that of Alice Claypoole Gwynne Vanderbilt, the wife of Cornelius Vanderbilt II, who lived in the Breakers for a number of years.

How to find it: The Breakers, at 44 Ochre Point Avenue on the southeast corner of Newport, is now a museum owned and run by the Preservation Society of Newport—which operates a number of the Newport mansions—and is open to the public for tours year-round. From I-95, take exit 9 onto RI 4 southbound. RI 4 becomes Tower Hill Road where it merges with US 1. Continue a short distance on Tower Hill Road until the cloverleaf intersection; there, turn onto RI 138, which crosses the Jamestown Bridge into Jamestown and then the Claiborne Pell Bridge into Newport and Middletown. After crossing the latter bridge into Newport, take a right onto Farewell Street (RI 138A), which becomes Thames Street. At the intersection of Thames Street and Memorial Boulevard, go left onto Memorial Boulevard (which remains RI 138A). Take a right onto Annandale Road, a left onto Narragansett Avenue, and then

The ghosts of the Vanderbilt family might still be celebrating the Roaring Twenties in their magnificent Newport mansion, the Breakers.

a quick right onto Ochre Point Avenue. The Breakers is at the corner of Ochre Point Avenue and Sheppard Avenue, on the edge of Salve Regina University, overlooking the Atlantic Ocean. For more information, visit the Newport Mansions Web site at www.newport mansions.org.

Brenton Point (Newport)

Brenton Point was once home to an enormous, beautiful mansion—with a unique, conical tower reminiscent of what might have housed Rapunzel—known as Brenton Point's Reef. Now its grounds are a state park filled with the ruins of its former glory. The cause of Brenton Point's downfall, according to local legend, is an ancient

Egyptian curse placed on the property as well as its original owner, the lawyer and renowned Egyptologist Theodore M. Davis.

Davis purchased the property, named after early Rhode Island settler William Brenton, in 1876 and soon erected the Reef— complete with extensive gardens, a windmill, and a large stable— with the wealth he had amassed through his excavation of several Egyptian tombs in the Valley of the Kings. One of those tombs was Amenhotep III, widely believed to be the father of Tutankhamen— popularly known as King Tut. It is a widely held belief that any man who desecrates the tombs of the Egyptian pharaohs would be cursed; considering the fate that befell Davis and his property, which was built with money accrued from his Egyptian expeditions and filled with the spoils of those excavations, the idea of a curse does not seem strange or extraordinary. Soon after the buildings were constructed, the windmill caught fire and burned down in a storm; not much later, the stables fell to the same fate.

Davis passed on in 1910. When his wife passed away in 1915, the property was sold to the Budlong family. Almost immediately, the Budlongs became embroiled in a long and difficult divorce, and the house was, for all practical reasons, abandoned; not even the Budlong children would use the large, impressive mansion to live in or to entertain friends. The Budlongs were tight-lipped about what it was about the house that scared them away and kept it vacant, but there were whispers of ghostly activity. The Reef itself burned down in 1960, dilapidated and unused for many years, and in 1969 the Budlong family willingly turned the entire property over to the state of Rhode Island for use as a state park.

Today the park is a popular and much-visited destination, with gorgeous Atlantic views from its Ocean Avenue location. The park's offices are located in the property's old servants' quarters—the one building that has remained perfectly intact through the years. Perhaps the lack of Egyptian ornamentation in the servants' quarters is what saved it from the same fate as the mansion, windmill, and stables. Whether the property is still considered cursed is unclear, but reports continue of ghostly voices flitting through the trees near the windmill and the sound of phantom horses trotting around the stables. Many park rangers, although they won't disclose why, have refused to enter the Brenton Point property after dark.

How to find it: Brenton Point State Park, open to the public from sunrise to sunset, is located on Ocean Avenue in Newport. From I-95, take exit 9 onto RI 4 southbound. RI 4 becomes Tower Hill Road where it merges with US 1. Continue a short distance on Tower Hill Road until the cloverleaf intersection; there, turn onto RI 138, which crosses the Jamestown Bridge into Jamestown and then the Claiborne Pell Bridge into Newport and Middletown. After crossing the latter bridge into Newport, take a right onto Farewell Street (RI 138A), which becomes Thames Street. At the intersection of Thames Street and Memorial Boulevard, take a left onto Memorial Boulevard (which remains RI 138A). Go right onto Bellevue Avenue and follow Bellevue until it ends, taking a right onto Ocean Avenue. For more information about Brenton Park, call 401-849-4562, or visit the Rhode Island State Parks Web site at www.riparks.com/brenton.htm.

Brinley Victorian Inn (Newport)

Actually two adjoining 19th-century homes (built in 1850 and 1870, respectively) that contain a total of 17 lavishly furnished guest-rooms, the Brinley Victorian Inn is said to be home to a very active spirit whose exploits come very close to what is thought of as pol-tergeist activity. Indeed, I would be tempted to label the distur-bances witnessed at the inn as symptomatic of a poltergeist infestation if it weren't for the claim of the inn's owner, John Sweetman, that he had seen the apparition of a woman wearing a long, black, Victorian dress struggling up the inn's main staircase—an apparition apparently matching in appearance a woman whose portrait hangs in the building's library. Considering that the Brinley Victorian Inn's unexplained phenomena are apparently linked to the whims of an alleged spirit, it's probably safe to assume that the inn is home not to a poltergeist but is, rather, the scene of a tradi-tional haunting—albeit a very active and physical one.

Mark Jasper's *Haunted Inns of New England* chronicles many of the Brinley Victorian Inn's disturbances over the years. A sampling:

John and Jennifer [Sweetman] were upstairs in their room when they heard the front door slam followed by the sound of someone running up the staircase. This was in turn followed by a rattling sound coming from the bedroom doorknob. . . . John walked out of his room and downstairs to investigate. He could find no one.[269]

Anna [Sweetman] said that one time a housekeeper and she were about to clean room 8. When they knocked on the door they heard the sound of paper bags being crinkled and people moving about. They unlocked the door and found themselves staring at an empty room.[270]

[In room 8] Anna began talking to the ghost. "Are you a boy or a girl?" she asked. Suddenly the coat hangers began wildly banging together.[271]

After the rooms are cleaned, mints in green wrappers are placed on the pillows. Frequently these mints would just disappear. And, one time when a plumber punched a hole in the wall in Anna's room, 20 unopened mints in pristine condition fell out of the wall. Jennifer thought it was possible they had mice and hired an exterminator to investigate. The exterminator examined the house and assured Jennifer they did not have a pest problem.[272]

These stories alone chronicle the experiences shared by the family that owns the inn. Many more unexplainable events have been experienced by various Brinley Victorian Inn guests over the years. For example, they've heard the sound of footfalls echoing throughout the halls and even in their rooms while they thought they were alone, they've witnessed objects move on their own—including the aforementioned mints in green wrappers[273]—and some have even come back to their rooms to find their dresser drawers or suitcases emptied onto the floor.

How to find it: The Brinley Victorian Inn is located at 23 Brinley Street in Newport. From I-95, take exit 9 onto RI 4 southbound. RI 4 becomes Tower Hill Road where it merges with US 1. Continue a short distance on Tower Hill Road until the cloverleaf intersection; there, turn onto RI 138, which crosses the Jamestown Bridge into Jamestown and then the Claiborne Pell Bridge into Newport and Middletown. After crossing the latter bridge into Newport, go right onto Farewell Street (RI 138A). Farewell Street will become Thames Street. Take a left onto Touro, a left onto Kay Street, and a right onto Brinley Street. For more information or to make reservations, call 401-849-7645 or 800-999-8523, or visit the inn's Web site at www.brinleyvictorian.com.

Burning Eyes of Block Island (Block Island)

For as long as Block Island has been inhabited by New Englanders, there have been unexplained reports of strange red or orange glowing eyes appearing on the back porches or in the backyards of Block Island residences in the dark of night. According to Dennis William Hauck's *Haunted Places: The National Directory*, the bodies of loved ones who died during a hard, cold New England winter used to be stored behind houses until the ground could thaw enough to bury them. Hauck draws a connection between this now-defunct practice and the fact that the burning eyes have typically appeared behind such a residence. Perhaps the spirits of those who were temporarily interred behind the houses still linger to haunt their final resting places.[274]

How to find it: Block Island—which is about 9 miles south of Charlestown, Rhode Island, and roughly 12 miles east of Long Island, New York—is accessed by ferry, boat, or plane.

Colt-Andrews School (Bristol)

Today's Colt-Andrews School is the conjoining of two formerly unconnected buildings: the Colt building, founded in 1906 by Samuel Pomeroy Colt (nephew of the creator of the famous Colt revolver), and the Andrews School, founded in 1938 by Robert D. Andrews. Apparitions of the buildings' founders reportedly have been seen by maintenance staff and teachers after hours in each of their respective buildings. Furthermore, the smell of women's perfume sometimes permeates the boys' bathroom, and disembodied voices have been heard by students in the same boys' bathroom, apparently giving the young children quite a scare.

How to find it: The Colt-Andrews School is located at 570 Hope Street in Bristol. From I-195, take exit 8 onto RI 114 southbound. Follow RI 114 into Bristol, at which point it will become Hope Street. For more information about the elementary school, call 401-254-5991.

Colt State Park (Bristol)

It would appear that Bristol's Samuel Pomeroy Colt was a man of legacy in more ways than one, for many of the various locations and landmarks that bear his name have gained a reputation for unexplainable phenomena.

In 1887 Colt bought three adjacent farms and converted them into a kind of private nature reserve for his family, who stayed there until 1965, when the state of Rhode Island purchased the property and converted it into a state park. Countless park visitors enjoy its quiet serenity, but more than a few have been rattled by the sight of two little girls walking hand in hand along the beach who suddenly vanish into thin air. It is said that many visitors have also heard the disembodied giggles of little girls echoing throughout the park's woods, though a source of these voices could not be found. Local legend states that two young girls—possibly sisters[275]—drowned on the property sometime in the 1970s, but none of the sources of this tale cites where their information comes from. While the tragic story might very well be true, it is equally likely that the tale represents nothing more than a legend conjured up to explain away the park's unnerving apparitions.

The property's stable is also reportedly home to a mischievous spirit who turns lights on and off while the building is empty and opens locked doors. It is said that a stable hand died inside the building, and this is the origin of the stable's unexplained activity, but the validity of this claim is no more certain than that of the beach's two spectral little girls.

How to find it: Colt State Park is a patch of preserved land off Asylum Road on the western shore of Bristol. From I-195, take exit 8 onto RI 114 southbound. Follow RI 114 into Bristol, at which point it becomes Hope Street. Follow RI 114 for a total of just over 12 miles; turn onto Asylum Road for about ¼ mile, and turn right into the state park. For more information, call 401-253-7482, or visit the park's Web site at www.riparks.com/colt.htm.

Inn at Villalon (Middletown)

This stately mansion in Middletown, not far from the border of Newport—a town known for its grand (and haunted) mansions—was constructed for a wealthy arms manufacturer named Hamilton Hoppin in 1856. The property was purchased by the Fabricant family in 1994, who converted it into a 12-guestroom hotel and re-named the mansion the Agincourt Inn. They, in turn, recently sold it to the current innkeepers, Stefan and Claudia Wessel, who gave the property its present name. After the conversion, it became very clear to the innkeepers and their living guests that they might not be the only occupants of the luxurious Victorian mansion.

The Inn at Villalon's alleged ghosts don't seem to be the shy type—they purportedly often move personal affects around right in front of guests and staff. Moreover, several different apparitions have been reported at the inn, including those of Hamilton Hoppin and his brother who materialized in the dining room, having a conversation in plain view of multiple witnesses and apparently oblivious to the living souls all around them;[276] a phantom car—said to have belonged to a reviled doctor who was shot and killed en route to the inn one evening—that pulls up to the front of the inn before vanishing into thin air;[277] spectral forms of slaves that appear in the basement, which was said to have been a stop on the Underground Railroad; men and women dressed in 19th-century garb who seem to be living souls until they vanish right before guests' eyes; and a tomahawk-carrying Narragansett tribesman in full war paint who appeared at the bedside of Selma Fabricant in the middle of the night (it has been said that the inn was built on an old Native American trail).[278] Considering the multitude of various unexplained phenomena reported at the inn over the 15 years it has been open as a place of lodging, it might not be a stretch to consider this luxurious lodging house one of the most haunted sites in New England.

How to find it: The Inn at Villalon (formerly the Agincourt Inn) is a luxurious Victorian-style mansion located at 120 Miantonomi Avenue in Middletown, very near the Newport border (although the inn is on the Newport island, it is considered to be part of Middletown). From I-95, take exit 9 onto RI 4, southbound. RI 4 will end and become Tower Hill Road where it merges with US 1. Continue a short distance on Tower Hill Road until the cloverleaf intersection; there, turn onto RI 138, which crosses the Jamestown Bridge into Jamestown, and then the Newport Bridge into Newport and Middletown. At the intersection of Admiral Kalbfus Road, Broadway, Main Street, and Miantonomi Avenue, which divides Middletown and Newport, keep straight on Miantonomi. For more information or to make reservations, call 401-847-0902 or 800-352-3750, e-mail VillalonInn@aol.com, or visit the inn's Web site at www.villaloninn.com.

La Petit Auberge (Newport)

This gourmet French restaurant has gained a reputation lately for serving unexpected chills along with fine food. Reportedly, silverware occasionally rattles on tables, often even when guests are seated, and there have been reports of apparitions wearing very old-fashioned clothing who materialize and then vanish just as suddenly as they appeared.

How to find it: La Petit Auberge is located at 19 Charles Street in Newport. From I-95, take exit 9 onto RI 4 southbound. RI 4 becomes Tower Hill Road where it merges with US 1. Continue a short distance on Tower Hill Road to the cloverleaf intersection; there, turn onto RI 138, which crosses the Jamestown Bridge into Jamestown and then the Claiborne Pell Bridge into Newport and Middletown. After crossing the latter bridge into Newport, go right onto Farewell Street (RI 138A), which becomes Thames Street. Then turn left onto

Marlborough Street; La Petit Auberge is on the corner of Charles and Marlborough streets. For more information, call 401-849-6669.

Nathaniel Porter Inn (Warren)

The Nathaniel Porter Inn was established as a place of lodging in 1980, but the structure itself dates all the way back to 1750, when it was a cooper's shop. Since its inception as an inn and restaurant, visitors have reported experiencing a multitude of unexplained phenomena. Lights are said to turn on and off even though the light switch has been in plain view and no one touched it,[279] witnesses claim to have heard both male and female voices calling out to them (sometimes even calling their name), and the apparitions of several different forms have been viewed in the building: a man wearing 18th-century garb has been reported to materialize, then walk through a wall; the apparition of a former housekeeper named Martha sometimes appears carrying a candle from guestroom to guestroom just before vanishing (sometimes the candle is said to appear by itself, without a human form holding it, bobbing in midair and moving from room to room); and sometimes the form of a woman is reported sitting in a chair and staring out the window—local legend states that she is staring out at where her child was playing before the young one met an unfortunate fate.[280]

How to find it: The Nathaniel Porter Inn is located at 125 Water Street in Warren. From I-195, take exit 8 onto RI 114 southbound. Follow RI 114 into Warren, and go right onto Water Street. For more information, call 401-289-0373.

Palatine Light (Block Island)

For still, on many a moonless night
from Kingston Head and from Montauk light
the spectre kindles and burns in sight.

Now low and dim, now clear and higher,
Leaps up the terrible Ghost of Fire,
Then, slowly sinking, the flames expire.

—*John Greenleaf Whittier, "Palatine"*[281]

Sometime in the middle of the 18th century, a Dutch ship called the *Princess Augusta* that was heading for the American colonies full of passengers—German immigrants known as "Palatines"—saw its crew mutiny and run the ship aground on rocks near Block Island.[282] Having watched from afar, a group of pirates jumped on the rare opportunity to raid an immobilized ship—they stole the valuables of the passengers and made them disembark onto the island while they torched the ship. One woman, according to legend, refused to leave the deck of the ship, and the ship was set ablaze with her on it. She stood on the fiery deck screaming as the rising tide lifted the beached *Princess Augusta* out into the ocean, where it quickly sank to its watery grave in the Atlantic.

Over the past couple of centuries, many strange lights—some of them reportedly resembling a burning ship—have been seen off the coast of Block Island. In the couple of years following the disaster, witnesses claimed to have seen a ship matching the description of the *Princess Augusta* careening toward shore only to burst into flames and then suddenly disappear.[283] The most famous such incident occurred in 1969, when dozens of witnesses saw a burning ship off the island's coast.[284] When the Coast Guard later went out to investigate the site of the reported ship, there was no sign of any vessel—no burnt hull, no flotsam, nothing.

How to find it: Block Island—which is about 9 miles south of Charlestown, Rhode Island, and roughly 12 miles east of Long Island, New York—is accessed by ferry, boat, or plane.

Roger Williams University (Bristol)

An 1890 barn that was relocated from nearby Gloucester to the university as an architectural project is now the Roger Williams University Theater. It would appear, if the stories are true, that when the Department of Historical Preservation moved the building, one of its former residents might have come along for the ride. The apparition of what appears to be a farmhand—who, local legend states, came back to the farm after a winter's night of hard drinking and fell asleep in the barn loft only to freeze to death—has reportedly appeared to cast, crew, and students at the Barn, and has even wreaked havoc on the electrical system if someone sits in what is now known as Banquo's seat. Although the identity of the purported farmhand is not known, somewhere along the line he picked up the name "Banquo" after a character in Macbeth.[285] Reportedly, the most frequently occurring brand of mischief of this Banquo's ghost involves making the stage curtains ripple and move as if a performer were about to enter through them to the stage.[286]

How to find it: Located at 1 Old Ferry Road in Bristol, at the intersection of RI 114 and RI 136, Roger Williams University is a liberal arts college whose picturesque campus boasts gorgeous views overlooking Hope Bay. From I-195, take Massachusetts exit 2 toward Newport. This exit will lead into RI 136 south; follow RI 136 south for about 9 miles. The entrance to Roger Williams University will be on the left-hand side of the road. The Barn is a large yellow building that can easily be seen from the campus entrance and from RI 114. For more information about Roger Williams University, call 800-458-7144, or visit the university's Web site at www.rwu.edu; to contact the theater directly, call 401-254-3666.

Spring House Hotel (Block Island)

Constructed in 1852 as a weekend getaway for the rising upper-middle class (as well as the established upper class) of the Northeast, the Spring House Hotel—overlooking the pristine beaches of secluded Block Island—has been a thriving, opulent, and luxurious place of lodging practically since the moment it opened its doors. To ensure that New England's elite kept coming back to the resort year after year, the ownership set strict standards of cleaning and maintenance for its staff. Reflecting this policy, the hotel's clever tagline is, "The only thing we overlook is the ocean."

If the stories are to be believed, it appears that one of these meticulous employees—a chambermaid supervisor named Clossie—still looks after the hotel's maintenance. Staff members often find items rearranged within rooms, and appliances such as fans have been known to turn themselves on right before the eyes of witnesses. According to David Pitkin's *Ghosts of the Northeast,* one chambermaid had just finished her inspection rounds one evening, closing and locking every door behind her as she went; when she turned around and looked behind her, to her astonishment every door had been flung wide open, almost as if Clossie were doing her own rounds behind the living chambermaid.[287] No explanation is given in the various accounts of the Spring House Hotel's haunting as to why the building's former head chambermaid is given credit for the hotel's unexplained phenomena; it's likely that the Clossie story was simply a legend that took form and made enough sense to continue on.

Room M13 seems to be the center of the hotel's paranormal activity, for it's in this room that a young boy kept his parents awake at night talking to an old woman that neither parent could see, and it's in this room that a woman was awakened by her bed shaking violently in the middle of the night.[288] But other rooms aren't without their unexplained occurrences: Items have been known to rearrange themselves in practically every room of the hotel. And in room 315 one employee was startled when she looked in the mirror to see an old man sitting on the bed behind her; when she turned around, the man was, of course, gone.[289]

How to find it: The Spring House Hotel is a sprawling, luxurious hotel with breathtaking ocean views, located at 52 Spring Street on Block Island. Block Island—which is about 9 miles south of Charlestown, Rhode Island, and roughly 12 miles east of Long Island, New York—is accessed by ferry, boat, or plane. The Spring House Hotel is on the east side of the island, on Spring Street, less than 1/2 mile south of the ferry station. For more information, or to make reservations, call 401-466-5844, or visit the hotel's Web site at www.springhousehotel.com.

St. Andrew's School (Barrington)

Founded in 1893 by Reverend William Merrick Chapin, the school's first headmaster, St. Andrew's School is now a co-ed suburban parochial school that was once a rural self-sustaining community for homeless boys and orphans, complete with its own farmland. It is said that Pastor Chapin still roams the grounds, and his apparition—identifiable by a flowing red cape[290]—has reportedly been seen by students, staff, and visitors alike.

Paranormal investigator Thomas D'Agostino once visited St. Andrew's, and he was working in the auditorium/gymnasium when he personally experienced an inexplicable phenomenon. As he was investigating, the room's piano struck four or five notes in succession, despite the fact that D'Agostino was alone in the room. D'Agostino initially shrugged off the occurrence as a mischievous student's prank—until the piano again played the same group of notes. It was then that D'Agostino realized that the closest door was about 30 feet away from the piano; it would have been impossible for anyone to run in, hit the piano's keys, and run out without being seen. A subsequent conversation with a school maintenance worker confirmed to D'Agostino that several people had experienced the exact same phenomenon in the auditorium.[291]

How to find it: St. Andrew's is located at 63 Federal Road in Barrington. From I-195, take exit 8 onto RI 114 southbound. Follow RI 114 to Federal Road, which will be a right-hand turn. The school will be about 1,000 feet down the road.

notes

1. Thomas A. Verde, *Maine Ghosts & Legends: 26 Encounters with the Supernatural* (Camden, ME: Down East Books, 1989), 40.
2. Ibid., 39.
3. Susan Smitten, *Ghost Stories of New England* (Edmonton, Canada: Ghost House Books, 2003), 111.
4. "Prospect Harbor Light," New England Lighthouses: A Virtual Guide, http://lighthouse.cc/prospect harbor.
5. Verde, 23.
6. Ibid., 24.
7. Dennis William Hauck, *Haunted Places: The National Directory— Ghostly Abodes, Sacred Sites, UFO Landings, and Other Supernatural Locations* (New York: Penguin Books, 1996; reissue 2002), 198.
8. Smitten, 122–123.
9. Verde, 68.
10. Ibid., 67.
11. Ibid., 69.
12. Ibid., 105.
13. Ibid., 204.
14. Ibid., 203.
15. Ibid., 198.
16. Bill and Nancy Washell, "Joshua Chamberlain House and Museum," *Encyclopedia of Haunted Places: Ghostly Locales from Around the World,* edited by Jeff Belanger (Franklin Lakes, NJ: New Page Books, 2005), 26–27.
17. Smitten, 110.
18. Ibid., 107.
19. Verde, 97.
20. Ibid., 96.
21. Ibid., 96.
22. Ibid., 84.
23. Ibid., 100.
24. Ibid., 99.
25. Ibid., 101.
26. Smitten, 106.
27. Ibid., 102.
28. Ibid., 103.
29. Verde, 119.
30. Ibid., 118.
31. Ibid., 119.
32. Ibid., 121.
33. Troy Taylor, "The Ghosts of Kennebunkport," Ghosts of the Prairie, www.prairie ghosts.com/kenport.html.
34. Verde, 122.
35. "Captain Lord Mansion," Haunted Houses.com, www.hauntedhouses.com/ states/me/captain_lord _mansion.cfm.

36. Smitten, 55.

37. Ibid., 52.

38. Mark Jasper, *Haunted Inns of New England* (Yarmouth Port, MA: On Cape Publications, 2000), 150.

39. Verde, 126.

40. Jasper, 153–154.

41. Ibid., 136.

42. Ibid., 158.

43. Ibid.

44. Ibid., 137.

45. Ibid.

46. Joseph A. Citro, *The Vermont Ghost Guide* (Hanover, NH: University Press of New England, 2000), 23.

47. Hauck, 414.

48. Joseph Citro, *Passing Strange: True Tales of New England Hauntings and Horrors* (Boston: Houghton Mifflin, 1997), 264.

49. Smitten, 59.

50. Thomas D'Agostino, "The Ice House Restaurant," *Encyclopedia of Haunted Places,* 41.

51. "History of the Old Stagecoach Inn Vermont Bed and Breakfast, Waterbury," Old Stagecoach Inn, www.old stagecoach.com/history/history-old-stagecoach-inn-vermont-bed-and-breakfast.asp.

52. Joseph Citro, *Green Mountain Ghosts, Ghouls & Unsolved Mysteries* (Boston: Houghton Mifflin, 1994), 47.

53. Ibid., 49.

54. Ibid., 44.

55. Ibid., 45.

56. Ibid., 44.

57. Gordon Alexander, "Albany, Vermont—Where Things Go Bump in the Night, or Mother-In-Law's Revenge," Log Cabin Chronicles, www.tomi fobia.com/galexander/go _bump.html.

58. Citro, *The Vermont Ghost Guide,* 1.

59. Hauck, 415.

60. Jasper, 117.

61. Ibid., 121.

62. Thomas D'Agostino, "The Bowman House and Laurel Glen Mausoleum," *Encyclopedia of Haunted Places,* 42.

63. Jasper, 121.

64. Ibid.

65. Citro, *The Vermont Ghost Guide,* 6.

66. "Haunted Places in Vermont," The Shadowlands, www.theshadowlands.net/places/vermont.htm.

67. Citro, *The Vermont Ghost Guide,* 5.

68. "Haunted Places in

Vermont," The
Shadowlands.

69. Citro, *Green Mountain
Ghosts,* 53.

70. Smitten, 14.

71. Ibid., 16.

72. Ibid., 210.

73. Ibid., 210.

74. Ibid., 211.

75. Thomas D'Agostino,
Haunted New Hampshire
(Atglen, PA: Schiffer
Publishing, 2006), 11.

76. Ibid.

77. Citro, *Passing Strange,* 81.

78. Ibid., 82.

79. Ibid.

80. D'Agostino, *Haunted New
Hampshire,* 48.

81. Ibid., 7.

82. Krista Marrs, "Kimball
Castle in New Hands: Plans
Outlined," *Laconia Citizen,*
June 20, 2001.

83. D'Agostino, *Haunted New
Hampshire,* 20.

84. Ibid., 117.

85. Balzano, "The Country
Tavern," *Encyclopedia of
Haunted Places,* 34.

86. Hauck, 271.

87. D'Agostino, *Haunted New
Hampshire,* 122.

88. Ibid., 99.

89. Ibid., 80.

90. "Haunted Places in New
Hampshire," The Shadow-
lands, www.theshadow

lands.net/places/new
hampshire.htm.

91. D'Agostino, *Haunted New
Hampshire,* 109.

92. Ibid., 21–22.

93. Ibid., 23.

94. Ibid., 156.

95. Tricia Thibodeau, "Vale
End Cemetery," TrueGhost
.com, www.trueghost.com/
ValeEndCemetery.htm.

96. "Spirits of the Windham
Restaurant," Windham
Restaurant, www.windham
restaurant.com/spirit.htm.

97. Ibid.

98. Ron Kolek, "Windham
Restaurant," *Encyclopedia
of Haunted Places,* 34.

99. D'Agostino, *Haunted New
Hampshire,* 33.

100. Ibid.

101. D'Agonstino lists Moulton's
first name as "Jonathon,"
although on the man's
tombstone, in Hampton's
Pine Grove Cemetery (and
in other sources, such as
Hauck's *Haunted Places:
The National Directory*),
it is spelled "Jonathan."

102. D'Agostino, *Haunted New
Hampshire,* 58.

103. Ibid., 59.

104. "Rockingham Hotel," City
Guide to Portsmouth, NH,
and the Seacoast, www
.portsmouthnh.com/

harbourtrail/rockingham
.cfm.

105. D'Agostino, *Haunted New
     Hampshire,* 144.

106. Hauck, 272.

107. D'Agostino, *Haunted New
     Hampshire,* 146.

108. Ibid.

109. Ibid., 38.

110. Ibid.

111. Jasper, 112.

112. Smitten, 112.

113. Jeremy D'Entremon,
     "Baker's Island Light," New
     England Lighthouses: A
     Virtual Guide, www.light
     house.cc/bakers/index
     .html.

114. Cheri Revai, *Haunted
     Massachusetts: Ghosts and
     Strange Phenomena of the
     Bay State* (Mechanicsburg,
     PA: Stackpole Books, 2005),
     41.

115. Ibid., 40.

116. Ibid., 52.

117. Ibid., 53.

118. Ibid., 55.

119. Ibid., 54–55.

120. Jasper, 14.

121. Revai, *Haunted
     Massachusetts,* 51.

122. Balzano, "The Charlesgate
     Hotel," *Encyclopedia of
     Haunted Places,* 31.

123. Holly Mascott Nadler,
     *Ghosts of Boston Town:
     Three Centuries of True
     Hauntings* (Camden, ME:

Down East Books, 2002),
99.

124. Ibid.

125. Nadler, 103.

126. Revai, *Haunted
     Massachusetts,* 73–74.

127. Nadler, 105.

128. Ibid.

129. "About Concord's Historic
     Inn Hotel," Concord's
     Colonial Inn, http://
     concordscolonialinn.reach
     local.net/concord-ma
     -lodging-about-the-inn
     .asp.

130. Ibid.

131. Revai, *Haunted
     Massachusetts,* 65.

132. Hauck, 218.

133. Jasper, 3.

134. Ibid., 4.

135. Ibid., 5.

136. Nadler, 127.

137. Ibid., 125.

138. Revai, *Haunted
     Massachusetts,* 9.

139. Ron Kolek, "Houghton
     Mansion," *Encyclopedia of
     Haunted Places,* 29.

140. Revai, *Haunted
     Massachusetts,* 27.

141. Ibid.

142. Smitten, 118.

143. Ibid., 120.

144. Jasper, 10.

145. Smitten, 115.

146. Ibid., 118.

147. Revai, *Haunted
     Massachusetts,* 24.

148. Ibid.

149. Jasper, 54.

150. Dan Gordon and Gary Joseph, *Cape Encounters: Contemporary Cape Cod Ghost Stories* (Hyannis, MA: Cockle Cove Press, 2004), 116.

151. Hans Holzer, *Ghosts of New England: Spine-Tingling Encounters with the Ghosts of New England* (New York: Random House, 1997), 282.

152. Jasper, 26–29.

153. Holzer, 284.

154. Jasper, 39.

155. Ibid., 23.

156. Ibid., 25.

157. Gordon and Joseph, 84–85.

158. Ibid., 77.

159. Ibid., 83.

160. Ibid.

161. Jasper, 65.

162. Ibid., 50.

163. Ibid., 51.

164. Gordon and Joseph, 64.

165. Jasper, 39.

166. Ibid., 57.

167. Ibid., 35.

168. Although the name "Forget Me Not" is fitting for a supposedly haunted guest room, this probably represents more of a coincidence than some kind of cosmic synchronicity—all of the Wildflower Inn's rooms are named in honor of flowers.

169. Jasper, 35.

170. Citro, *Passing Strange*, 302.

171. "Haunted Places in Connecticut," The Shadowlands, www.the shadowlands.net/places/connecticut.htm.

172. It should be noted here that Aykroyd—who seems to know his paranormal phenomenon, as he has hosted a number of *Discovery* specials on a variety of topics—speaks in error about Dudleytown's location:

> Aykroyd: The other day I read that Harold Ramis, my colleague in *Ghostbusters,* said he doesn't believe in ghosts!
>
> *Playboy*: And that surprises you?
>
> Aykroyd: Yes, because he is a very smart person. I'm going to bring him up to Dudley Town, Massachusetts, and scare . . . him sometime. I'll take him to the most haunted place on Earth. He's my man. He's going. I can't believe he offhandedly says he doesn't believe in

ghosts when it's a reality of life on this planet.

173. David Sheff, "The *Playboy* Interview: Dan Aykroyd," *Playboy* (August 1993).

174. Gary P. Dudley, *The Legend of Dudleytown: Solving Legends through Genealogical and Historical Research* (Westminster, MD: Heritage Books, 2001).

175. Hauck, 93.

176. Cheri Revai, *Haunted Connecticut: Ghosts and Strange Phenomenon of the Constitution State* (Mechanicsburg, PA: Stackpole Books, 2006), 7.

177. Gary P. Dudley, "The Warrens," *The Legend of Dudleytown,* www.legend ofdudleytown.com/ warren.html.

178. Elaine Kuzmeskus, *Connecticut Ghosts* (Atglen, PA: Schiffer Publishing., 2006), 69.

179. Revai's book claims that Cheney committed suicide, but records show that she died of lung disease in New York City. This may be a moot point, because Gary Dudley insists that Mary Cheney never set foot in Dudleytown. This last point seems remarkably difficult to prove, however.

180. Descriptions of the Dudleytown legend by Revai and Kuzmeskus disagree on the order of these events: Revai claims that Brophy's wife was so overcome by grief when her children disappeared that she was finally overtaken by her illness. Kuzmeskus claims that Brophy's children disappeared shortly after his wife's demise.

181. Dudley insists that "Clarke" is the correct spelling and that Clarke purchased the property in 1900; Revai has the name as "Clark" and claims that the Clark family settled in Dudleytown in 1920; Kuzmeskus inexplicably lists the doctor as "Carter."

182. Kuzmeskus, 70.

183. Revai, *Haunted Connecticut,* 8.

184. Iveagh Hunt Sterry, *They Found a Way: Connecticut's Restless People* (Brattleboro, VT: Stephen Daye Press, 1938).

185. Dudley, "Dudleytown History," *The Legend of Dudleytown.*

186. Hauck, 93.

187. The Ghost Investigators Society, Ghostpix.com, www.ghostpix.com.

188. Hauck, 93.

189. Ed and Lorraine Warren, with Robert David Chase, *Ghost Hunters* (New York: St. Martin's Press, 1989).

190. Dudley, "Why is Dudleytown Haunted?" *The Legend of Dudleytown.*

191. Smitten, 76.

192. Revai, *Haunted Connecticut,* 24.

193. Ibid.,11.

194. Ibid., 80.

195. Citro, *Passing Strange,* 111.

196. Smitten, 66.

197. Ibid., 67.

198. Ibid., 68.

199. Ibid., 68.

200. Revai, *Haunted Connecticut,* 41.

201. Smitten, 12.

202. Ibid., 12.

203. Ibid., 13.

204. Revai, *Haunted Connecticut,* 89.

205. Ibid., 53.

206. "Haunted Places in Connecticut," The Shadowlands.

207. Church of Eternal Light, www.churchofeternallight .org

208. Revai, *Haunted Connecticut,* 47.

209. Ibid., 48.

210. David E. Phillips, *Legendary Connecticut* (Willimantic, CT: Curbstone Press, 1992).

211. Revai, *Haunted Connecticut,* 11.

212. "Seventh Day Baptist Cemetery," Creepy Connecticut .Net, www.creepyconnecti cut.net/id72.html.

213. Where the name "Huguenot House" came from is as much a mystery as the strange sights and sounds that people have experienced within it. Dolores Riccio and Joan Bingham speculate in *Haunted Houses USA* (NY: Penguin Books, 1989) that France's Huguenot sect might have been the ancestors of the Belmont family.

214. Smitten, 23.

215. "Haunted Places in Connecticut," The Shadowlands.

216. Smitten, 168.

217. Ibid., 169.

218. Ibid., 170.

219. "Haunted Places in Connecticut," The Shadowlands.

220. Revai, *Haunted Connecticut,* 64.

221. Ibid., 44.

222. Gerry David and Sue Hardy, *50 Hikes in Connecticut,* Fifth Edition (Woodstock, VT: Countryman Press, 2002), 164.

223. Revai, *Haunted Connecticut,* 32.
224. Ibid., 37.
225. Ibid., 37.
226. Ibid., 38.
227. Ibid., 70.
228. Ibid., 71.
229. David Pitkin, *Ghosts of the Northeast* (Salem, NY: Aurora Publications, 2002).
230. Holzer, 339.
231. Ibid., 340.
232. Revai, *Haunted Connecticut,* 82.
233. Kuzmeskus, 78.
234. Revai, *Haunted Connecticut,* 85.
235. Jasper , 87.
236. Revai, *Haunted Connecticut,* 90.
237. Ibid., 91.
238. Ibid., 93.
239. There is some debate as to whether the term comes from the language of the Pequot, Mohegan, or Narragansett tribe.
240. Revai, *Haunted Connecticut,* 50.
241. Ibid., 99.
242. Smitten, 152.
243. Jasper, 104.
244. Thomas D'Agostino, *Haunted Rhode Island* (Atglen, PA: Schiffer Publishing, 2005), 15.
245. Smitten, 22.
246. D'Agostino, *Haunted Rhode Island,* 52.
247. Ibid., 23–24.
248. Ibid., 24.
249. Ibid., 107.
250. Laura Meade Kirk, "The Scariest Places in a State Packed with Ghost Stories," *Providence Journal,* October 26, 2003 (www.projo.com/yourlife/content/projo_20031026_spooky.a6469.html).
251. Ibid.
252. D'Agostino, *Haunted Rhode Island,* 56.
253. Ibid., 16.
254. Several accounts state that the standing governor refused to compensate Sprague for his men's lodging in the tavern, perhaps as revenge for the tavern's initial support of Thomas Dorr. In any case, it would certainly appear that the Sprague name has a curse on it—at least within the confines of the state of Rhode Island (see page 201, the Sprague Mansion).
255. D'Agostino, *Haunted Rhode Island,* 19.
256. Smitten, 217.
257. D'Agostino, *Haunted Rhode Island,* 134.
258. Ibid.
259. Ibid., 37–38.
260. Smitten, 36.
261. Ibid., 32.
262. Ibid., 33.

Whittier, John Greenleaf. "Palatine." *The Poetical Works.* Boston: Houghton Mifflin, 1881.

The Windham Restaurant. www.windhamrestaurant.com.

Taylor, Troy. "The Ghosts of Kennebunkport." Ghosts of the Prairie. www.prairieghosts.com.

Thibodeau, Tricia. "Vale End Cemetery." TrueGhost.com. www.trueghost.com/valeendcemetery.htm.

Verde, Thomas A. *Maine Ghosts & Legends: 26 Encounters with the Supernatural.* Camden, ME: Down East Books, 1989.